IN THE BEGINNING

AMERICAN ACADEMY OF RELIGION
AIDS FOR THE STUDY OF RELIGION SERIES

Charles Hardwick, Editor

Number 11

IN THE BEGINNING
Creation Myths from
Ancient Mesopotamia, Israel and Greece

by
Joan O'Brien and Wilfred Major

JOAN O'BRIEN
WILFRED MAJOR

IN THE BEGINNING
Creation Myths from Ancient Mesopotamia, Israel and Greece

SCHOLARS PRESS

IN THE BEGINNNG
Creation Myths from
Ancient Mesopotamia, Israel and Greece

by
Joan O'Brien and Wilfred Major

© 1982
The American Academy of Religion

Library of Congress Cataloging in Publication Data

O'Brien, Joan V.
    In the beginning.

    (Aids for the study of religion ; no. 11)
    (ISSN 0145- 3246)
    Bibliography: p.
    1. Creation. I. Major, Wilfred. II. Title. III. Series.
BL226.027   291.2'4   81-21311
ISBN 0-89130-559-9   AACR2

Manufactured in the U.S.A.

Recently, some anthologies have appeared which contain creation myths from all over the world. These publications indicate a widespread interest in creation myths, an interest whetted by the popular belief that people's deepest insights are reflected in these myths. But such collections also result from the current interest in a structural approach to mythology. The structuralists study myths from diverse societies to discover common transcultural patterns in human thought. Such studies have advanced our understanding of universal story-patterns.

There is an element in creation myths, however, that the structural approach often slights. This is the myths' capacity to reveal distinctive traits of a specific culture. Why, for instance, do the Mesopotamian myths picture human beings as the drudges of the world, while the Israelite Priests make them the rulers? Why is Hesiod's Greek account distinctive in viewing irrational Eros as one of the primeval forces of the universe? Another approach is needed, so that students can grapple with two sets of questions simultaneously: those relating to trans-cultural patterns and those that plumb the imaginative genius of a given people, and its mythmakers. To provide the materials for this dual task, we have developed this textbook of creation myths set in their cultures.

The book can be used in four academic areas: classical mythology, comparative religion, comparative mythology, and women's studies. The teacher of classical mythology who wishes to treat part of a course comparatively will find ample mate-rial for such a unit. The religion class can study the myths for theological similarities and differences. Comparatists can treat these myths in depth against the background of their respective cultures. And a womens' studies class can use these materials to study the image of woman in myth.

Since Israelite and Greco-Roman cultures have had such a profound impact on our own civilization, texts from Genesis and Hesiod are logical choices for the book. The Mesopotamian myths are a less obvious choice. They antedate both the biblical stories and Hesiod and are of little direct importance for Hesiodic studies. The Kumarbi myth of the Hurrians, known to us through Hittite sources, is a clearer antecedent to Hesiod. But student interest in the antecedents of the biblical material led us to choose the Babylonian myths rather than the more esoteric Hittite ones. Thus, from Mesopotamia, we include *Atrahasis* for the creation of the human race, and the less representative but more complete *Enuma Elish* for the origin of the cosmos.

Egypt is an obvious omission. Why are Egyptian myths not included in addition to or in place of the Mesopotamian? Egypt indeed loomed large on the ancient horizon and its mythology is rich. The addition of Egyptian myths would be desirable, if pedagogically practical. Three cultures, however, are as many as students can comfortably handle in detail and we chose Mesopotamia rather than Egypt for two interrelated reasons. First, the similarities between Mesopotamian and Israelite myths illustrate the comparative method. The second reason is historical. It was the similarities between the Mesopotamian Flood story and the Noah story that first convinced the great nineteenth century biblical scholars of the existence of myth in the Bible. A similar juxtaposition of Mesopotamian and Israelite myths should, we believe, awaken student imaginations today.

The texts are the core of the book. Wherever possible, we have tried to present fresh contemporary translations. Our aim in these translations has been to capture the spirit of the original without sacrificing fidelity to the text. For the same reason, we have kept scholarly apparatus to a minimum. We have newly translated the selections included from Hesiod's *Theogony* and *Works and Days*; Assyriologist Tikva Frymer-Kensky has provided a fresh rendering of *Atrahasis*; and Craig McVay has made a new translation of the opening passage of Ovid's *Metamorphoses*. In the case of the fragmentary Akkadian epic, *Atrahasis*, brackets and other scholarly apparatus were unavoidable. These let the reader know where the text breaks off and the translator is emending. Perhaps this apparatus will help the student gain some insight into the difficulties the translator encounters. Of the texts used in the book, only the biblical texts and *Enuma Elish* are presented in standard translations.

We adopted the translation of *The New English Bible* because of
its simple, clear, but fairly literal language. We used
Speiser's translation of *Enuma Elish* because Speiser is one of
the giants in ancient Near Eastern scholarship and his translation, although somewhat dated, is the best one currently available. To aid student understanding of these texts, we have
provided introductions. Each introduction gives information
about the origin of the text, and the style and viewpoint of
the mythographer.

Next to the texts themselves, Part Three, the essays on
cultural backgrounds, should be the most valuable part of the
book. There are four such essays: one on each of the cultures
from which our myths are drawn, and an essay on the status of
women in the three civilizations. Any teacher who has tried to
teach a unit of comparative mythology knows how widely student
questions can range: from relative dating of Hammurabi and
Abraham, to a people's climate, government, religion, or customs.
We have incorporated into the essays answers to some of the most
frequently asked questions of this kind. The primary purpose of
these essays, however, is to provide the students with a context
for understanding the myths included in this book. Thus, our
aim has been to highlight the ideas and experiences which seemed
most important to the cultures rather than to present detailed
sketches of their history. A culture based on writing would
differ from a culture based on monotheism or again from a
culture based on conflict. Such labels for Mesopotamia, Israel,
and Greece, respectively, must be used cautiously, but the
distinctions they imply should help students perceive cultural
differences in the myths and evaluate them critically.

Although each essay presented its own peculiar problem,
the overview of ancient Mesopotamia was particularly difficult.
First of all, scholars are continually reassessing this civilization in light of recent discoveries and wide gaps still exist in
the available evidence. In addition, ancient Mesopotamia is
generally less familiar to the reader than is ancient Israel or
Greece. Finally, there are relatively few overviews of ancient
Mesopotamia. Although we cannot hope to provide a comprehensive
survey of such a heterogeneous culture as that of Mesopotamia,
we thought it necessary to include a brief sketch of its
history, city life, and religion so that the student could make
sound judgments on the cultural significance of the selections.

For the biblical material, the situation was quite different.
So much material is available on Israel in popular as well as

scholarly form that our job was to let a few salient examples
typify the Israelites and thereby provide the background
necessary for understanding our selections. Thus, our general
historical overview focuses particularly on the early period in
which the myths were formed, on the period of the United Kingdom
during which the author of Adam and Eve probably lived, and on
the period of the exile when the Priests flourished. Finally,
we decided not to include a separate section on the religion of
the Israelites since their religion permeated every aspect of
their state and culture. Instead, since so many of their religious practices and beliefs were intertwined with political and
social circumstances, we were able to incorporate most of the
theological material into the historical sketch.

Two conditions shaped our essay on Greek culture. On the
one hand, information on ancient Greek culture is both readily
available and widely used in mythology classes. On the other
hand, Hesiod, the Greek poet whose works appear in this book, is
relatively obscure in comparison to Homer. In fact, even
scholars have paid scant attention to Hesiod and his times.
It seemed more useful, therefore, to concentrate on Hesiod's
world and its relation to the mainstream of Greek culture
exemplified by Homer.

The essay on Women in the Three Cultures examines the
position of women in ancient Mesopotamia, Israel, and Greece
as background for understanding many of the myths included in
this book. Since our own culture is currently reevaluating the
status of women, it seemed important to consider the relationship between mythic representation of women and such historical
evidence as is available. Such information is essential if we
are to evaluate the relevance of these myths for our own age.
Since the older scholarship neglected this question, our essay
is necessarily tentative; and since much of the scholarship on
this issue is in progress, our essay is heavily bibliographical.

Everything else in this book is ancillary to the texts and
the cultural essays. The introduction to the book is about the
meaning and scope of creation myths. The conclusion is
pedagogical, showing how one may (and may not) compare myths
from different cultures. It ends with some charts, illustrating
the similarities and differences in the myths we have presented.
The study questions deal with both events and interpretation and
often focus on comparative issues. The notes on the texts are
of two kinds: some provide necessary material for understanding
obscure points in the text, others point out parallels. We have

limited those of the first category to comments we feel would be useful for class discussions. The annotated bibliographies provide teacher and students with tools for further investigation. The Appendix, "Ovid's Creation Story," contains a brief introduction to the Roman poet and the opening sequence of the *Metamorphoses*. Despite its late date and Roman setting, Ovid's version contains so many parallels to the stories in this book and so many Greek motifs that we felt it should be included. Teachers may want to use this story more centrally than its position in an appendix would suggest.

The book has been designed to allow a maximum of flexibility to the teacher. Topics are presented in logical order. We have kept the units as independent as possible, however, to allow for the option of using the material both selectively and in any order. Also, we have tried to avoid imposing arbitrary distinctions, e.g., between myth, legend, and saga. Ideally, both the teacher and student should be free to develop their own definitions.

We hope the reader will find materials here to accomplish several goals: (1) to see how different peoples shape and/or change myths in response to theological and cultural experiences; (2) to understand that even in the so-called "high-religions," myth-makers borrow and adapt materials freely; (3) to place biblical mythology in the context of the ancient Near East; (4) to see the need for caution in drawing conclusions about one myth as the source of another; (5) to appreciate the social dimension of myth as it helps shape social institutions, values, and prejudices; (6) to learn that ancient peoples, and by extension, all peoples use myth as a necessary element in their religious thinking and in their attempts to come to terms with human existence.

Acknowledgments

Since this book is transcultural in content, we could not have completed it without the generous help of specialists. We thank, first of all, Marcel Sigrist and Roger Karban for their invaluable assistance when we were preparing the chapters on Mesopotamia and Israel respectively; Marvin H. Pope, William W. Hallo, Brevard S. Childs, and Tikva Frymer-Kensky for reading parts or all of these same chapters; Erling B. Holtsmark and Rick Williams for reading the chapter on Greece; Froma Zeitlin, Rosemary Radford Ruether, and Judith Ochshorn for reading the chapter on Women; Salle Ann Schlueter for her help on Ovid; and, above all, Robert Griffin for his incisive criticism of the whole manuscript.

We are grateful to Alan Cohn and Angela B. Rubin of the Southern Illinois University at Carbondale Humanities library for their professional assistance in searches large and small; to Davis Perkins, Charles Winquist, and Charles H. Bowman of Scholars Press, and Charley D. Hardwick, Editor of the Aids to Religion Series, for their patient, cordial help; to Oxford University Press for permission to reprint biblical material and to Princeton University Press for permission to reprint selections from *Enuma Elish*; to colleagues George K. Plochmann, Carroll Grimes, Charles Speck, and John E. Becker for insights and encouragement; to graduate assistants Dennis Frazier, Craig McVay, Sandra Moffitt, Sue Burnham, and Emilie Babcox for editorial and research help; to secretaries Elline Long, Joan Bergt, Sue Culbertson, and Joyce Ambler for endless efforts, and especially to Caryl Maltby for preparing the final photo-ready copy of the manuscript; to many students, especially to Joanne Pappelis and David Gibson. For financial assistance, we express gratitude to Michael Dingerson and the Office of Research and Development, to Lon R. Shelby and James F. Light, Deans of the College of Liberal Arts and especially to Eugene F. Timpe and Helmut Liedloff, chairmen of the Department of Foreign Languages and Literatures at SIU-C, who created as conducive an atmosphere as their resources allowed.

TABLE OF CONTENTS

PREFACE v

INTRODUCTION TO CREATION MYTHS 1

PART ONE: CREATION OF THE COSMOS

Chapter 1: From Mesopotamia: *Enuma Elish* 9

Chapter 2: From Israel: The Creation Hymn
                (Genesis 1:1-2:4a). 33

Chapter 3: From Greece: Hesiod's *Theogony*. 47

PART TWO: CREATION OF THE HUMAN RACE

Chapter 4: From Mesopotamia: *Atrahasis* 69

Chapter 5: From Israel: Adam and Eve
             (Genesis 2:4b-3:24) 89

Chapter 6: From Greece: Pandora and the Five Ages
             (Hesiod's *Works and Days*, 47-201). .107

PART THREE: THE CULTURAL BACKGROUND

Chapter 7: Mesopotamia: A Culture Based on Writing . . .125

Chapter 8: Israel: A Culture Based on Monotheism 145

Chapter 9: Greece: A Culture Based on Conflict 159

Chapter 10: Women in the Three Cultures 173

CONCLUSION ON COMPARING MYTHS 195

SELECTED BIBLIOGRAPHY 201

APPENDIX: Ovid on Creation (*Metamorphoses* 1:1-150) 207

in memoriam

CLAIRE HAHN-BECKER

and

WILFRED and IRENE MAJOR

INTRODUCTION TO CREATION MYTHS

Ancient creation myths conjure up different ideas for different modern readers. For some, they suggest quaint stories about why snakes crawl on their bellies, why men have to work, and why women have pain in childbirth. For some, they suggest ancient descriptions of the origins of practically everything from pick-axes to toothaches or the primitive science which saw the earth as a flat disc populated by centaurs, nymphs, satyrs, and other strange creatures. For some, they suggest outmoded social structures which institutionalize slavery, unequal social status, or divine beings who have no moral restrictions. For others, however, these time-bound stories also reveal a search for the ultimate meaning of the world and human existence. In searching for origins, after all, ancient people were searching for a definition of themselves and their world just as we do today in our scientific, theological, and philosophical speculations.

We can observe this simultaneous existence of the sublime and the ridiculous, the simple and the profound in all myths, modern and ancient. We can even mistake one for the other, especially in ancient stories whose assumptions are very different from ours. But this problem is especially acute in ancient creation myths since their examination of origins necessarily involves scientific and social assumptions which we often view as outmoded. Ancient science, however, was much more complex and sophisticated than the brief simplified views of it which creation myths contain. For instance, our ancient ancestors developed astronomy to a very accurate level. Even when they described the earth and the sky as a plate with a bowl on top, they were trying to explain a complex reality in simple imagery, not unlike the models that scientists use today to explain our own view of the solar system. Although ancient science is outmoded, it played a vital role in our ancestors' beliefs.

1

Likewise, ancient creation myths often juxtapose ephemeral social roles and institutions with valid, perennial truths. Bronislaw Malinowski long ago observed that a creation myth, in depicting the ideal social structures of a society, performed a necessary, cohesive social function. More recently, however, scholars have pointed out the adverse effects that such myths can have in justifying prejudices about "inferior" groups in society. We will consider the pernicious effects of "myths as social charter" on women in Chapter 10, but here it is sufficient to observe that no myth can totally transcend the viewpoint and prejudices of its mythmaker. Memorable myths promulgate outmoded social beliefs as well as wisdom.

If our interest in ancient science and sociology is mostly historical, we have many other reasons for reading ancient creation myths. The most obvious reason, of course, is that we enjoy them. They are good stories, set in mysterious primeval surroundings, filled with fantasy, excitement, and astute insights into character and motivation. Part of the pleasure which they provide us, however, is the insight they give into the age-old wisdom of our ancestors as they pondered the beginnings of the universe and the roles we mortals play in it. We view the deep past across an abyss, as it were. And it is this encounter with the totally other, an image or way of seeing the world that is at once recognizably human but so different from our own characteristic modes of thought as to shock us into an enlarged view of what it means to be human, that makes the study of these myths so exciting and educational. They raise questions that we usually confront in times of crisis such as the death of a loved one: why are we born to die? can we transcend death in an afterlife? is there a god or gods whose "vast eternal plan" helps us find meaning in our mortality?

We can analyze myths in many different ways to discover their insight into these questions. But scholars today tend to use one or more of four basic approaches. Fundamentalists believe that creation myths are historical accounts of the origins of things; moral fictionists believe the myths provide useful lessons for living; structuralists have pointed out the universal patterns of thought which myths contain; and symbolists believe the myths contain truth which is symbolic rather than historical.

Today's fundamentalists focus, of course, on the biblical narratives, especially those concerning the creation of the human race and the flood. Over a hundred years ago, however, their

position suffered a severe blow with the discovery of the
"Babylonian Noah Story," later identified as Tablet XI of the
Epic of Gilgamesh. This story, much older than the biblical
account of the flood, resembles it in so many details that
scholars quickly realized the story of Noah was neither totally
original nor a literal rendering of an historical event.
Although many readers still look for historical truth in these
stories, most biblical scholars and mythologists no longer find
this fundamentalist approach adequate.

A more valid but still limited approach is that of the moral
fictionists. For them, creation myths provide a frame of reference for thinking about moral problems. Although on first
thought, Kronos' gobbling down of his children seems a rather
dubious moral exemplum, the bestiality of this divine father
helps us to define tyrannical authority, the world as we would
least like it to be, and to appreciate the civilized rule of
Zeus when he overthrows his savage father (Hesiod, *Theogony*
459-506). When viewed as moral fictions, then, myths are
propaganda justifying the status quo. But such interpretations
do not explain why myths are so convincing.

Generally speaking, then, we may limit our detailed discussion to the structuralist and symbolist approaches because they
explore the profound questions raised by these myths. Although
adherents of these two schools tend to emphasize their differences from each other, they have much in common. Both understand that the subject matter of creation myths is human interaction with a transcendent and divine realm; and both see the
purpose of the myths in their suggestion of the interrelationship
of time and eternity, mortality and immortality. There seems to
be no reason, then, why we cannot be eclectic, taking something
of value from both approaches.

The symbolists believe that creation myths contain symbolic
rather than historical truth. Our languages, symbolists argue,
have difficulty expressing even human emotions. A lover, for
instance, will give a rose to express what words cannot. If
such symbols are necessary to convey the deepest human relationships, they are even more essential to describe our interaction
with a transcendent world. Mythic language is symbolic, then,
because ordinary language is incapable of describing encounters
between divinity and humanity or of expressing the relationship
between time and eternity. Since creation myths attempt to
express what is beyond the limits of ordinary language, they

use concrete particulars from everyday experience as well as
analogies, paradoxes, riddles, and symbols to suggest a higher
level of reality in which the human and divine worlds intertwine.
When these myths are particularly good and express a felt truth,
we recognize in them our own beliefs and hopes.

For example, even if the story of Adam and Eve cannot be
taken as an historical or scientific account of the first human
beings, it nevertheless expresses something of "the mysterious
possibilities of human freedom, which we cannot fully explain,
but which we can in part understand" (Langdon Gilkey, *Maker of
Heaven and Earth*, p. 223). God depicted as a craftsman, marriage-
broker, judge, and gentleman out for an evening stroll is set
alongside the couple's simultaneous innocence and sinfulness.
Symbols like the serpent and the forbidden fruit partially
reveal and partially hide the author's intent. The explanations
of God's punishments to the man and the woman are, on the one
hand, naive descriptions of the status quo in which men worked
by the sweat of their brow and women suffered both the pain of
childbirth and virtual slavery. On the other hand, these
explanations are profoundly evocative: pain in childbirth is
suggestive of the whole spectrum of poignant dilemmas and limitations associated with parenthood, which Israelite society
connected primarily with women; the sweat of the brow expresses
the anxieties and cut-throat competition which that society
connected with the man's lot. Although we may reject the
division of labor described in the myth, we recognize the
punishments as the underside of the gift of life. Thus, this
symbolic, paradoxical story expresses both the mystery of human
life and the limitations imposed on it.

Claude Lévi-Strauss is the chief spokesman for the structural
position, and he denies the symbolist's contention that these
myths tell us anything instructive about the order of the world,
the origin and destiny of the human race, or the nature of reality. The great virtue of these myths, he contends, is that they
tell us not how things are but how human beings think. From his
analysis of American Indian myths, Lévi-Strauss has shown that
these myths provide insight into the beliefs, customs, and institutions of their respective tribes. Furthermore, the striking
resemblances between myths from different societies help us
discover structures of the human mind which remain so constant
over barriers of time and space "that we can assume them to be
fundamental" to all human beings ("Structuralism and Myth,"

pp. 67-68). The patterns of tribal myths, therefore, can illuminate our understanding of the way the mind structures reality.

In approaching the story of Adam and Eve, the structuralist would first point to the striking similarities between this story and stories like *Atrahasis*. This Mesopotamian story describes how human beings are created out of clay, divine blood, divine spittle, and the flesh of a slain god. They are created to replace the gods who have been wearily digging the canals for the Tigris and Euphrates rivers. By the end of the story, a relationship between divine leisure and human work has been developed which suggests the interdependence of the divine and human worlds. *Atrahasis* and the biblical story are similar, a structuralist would say, because they both consider, from their own perspectives, the same sets of binary relationships: gods and mortals, work and leisure, male and female, freedom and necessity, human life and transcendence. Different narrators, with different cultural backgrounds, stress different elements: the Israelite stresses God's power and benevolence, human freedom and necessity, male and female; the Mesopotamian stresses divine power and capriciousness, work and leisure, and the oppositions within the divine world. Still, the similarities between the two stories show the human mind wrestling with the same basic tensions.

In this brief analysis, we have seen the different ways symbolists and structuralists approach myths of human creation. Their differences are just as apparent in their analyses of cosmogonic myths. Since cosmogonies situate everything and everybody in the universe and articulate a people's view of the interrelationship of the universe, the gods, and their creatures, they are the most all-encompassing myths. The symbolists look at cosmogonies for unique symbols which provide windows, however dark, into objective reality. In the Mesopotamian *Enuma Elish*, for instance, the fertile mingling of the divine waters suggests the awesome power of a nature that is passively unaware of its consequences; in the Israelite Creation Hymn, God's sweeping over the waters like a mighty wind suggests the majesty of God penetrating all creation; and in the Greek *Theogony*, Eros' presence among the primal creative forces suggests the power of erotic love, driving each being to seek fulfillment through sexual or spiritual intercourse, and creating itself in the very act of destroying its innocence. The three images are powerful symbols that reveal different beliefs of the three traditions.

Although the structuralist would acknowledge the richness of these symbols, he would be more interested in finding how binary structures, found in cultures all over the world, are evident in these myths. In *Enuma Elish*, there is the conflict between gods identified with the material world and gods of intellect, between passive older gods and young active ones. In the biblical account, Yahweh's breath is the spiritual pole enlivening material creation. And the presence of Eros at the beginning of the Greek account expresses the author's fear that reason is subservient to irrational forces in divine as well as in human affairs. All three traditions, then, work with the same oppositions between matter and spirit, arranging them in different ways. Furthermore, every new narrator of an old story changes and adapts it to his own cultural perspective. So Lévi-Strauss argues that "a myth no sooner comes into being than it is modified through a change of narrator" (p. 77).

The foregoing brief descriptions suggest the kinds of questions the structuralists and symbolists raise and indicate how the two groups differ in methods and goals. The structuralist looks for the unifying structures common to the human mind; the symbolist for the unique symbols which embody emotional truths about human belief in a transcendent world. We have given only an outline of the two approaches in order to suggest how each can be applied to the myths in this book. (For fuller explanations, see the works of Langdon Gilkey, John Macquarrie, Claude Lévi-Strauss, Paul Tillich and David Tracy in the Bibliography.)

We can interpret creation myths in many different ways, but whatever method we use or perspective we adopt, we will surely find that these myths are great persuaders. They teach us much about ourselves as well as about those who wrote them, and they reveal that human beings have always searched for meaning and purpose in life. Thus these stories are indeed relevant, for if nothing else they question sentimentalities such as the fashionable current myths of absurdity and apocalypse which, despite any element of truth they may contain, inevitably tend to undermine human community and the potential for individual happiness.

PART ONE: CREATION OF THE COSMOS

Chapter 1

From Mesopotamia: *Enuma Elish*

INTRODUCTION p. 10
OUTLINE p. 15
SELECTIONS p. 16
NOTES p. 27
STUDY QUESTIONS p. 31

INTRODUCTION TO *ENUMA ELISH*

The Assyrians dominated Mesopotamia during the second millennium. Throughout the area, they were well known for their harsh
policies. They were ruthless warriors when they attacked a city
and stern taskmasters after they had subjugated it. More than
once, they forced the whole population of a city into exile
because their demands were not met. (See Chapter 7.)

The Assyrians even attacked Babylon, which was known throughout Mesopotamia as a sacred city. When they captured it (about
1200 B.C.), they carried off the city's statue of Marduk, its
patron god and protector. For the Babylonians, such an occur-
rence was devastating. Their once prestigious city was at the
mercy of the savage Assyrians. But even worse, their patron god,
Marduk, had abandoned them and proven himself inferior to the
Assyrian god.

It took Babylon nearly one hundred years to recover from
this disaster. Finally, when King Nebuchadnezzar I recaptured
the statue (around 1100 B.C.), the city could regain its pride.
It was, of course, a time for great celebration in Babylon.
Triumphal processions, festivals, and thanksgiving rituals filled
the city. From the Babylonian point of view, not only was
Marduk's statue back where it belonged, but also Marduk himself
had triumphed over his enemies. He had returned to protect
Babylon again and bestow his favors on the city which he had
founded.

Enuma Elish was probably written in this festive atmosphere
by a group of priests dedicated to Marduk (W. G. Lambert, "Reign
of Nebuchadnezzar"). At least the purpose of the poem confirms
this assumption. Taken as a whole, *Enuma Elish* is a celebration
of Marduk's powers and accomplishments, including his conquest
of Tiamat, his rise to kingship over the other gods, his creation
of the world and the human race, and his building of Babylon
itself.

The poem, then, is not primarily an account of the creation of the universe. It is rather a propagandistic story meant to spread the cult of Marduk. Its insistence on Marduk's supremacy even deviates from traditional Mesopotamian mythology. In other creation accounts, for example, Marduk plays a minor role if he is mentioned at all. Instead, Enlil is usually credited with the creation of the earth, Ea with the creation of the human race, and Anu with the supreme authority over the other gods.

But when the priests who wrote *Enuma Elish* use such traditional material, they alter it to buttress their different perspective. Marduk takes over many of the functions of Anu, Ea, and especially Enlil. At his birth, Marduk is called the greatest of the gods, twice as strong and ten times more brilliant than the others. At the end of the poem, he has become the ruler of the world, and the gods give him fifty names to indicate his many spheres of influence. Even the mighty gods Enlil and Ea willingly offer Marduk their own names as an indication of his control over them.

This elevation of Marduk leads to other distortions as well. Unlike other Mesopotamian god-lists, which account for large numbers of gods, the opening genealogy of *Enuma Elish* mentions only those who are direct ancestors of Marduk. It begins in the traditional way with a list of paired male and female deities, Apsu and Tiamat, Lahmu and Lahamu, Anshar and Kishar. But after these pairs, it focuses only on Anu and Ea, Marduk's male progenitors. Enlil's name is conspicuously absent from this heavily edited list.

Enuma Elish, then, is not a typical Mesopotamian creation account. Yet despite this problem, it is still worthy of study because it contains the fullest account of creation which scholars have unearthed from ancient Mesopotamia. Although other poems, such as "The Origin of the Pickaxe" and "The Worm and the Toothache," tell creation stories, none of them has as much detail as *Enuma Elish*.

Creation Topics in *Enuma Elish*

In the polytheistic world of the ancient Near East, creation myths frequently included a theogony, a cosmogony, and a story of succession. *Enuma Elish* is a clear example of this kind of creation account. Although it develops the theme of succession in more detail, the poem does contain a limited theogony, or origin of the gods, which reveals some interesting patterns.

Each new generation of gods surpasses its elders in wisdom,
strength, and personality. The early gods' personalities are
limited by the natural phenomena which they represent. Apsu,
for example, is the underground fresh water and wants only to
rest undisturbed. Tiamat, the salt water ocean, is not easily
aroused, but once she is angered her power is nearly unstoppable.
At the beginning of the poem, Apsu and Tiamat are sexually
united as they mingle their waters together. Both are passive
partners in this encounter and seem unaware that new gods are
born as a result of their union. Unlike anthropomorphic gods,
they do not make personal choices because they are bodies of
water.

The later generations of gods, however, are not so closely
tied to natural phenomena. They act in more human ways, playing,
dancing, making noise, and planning for the future. Unlike Apsu
and Tiamat, they are gods with personality from the time of
their birth. (See Chapter 7.) For example, Ea is first
characterized as a god of intelligence and craftiness. He shows
his shrewd understanding of character when he puts Apsu to sleep
and slays him. Ea easily wins this contest because he recognizes
that Apsu's greatest weakness is his desire for rest. Only after
he slays Apsu and takes control of the fresh water is Ea identified with any natural phenomenon. Even then, he is clearly
not the water itself, but the ruler of the water.

The cosmogony (origin of the world) in *Enuma Elish* is also
incomplete. It does not account for the creation of plants and
animals or other important creatures. Rather, it emphasizes
the process of creation instead of its results. Although this
process is not systematic, two methods of creating are frequently
seen throughout this poem: sexual generation and craftsmanship.

In *Enuma Elish*, sexual generation produces not only the gods
but also some features of a partly formed earth. Apsu and
Tiamat, for example, are the fresh and salt water. Their children, Lahmu and Lahamu, are silt deposits which build up at the
mingling of the waters and will eventually produce land. Anshar
and Kishar are the horizons which mark the border between the
earth and the sky. Finally, Anu is the sky itself. (See Notes
to *Enuma Elish*.) This mythic image of a primitive earth in the
process of formation is based on the experience of the
Mesopotamian people. They could directly observe, for example,
the silt deposits adding to the land at the juncture of the
rivers and the Persian Gulf. The priests of Marduk, however,
were not interested in developing this idea, for the cosmogony

abruptly stops at this point. No surface is given to the earth;
no plants, animals, or humans are formed. All of these essential
features must wait for Marduk to create them as an awesome
display of his mighty powers.

The other method of creation, craftsmanship, is used frequently throughout the poem. Anu, for example, creates the four
winds for his baby grandson to play with; Tiamat makes seven
monsters as engines of war; and Marduk fashions human beings
from the body of a dead god. All of these things are formed
from pre-existing material while the creator-gods act as craftsmen, molding the new object into shape.

The fullest example of this method occurs when Marduk forms
the surface of the earth out of Tiamat's body. The scene clearly
describes a master craftsman at work. Marduk steps back occasionally to get a fuller view of his new creation. The other
gods, watching him work, marvel at the thing as it takes shape.
But Marduk's motive is just as important as his method here.
Since he has only recently gained kingship over the gods by
defeating Tiamat, he must now do something with her body. So
he uses it to separate her waters and prevent her from returning
to life. Marduk creates the world, then, for a pragmatic
purpose, to keep himself in power. Likewise, he creates the
human race to forestall a possible revolt by the defeated gods.
Finally, he gives the younger gods large responsibilities to
keep them out of trouble.

In *Enuma Elish*, then, we see two very different views of
the creation of the world. In the genealogy which begins the
poem, we see the world being formed naturally as the gods breed
new generations of themselves. In this view, the world is
virtually a living being, divine and constantly expanding. In
the later creations, we see personal deities creating things at
will for their own purposes. These gods do not follow any
unified plan, nor do they worry about the conflict which their
new creation may cause.

All of this suggests a chaotic and unpredictable universe.
There is no necessary end to the process of creation, no permanent resolution of the inevitable conflicts which result from
continual formation of new parts of the world. Within this
context, the theme of royal succession emerges as the most
important element. Obviously, a world as unpredictable as the
one described in *Enuma Elish* needs stability and control, but
such an order is lacking until Marduk assumes the powers of
kingship over all the gods.

Before Marduk's reign, a generation gap divides the gods
into two opposing groups. The older gods, headed by Tiamat, are
passive in nature and dislike change. The younger generation,
led by Anu, are noisy, disorderly, and always active. Inevitably, a full-scale war breaks out between the two groups. Since
Tiamat proves to be too strong for the younger generation, Anu
seeks the help of Marduk. In return for his aid, Marduk receives
absolute control over the other gods.

Marduk's conquest of Tiamat, however, is only the beginning
of the new order which he establishes. His fabulous creations
of sky, earth, and the human race bring the older generation
under his control. But more importantly, Marduk uses his power
to establish a lasting order among the younger generation.
Marduk channels their ceaseless activity by assigning to each his
own station (a planet or star) from which he can use his energy
constructively. By these maneuvers, Marduk successfully deals
with the conflicts which would otherwise threaten his reign and
the stability of the world. The gods now work harmoniously with
one another in a well-ordered world and pay homage to the genius
of Marduk.

Such a story can be interpreted in many ways. On a mythic
level, it can be seen as a resolution of the conflict between
chaos and order which is prominent in many creation stories
worldwide. From this viewpoint, Tiamat and her followers are
the representatives of chaos. Marduk, the representative of
order, shapes this chaotic mass into a stable universe. On an
historical level, the poem can be seen as an explanation of the
development of kingship in Mesopotamia. The various ways in
which the gods are organized echo the governmental structures of
Mesopotamia from its earliest times. (See Jacobsen, *Treasures of
Darkness*.) But whatever else it may be, *Enuma Elish* is primarily
a celebration of Marduk as god of Babylon and the most powerful
of all the Mesopotamian deities.

OUTLINE OF *ENUMA ELISH*

A. The Beginnings (I:1-104)*
   1. Early Generations of Gods (I:1-20)
   2. War between Apsu and Ea (I:21-78)
   3. Birth of Marduk (I:79-104)

B. War between Tiamat and Marduk (I:105-IV:122)
   1. Tiamat's Preparations for War (I:105-161)*
   2. Anshar's Attempts to Stop Tiamat (II:1-III:138)
   3. Marduk's Victory (IV:1-122)*

C. Marduk's Creations (IV:123-VI:44)*
   1. Creation of Sky and Earth (IV:123-46)
   2. Creation of Stars and Gods' Stations (V:1-22)
   3. Creation of Human Race (VI:1-44)

D. Building of Babylon (VI:45-81)

E. Glorification of Marduk (VI:82-VII:144)
   1. Praises of Marduk's Weapon (VI:82-102)
   2. Humanity's Duties to Marduk (VI:103-20)
   3. Marduk's Fifty Names (VI:121-VII:144)

F. Epilogue (VII:145-57)

Starred passages are included in the readings which follow.

ENUMA ELISH (When on High)

Early Generations of Gods (I:1-20)

When on high the heaven had not been named,   I:1
Firm ground below had not been called by name,
Naught but primordial Apsu, their begetter,
And Mummu-Tiamat, she who bore them all,
Their waters commingling as a single body;   5

Sacred place

No reed hut had been matted, no marsh land had appeared,
When no gods whatever had been brought into being,
Uncalled by name, their destinies undetermined--
Then it was that the gods were formed within them.
Lahmu and Lahamu were brought forth, by name they were called.[10]
Before they had grown in age and stature.
Anshar and Kishar were formed, surpassing the others.
They prolonged the days, added on the years.
Anu was their heir, of his fathers the rival;
Yea, Anshar's first-born, Anu, was his equal.   15
Anu begot in his image Nudimmud.
This Nudimmud was of his fathers the master;
Of broad wisdom, understanding, mighty in strength,
Mightier by far than his grandfather, Anshar.
He had no rival among the gods, his brothers.   20

War between Apsu and Ea (I:21-78)

The divine brothers banded together,
They disturbed Tiamat as they surged back and forth,
Yea, they troubled the mood of Tiamat
By their hilarity in the Abode of Heaven.

From "*Akkadian Myths and Epics*," transl. by E. A. Speiser in *Ancient Near Eastern Texts Relating to the Old Testament*, ed. by James B. Pritchard 3rd edn. with Supplement (copyright (c) by Princeton University Press): pp. 60-68. Reprinted by permission of Princeton University Press.

Apsu could not lessen their clamor   25
And Tiamat was speechless at their ways.
Their doings were loathsome unto. . . .
Unsavory were their ways; they were overbearing.
Then Apsu, the begetter of the great gods,
Cried out, addressing Mummu, his vizier: 30
"O Mummu, my vizier, who rejoicest my spirit,
Come hither and let us go to Tiamat!"
They went and sat down before Tiamat,
Exchanging counsel about the gods, their first-born.
Apsu, opening his mouth,   35
Said unto resplendent Tiamat:
"Their ways are verily loathsome unto me.
By day I find no relief, nor repose by night.
I will destroy, I will wreck their ways,
That quiet may be restored. Let us have rest!"   40
As soon as Tiamat heard this,
She was wroth and called out to her husband.
She cried out aggrieved, as she raged all alone,
Injecting woe into her mood:
"What? Should we destroy that which we have built?   45
Their ways indeed are most troublesome, but let us attend kindly!"
Then answered Mummu, giving counsel to Apsu;
Ill-wishing and ungracious was Mummu's advice:
"Do destroy, my father, the mutinous ways.
Then shalt thou have relief by day and rest by night!"   50
When Apsu heard this, his face grew radiant
Because of the evil he planned against the gods, his sons.
As for Mummu, by the neck he embraced him
As that one sat down on his knees to kiss him.
Now whatever they had plotted between them,   55
Was repeated unto the gods, their first-born.
When the gods heard this, they were astir,
Then lapsed into silence and remained speechless.
Surpassing in wisdom, accomplished, resourceful,
Ea, the all-wise, saw through their scheme.   60
A master design against it he devised and set up,
Made artful his spell against it, surpassing and holy.
He recited it and made it subsist in the deep,
As he poured sleep upon him. Sound asleep he lay.
When Apsu he had made prone, drenched with sleep,   65
Mummu, the adviser, was powerless to stir
He loosened his band, tore off his tiara,

Removed his halo and put it on himself.

Having fettered Apsu, he slew him.

Mummu he bound and left behind lock.   70

Having thus upon Apsu established his dwelling,

He laid hold on Mummu, holding him by the nose-rope.

After Ea had vanquished and trodden down his foes,

Had secured his triumph over his enemies,

In his sacred chamber in profound peace had rested,   75

He named it "Apsu," for shrines he assigned it.

In that same place his cult hut he founded.

Ea and Damkina, his wife, dwelled there in splendor.

Birth of Marduk (I:79-104)

In the chamber of fates, the abode of destinies,

A god was engendered, most able and wisest of gods.   80

In the heart of Apsu was Marduk created,

In the heart of holy Apsu was Marduk created.

He who begot him was Ea, his father;

She who bore him was Damkina, his mother.

The breast of goddesses he did suck.   85

The nurse that nursed him filled him with awesomeness.

Alluring was his figure, sparkling the lift of his eyes.

Lordly was his gait, commanding from of old.

When Ea saw him, the father who begot him,

He exulted and glowed, his heart filled with gladness.   90

He rendered him perfect and endowed him with a double godhead.

Greatly exalted was he above them, exceeding throughout.

Perfect were his members beyond comprehension,

Unsuited for understanding, difficult to perceive.

Four were his eyes, four were his ears;   95

When he moved his lips, fire blazed forth.

Large were all four hearing organs,

And the eyes, in like number, scanned all things.

He was the loftiest of the gods, surpassing was his stature;

His members were enormous, he was exceeding tall.   100

"My little son, my little son!

My son, the Sun! Sun of the heavens!"

Clothed with the halo of ten gods, he was strong to the utmost,

As their awesome flashes were heaped upon him.

sky God

Tiamat's Preparations for War (I:105-61)

Anu brought forth and begot the fourfold wind   105
Consigning to its power the leader of the host.
    He fashioned . . ., stationed the whirlwind,
He produced streams to disturb Tiamat.
The gods, given no rest, suffer in the storm.
Their hearts having plotted evil,   110
To Tiamat, their mother, said:
"When they slew Apsu, thy consort,
Thou didst not aid him but remainedst still.
When the dread fourfold wind he created,
Thy vitals were diluted and so we can have no rest.   115
Let Apsu, thy consort, be in thy mind
And Mummu, who has been vanquished! Thou art left alone!
. . . thou pacest about distraught,
. . . without cease. Thou dost not love us!
. . . pinched are our eyes,   120
. . . without cease. Let us have rest!
. . . to battle. Do thou avenge them!
. . . and render them as the wind!"
When Tiamat heard these words, she was pleased
". . . you have given. Let us make monsters,   125
. . . and the gods in the midst. . . .
. . . let us do battle and against the gods . . . !"
They thronged and marched at the side of Tiamat.
Enraged, they plot without cease night and day,
They are set for combat, growling, raging,   130
They form a council to prepare for the fight.
Mother Hubur, she who fashions all things,
Added matchless weapons, bore monster-serpents,
Sharp of tooth, unsparing of fang.
With venom for blood she has filled their bodies.   135
Roaring dragons she has clothed with terror,
Has crowned them with haloes, making them like gods,
So that he who beholds them shall perish abjectly,
And that, with their bodies reared up, none might turn them back.
She set up the Viper, the Dragon, and the Sphinx,   140
The Great-Lion, the Mad-Dog, and the Scorpion-Man,
Mighty lion-demons, the Dragon-Fly, the Centaur--
Bearing weapons that spare not, fearless in battle.
Firm were her decrees, past withstanding were they.
Withal eleven of this kind she brought forth.   145

From among the gods, her first-born, who formed her Assembly,
She elevated Kingu, made him chief among them.
The leading of the ranks, command of the Assembly,
The raising of weapons for the encounter, advancing to combat,
In battle the command-in-chief--   150
These to his hand she entrusted as she seated him in the Council:
"I have cast for thee the spell, exalting thee in the Assembly
    of the gods.
To counsel all the gods I have given thee full power.
Verily, thou art supreme, my only consort art thou!
Thy utterance shall prevail over all the Anunnaki!"   155
She gave him the Tablet of Destinies, fastened on his breast:
"As for thee, thy command shall be unchangeable, Thy word shall
    endure!"
As soon as Kingu was elevated, possessed of the rank of Anu,
For the gods, his sons, they decreed the fate:
"Your word shall make the first subside,   160
Shall humble the 'Power-Weapon,' so potent in its sweep!"

   II:1-III:138. The scene now shifts to the new gods as they
discover Tiamat's plan and try to forestall it. The situation
is similar to the time when Apsu was planning to kill all his
children. But this time, the enemy, Tiamat, is much more formidable and better prepared. In their desperation, the new gods
make two unsuccessful attempts at stopping Tiamat before finding
a workable plan.

   As we might expect, Ea makes the first attempt to subdue
Tiamat. When he hears of her plans, he reports to his grandfather, Anshar. The old god recalls that Ea has killed Apsu
and bids him to do the same with Tiamat. Ea's attempt, however,
ends in failure and he returns defeated. Although Anshar is
disturbed by this news, he asks Anu to try again, but this time
he tells Anu to speak with the authority of Anshar so that
"Tiamat's mood may be calmed." Anu sets out to accomplish this
task but retreats sheepishly at the mere sight of the fierce
Tiamat. When Anshar is informed of this second failure, he
becomes so upset that his hair stands on end. Overcoming his
disappointment, however, he summons Marduk to come before him.

   Meanwhile, Ea's son Marduk has been waiting in the wings.
Thoroughly briefed by his father, Marduk is ready to take advantage of the situation. So when he steps forward and is asked
to kill Tiamat, he boasts that the rest of the gods are afraid
of a mere woman. He alone will slay her, he says, if he is
given absolute authority over all the gods.

   Anshar is apparently pleased with this brash suggestion and
immediately sends for Lahmu and Lahamu to ratify the decision.
On hearing the full story of Tiamat's behavior, Lahmu and Lahamu
are sorely distressed. They quickly go to Anshar's house where
they indulge in a large banquet and plenty of wine. After they
become "very languid," they agree to give Marduk the power he
requested. The story then continues as follows:

Marduk's Victory (IV:1-122)

They erected for him a princely throne.   IV:1
Facing his fathers, he sat down, presiding.
"Thou art the most honored of the great gods,
Thy decree is unrivaled, thy command is Anu.
Thou, Marduk, art the most honored of the great gods,   5
Thy decree is unrivaled, thy word is Anu.
From this day unchangeable shall be thy pronouncement.
To raise or bring low--these shall be in thy hand.
Thy utterance shall be true, thy command shall be unimpeachable.
No one among the gods shall transgress thy bounds!   10
Adornment being wanted for the seats of the gods,
Let the place of their shrines ever be in thy place.
O Marduk, thou art indeed our avenger.
We have granted thee kingship over the universe entire.
When in Assembly thou sittest, thy word shall be supreme.   15
Thy weapons shall not fail; they shall smash thy foes!
O lord, spare the life of him who trusts thee,
But pour out the life of the god who seized evil."
Having placed in their midst the Images,
They addressed themselves to Marduk, their first-born: 20
"Lord, truly thy decree is first among gods.
Say but to wreck or create; it shall be.
Open thy mouth: the Images will vanish!
Speak again, and the Images shall be whole!"
At the word of his mouth the Images vanished.   25
He spoke again, and the Images were restored.
When the gods, his fathers, saw the fruit of his word,
Joyfully they did homage: "Marduk is king!"
They conferred on him scepter, throne, and vestment;
They gave him matchless weapons that ward off the foes: 30
"Go and cut off the life of Tiamat.
May the winds bear her blood to places undisclosed."
Bel's destiny thus fixed, the gods, his fathers,
Caused him to go the way of success and attainment.
He constructed a bow, marked it as his weapon,   35
Attached thereto the arrow, fixed its bow-cord.
He raised the mace, made his right hand grasp it;
Bow and quiver he hung at his side.
In front of him he set the lightning,
With a blazing flame he filled his body.   40
He then made a net to enfold Tiamat therein.

The four winds he stationed that nothing of her might escape,
The South Wind, the North Wind, the East Wind, the West Wind.
Close to his side he held the net, the gift of his father, Anu.
He brought forth Imhulla "the Evil Wind," the Whirlwind, the   45
     Hurricane,
The Fourfold Wind, the Sevenfold Wind, the Cyclone, the Matchless
     Wind;
Then he set forth the winds he had brought forth, the seven of
     them.
To stir up the inside of Tiamat they rose up behind him.
Then the lord raised up the flood-storm, his mighty weapon.
He mounted the storm-chariot irresistible and terrifying.   50
He harnessed and yoked to it a team-of-four,
The Killer, the Relentless, the Trampler, the Swift.
Their lips were parted, their teeth bore poison.
They were tireless and skilled in destruction.
On his right he posted the Smiter, fearsome in battle,   55
On the left the Combat, which repels all the zealous.
For a cloak he was wrapped in an armor of terror;
With his fearsome halo his head was turbaned.
The lord went forth and followed his course,
Towards the raging Tiamat he set his face.   60
In his lips he held a spell;
A plant to put out poison was grasped in his hand.
Then they milled about him, the gods milled about him,
The gods, his fathers, milled about him, the gods milled about
     him.
The lord approached to scan the inside of Tiamat,   65
And of Kingu, her consort, the scheme to perceive.
As he looks on, his course becomes upset,
His will is distracted and his doings are confused.
And when the gods, his helpers, who marched at his side,
Saw the valiant hero, blurred became their vision.   70
Tiamat emitted a cry, without turning her neck,
Framing savage defiance in her lips:
"Too important art thou for the lord of the gods to rise up
     against thee!
Is it in their place that they have gathered, or in thy place?"
Thereupon the lord, having raised the flood-storm,   75
     his mighty weapon,
To enraged Tiamat he sent word as follows:
"Why art thou risen, art haughtily exalted,

Thou hast charged thine own heart to stir up conflict,
. . . sons reject their own fathers,
Whilst thou, who hast born them, hast foresworn love!   80
Thou hast appointed Kingu as thy consort,
Conferring upon him the rank of Anu, not rightfully his.
Against Anshar, king of the gods, thou seekest evil;
Against the gods, my fathers, thou hast confirmed thy wickedness.
Though drawn up be thy forces, girded on thy weapons,   85
Stand thou up, that I and thou meet in single combat!"
When Tiamat heard this,
She was like one possessed; she took leave of her senses.
In fury Tiamat cried out aloud.
To the roots her legs shook both together.   90
She recites a charm, keeps casting her spell,
While the gods of battle sharpen their weapons.
Then joined issue Tiamat and Marduk, wisest of gods.
They strove in single combat, locked in battle.
The lord spread out his net to enfold her,   95
The Evil Wind, which followed behind, he let loose in her face.
When Tiamat opened her mouth to consume him,
He drove in the Evil Wind that she close not her lips.
As the fierce winds charged her belly,
Her body was distended and her mouth was wide open.   100
He released the arrow, it tore her belly,
It cut through her insides, splitting the heart.
Having thus subdued her, he extinguished her life.
He cast down her carcass to stand upon it.
After he had slain Tiamat, the leader,   105
Her band was shattered, her troupe broken up;
And the gods, her helpers who marched at her side,
Trembling with terror, turned their backs about,
In order to save and preserve their lives.
Tightly encircled, they could not escape.   110
He made them captives and he smashed their weapons.
Thrown into the net, they found themselves ensnared;
Placed in cells, they were filled with wailing;
Bearing his wrath, they were held imprisoned.
And the eleven creatures which she had charged with awe,   115
The whole band of demons that marched on her right,
He cast into fetters, their hands he bound.
For all their resistance, he trampled them underfoot.
And Kingu, who had been made chief among them,

He bound and accounted him to Uggae. 120
He took from him the Tablet of Destinies, not rightfully his,
Sealed them with a seal and fastened them on his breast.

Creation of Sky and Earth (IV:123-46)

When he had vanquished and subdued his adversaries,
Had . . . the vainglorious foe,
Had wholly established Anshar's triumph over the foe, 125
Nudimmud's desire had achieved, valiant Marduk
Strengthened his hold on the vanquished gods,
And turned back to Tiamat whom he had bound.
The lord trod on the legs of Tiamat,
With his unsparing mace he crushed her skull. 130
When the arteries of her blood he had severed,
The North Wind bore it to places undisclosed.
On seeing this, his fathers were joyful and jubilant,
They brought gifts of homage, they to him.
Then the lord paused to view her dead body, 135
That he might divide the monster and do artful works.
He split her like a shellfish into two parts:
Half of her he set up and ceiled it as sky,
Pulled down the bar and posted guards.
He bade them to allow not her waters to escape. 140
He crossed the heavens and surveyed the regions.
He squared Apsu's quarter, the abode of Nudimmud,
As the lord measured the dimensions of Apsu.
The Great Abode, its likeness, he fixed as Esharra,
The Great Abode, Esharra, which he made as the firmament. 145
Anu, Enlil, and Ea he made occupy their places.

Creation of Stars and Gods' Stations (V:1-22)

He constructed stations for the great gods, V:1
Fixing their astral likenesses as the Images.
He determined the year by designating the zones:
He set up three constellations for each of the twelve months.
After defining the days of the year by means of heavenly figures,
He founded the station of Nebiru to determine 5
    their heavenly bands,
That none might transgress or fall short.
Alongside it he set up the stations of Enlil and Ea.
Having opened up the gates on both sides,
He strengthened the locks to the left and the right. 10

In her belly he established the zenith.
The Moon he caused to shine, the night to him entrusting.
He appointed him a creature of the night to signify the days:
"Monthly, without cease, form designs with a crown.
At the month's very start, rising over the land,   15
Thou shalt have luminous horns to signify six days,
On the seventh day reaching a half-crown.
At full moon stand in opposition in mid-month.
When the sun overtakes thee at the base of heaven,
Diminish thy crown and retrogress in light.   20
At the time of disappearance approach thou the course of the sun,
And on the thirtieth thou shalt again stand in opposition to
   the sun."

   23ff. At this point the text is fragmentary. But enough
remains to reveal that Marduk continues to create "marvelous
things." He pokes out Tiamat's eyes, and the Tigris and
Euphrates rivers flow from them. He forms mountains out of her
breasts. Then he drills holes in them, allowing springs to
gush forth. Finally, as a memorial to his conquest of Tiamat,
he turns her eleven monsters into statues and places them at
the gate of the Apsu. After these events are described, there
is a gap in the text. The story then resumes on Tablet VI:

Creation of Human Race (VI:1-44)

When Marduk hears the words of the gods,   VI:1
His heart prompts him to fashion artful works.
Opening his mouth, he addresses Ea
To impart the plan he had conceived in his heart:
"Blood I will mass and cause bones to be.   5
I will establish a savage, 'man' shall be his name.
Verily, savage-man I will create.
He shall be charged with the service of the gods
   That they might be at ease!
The ways of the gods I will artfully alter.
Though alike revered, into two groups they shall be divided."   10
Ea answered him, speaking a word to him,
Giving him another plan for the relief of the gods:
"Let but one of their brothers be handed over;
He alone shall perish that mankind may be fashioned.
Let the great gods be here in Assembly,   15
Let the guilty be handed over that they may endure."
Marduk summoned the great gods to Assembly;
Presiding graciously, he issues instructions.
To his utterance the gods pay heed.

The king addresses a word to the Anunnaki: 20
"If your former statement was true,
Do now the truth on oath by me declare!
Who was it that contrived the uprising,
And made Tiamat rebel, and joined battle?
Let him be handed over who contrived the uprising.   25
His guilt I will make him bear. You shall dwell in peace!"
The Igigi, the great gods, replied to him,
To Lugaldimmerankia, counselor of the gods, their lord:
"It was Kingu who contrived the uprising,
And made Tiamat rebel, and joined battle."   30
They bound him, holding him before Ea.
They imposed on him his guilt and severed his blood vessels.
Out of his blood they fashioned mankind.
He imposed the service and let free the gods.
After Ea, the wise, had created mankind,   35
Had imposed upon it the service of the gods--
That work was beyond comprehension;
As artfully planned by Marduk, did Nudimmud create it--
Marduk, the king of the gods divided
All the Anunnaki above and below.   40
He assigned them to Anu to guard his instructions.
Three hundred in the heavens he stationed as a guard.
In like manner the ways of the earth he defined.
In heaven and on earth six hundred thus he settled.

VI:45-VII:144. Now that Marduk has finished putting order
into the universe, the gods propose that a sanctuary (the city
of Babylon) be built for them all. After they complete the job,
they praise the weapons Marduk used to slay Tiamat. Then they
proclaim the duties of the human race which include paying homage
to Marduk and supplying sustenance to all the gods. Finally,
they praise Marduk by reciting his fifty names. Each name
indicates something of Marduk's accomplishments and powers. For
example, he is called "Ziukkinna" because he "established the
heavens," "Suhrim" because he defeated his enemies, and "Asaru"
because he created vegetation. Finally, the gods give Marduk
yet another title, "Fifty," to encompass all the characteristics
of his fifty names.

NOTES TO *ENUMA ELISH*

Title. The title, *Enuma Elish*, is derived from the first two words of the Babylonian text and means "When on high." This is the traditional way to name texts which are otherwise untitled.

Headings and Line Numbers. The headings used to divide the text are taken from the outline which precedes it. They are not part of the original text or Speiser's translation.

The line numbers follow those used by Speiser in his translation. The original text was written on seven clay tablets, which held approximately 170 lines of text each. The Roman numerals indicate the tablet number, and the Arabic numerals indicate the line numbers from the tablet. The numbers correspond approximately to those on the original tablets.

I:1-9. The rhetorical pattern in these opening lines is similar to those in other creation accounts such as the Creation Hymn (Genesis 1:1-2:4), Adam and Eve (Genesis 2:4-3:24), *Atrahasis*, and many others. See Conclusion on comparing myths for a detailed analysis.

The opening lines describe the primordial condition before any creation has occurred. According to Thorkild Jacobsen's *The Treasures of Darkness*, Apsu is the primeval fresh water and Tiamat the salt water. Such a division would be natural for people surrounded by the Tigris and Euphrates rivers and the Persian Gulf. Another interpretation by A. Kragerud ("The Concept of Creation in *Enuma Elish*") suggests that Apsu and Tiamat are the terrestrial and celestial waters.

Although identified as bodies of water in these lines, Apsu and Tiamat are also deities as their activities in the rest of the poem make clear. Tiamat also shows characteristics of a monster or dragon. See IV:71ff. and V:45ff.

I:1. Had not been named. Naming something meant bringing it into existence or exercising some control over it. There are frequent references to the importance of naming in *Enuma Elish*. See also Genesis 2:19ff. where Adam names the animals.

I:5. Their waters commingling. These are the waters of
Apsu and Tiamat. The mingling of waters of the male Apsu and
female Tiamat suggests a sexual union and the beginning of the
generation of the gods explained in I:10-20. See also Hesiod's
Theogony, 116ff.

I:6. Reed hut. Reed huts were typical Mesopotamian
dwelling places, but they were also used for cultic rituals.
The reference here may include both meanings.

I:10-22. These lines give a shortened version of the
typical Mesopotamian genealogy of the early deities. It may
be pictured as follows:

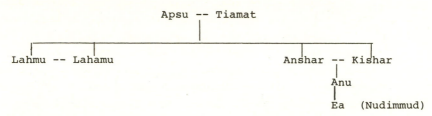

Other texts show many more gods. See Introduction to *Enuma
Elish*. Jacobsen identifies these early gods with natural
phenomena: Lahmu and Lahamu are the silt which formed in the
primeval oceans; Anshar and Kishar are the circular rims of
the sky (An) and the earth (Ki); Anu is the sky; and Ea is
the god of the fresh waters.

These lines show the cause of the conflicts which are to
follow. Essentially, there is a generation gap between "the
forces of motion and activity (the gods) and the forces of
inertia and rest (the older generation of powers)." (Jacobsen,
Treasures, p. 170). The movement caused by the gods who
"surged back and forth" is a constant source of irritation to
Apsu and Tiamat. In this passage Apsu is aroused to take
action. Later, Tiamat will do the same (I:108ff.).

I:30. Vizier. A vizier is an adviser and second in
command.

I:56. The gods, their first born. These are gods of
activity against whom Apsu is plotting.

I:60. Saw through their scheme. That is, Ea saw through
the scheme of Apsu and Mummu.

I:63. Made it subsist in the deep. Ea here casts his
spell on the waters of Apsu. Ea shows his cleverness in using
magic to sing Apsu to sleep and kill him. This makes it
possible for Ea to build his house on the Apsu (fresh water)
(I:70). The Apsu subsequently is the home of Ea's sacred abode.

I:72. Holding him by the nose-rope. Mummu here is apparently pictured as some kind of animal. Such imagery is frequent in *Enuma Elish*. See also descriptions of Tiamat (IV:71ff.).

I:77. Cult hut. The same word as in I:6, but the context here indicates that the reed hut is not a commoner's dwelling but a sacred place.

I:91. He rendered him perfect. According to Speiser, the word used here refers primarily to a craftsman's final inspection before his work is pronounced fit for use. Marduk's birth shows him with double the features of any other god ("four were his eyes, four were his ears") thus signifying that he is twice as great as the other gods.

I:109. The gods. These gods apparently live with Tiamat.

I:132. Mother Hubur. This is another name for Tiamat and suggests that she is the female counterpart of Ea.

I:155. Anunnaki. Anunnaki is a collective name for the gods who live below the earth. In *Enuma Elish*, however, the name is often applied to other groups of gods. See, for example, VI:20, 40.

I:156. Tablet of Destinies. These were apparently symbols of authority and control over the gods.

I:161. Power Weapon. Mesopotamian gods often had characteristic weapons. Later in *Enuma Elish* Marduk will make his own weapon, the bow and arrow (IV:35-38). See also the sword which God uses to guard the Garden of Eden (Genesis 3:24). See Speiser, *Genesis*, p. 25.

IV:4. Thy command is Anu. Marduk's command will have the same authority as Anu's. The lines which follow indicate this, especially the episode where Marduk is given the power to create by word (IV:19-26). This is the power Marduk wanted in return for fighting Tiamat although here it is displayed only in a bit of parlor magic.

IV:72. Framing savage defiance in her lips. Tiamat here taunts Marduk, a typical technique in single combat. But the insult her speech contains is not readily understandable.

IV:120. Uggae. Uggae is the god of death.

IV:144. Esharra. Heidel interprets Esharra as a poetic designation of the earth. Thus, he says, it is a canopy which covers the Apsu or fresh water (*Babylonian Genesis*). Kragerud, however, interprets it as the temple of Marduk. It would then parallel Ea's temple, the Apsu. Kragerud says the earth is pictured here as a series of temples surrounded by water.

IV:146. Anu, Enlil, and Ea he made occupy their places.
Anu was assigned the sky, Enlil the earth and atmosphere, and Ea
the fresh water. This is one of the few times that Enlil is even
mentioned in the poem. See Introduction to this chapter.

V:1-22. This passage contains some Mesopotamian astronomy,
explaining the origin of the stellar contellations and the cycles
of the moon. Throughout the ancient world, the Mesopotamians
were noted for their knowledge of astronomy.

V:6. Nebiru. The planet Jupiter.

VI:6. I will establish a savage, 'man' shall be his name.
"Savage" is Speiser's translation of *lullu* which means the
aboriginal human being. The Mesopotamians believed that the
first human beings were completely barbarous. See Introduction
to *Atrahasis*.

VI:28. Lugaldimmerankia. This epithet of Marduk means "the
king of the gods of heaven and earth."

STUDY QUESTIONS ON *ENUMA ELISH*

1. Early Generations of Gods (I:1-20)

    What exists at the beginning of this story? Identify Apsu
    and Tiamat. What are they doing? Note the emphasis on
    naming. What is the significance of having a name? How
    many generations of gods come into being? Is there any
    progression from one generation to the next? How are these
    gods created?

2. War between Apsu and Ea (I:21-78)

    What causes the trouble between the younger gods and Apsu?
    Why is Tiamat opposed to killing the younger gods? What
    does Apsu do? How do the younger gods react to the news
    that Apsu plans to kill them? How does Ea react? Is Apsu's
    death consistent with his personality? How does this show
    Ea's cleverness? What does Ea do with Apsu's body? What
    does he do with Mummu?

3. Birth of Marduk (I:79-104)

    How is Marduk greater than the gods born before him? In
    addition to his role as father, what else does Ea do to make
    Marduk great? What does Marduk look like? How does his
    appearance indicate his supremacy over the other gods?

4. Tiamat's Preparations for War (I:105-161)

    What is the cause of this war? Compare to the cause of the
    war between Apsu and Ea. Describe Tiamat's preparations for
    the war. Why is she a more formidable enemy than Apsu? Who
    is Kingu? What powers does Tiamat give him?

5. Marduk's Victory (IV:1-122)

    Describe Marduk's preparations for the war. What powers is
    he given? What weapons does he have? Who actually fights
    during the war? What happens to Kingu and Tiamat's other
    helpers? Why don't they fight? How does Marduk kill Tiamat?
    What does he do with Kingu? With the others who sided with
    Tiamat?

6. Marduk's Creations (IV:123-VI:44)

   Describe what Marduk does with Tiamat's body. What happens
   to Tiamat's blood? Why does Marduk post guards in the sky?
   How does Marduk put some order into the society of gods?
   Describe the process of creating the human race. What
   materials are used? What plan does Marduk use? Why does he
   create human beings? Who actually does the work of creation?

7. Important Names to Identify

   Anu, Apsu, Ea, Kingu, Marduk, Tiamat

8. General Questions

   Try to draw a picture of the world as it was created in this
   story. How does it differ from our conception of the world?
   What materials were used to make it?

   How do the gods fit into the world? Are they part of it or
   above it? Why is Marduk their king? What does he accomplish
   which no other god did?

   How do human beings fit into the world? What is their relationship to the gods? Why were they created?

   Compare *Enuma Elish* to the Israelite Creation Hymn and
   Hesiod's *Theogony* in terms of the kind of world which is
   created, the character of the creator gods, the wars, and
   the role of the human race in the newly created world.

Chapter 2

From Israel: The Creation Hymn (Genesis 1:1-2:4a)

INTRODUCTION p. 34
TEXT p. 39
NOTES p. 42
STUDY QUESTIONS p. 45

INTRODUCTION TO THE CREATION HYMN (GENESIS 1:1-2:4a)

Because they lived in a polytheistic world, the ancient
Israelites had great difficulty maintaining their faith in one
God. Their neighbors all believed that many gods inhabited the
upper, lower, and remote regions of the world. They also
performed many rituals designed to appease or befriend these
gods. The Israelites, of course, fought such beliefs and practices in an effort to keep their religion free of pagan ideas.
But at times, polytheism appeared more attractive than their
exclusive covenant with one God. So they adopted some pagan ways
which modified their traditional beliefs. In order to remain
faithful to their God, then, the Israelites needed frequent
reminders of the value of their religious views.

Such reminders were especially necessary when the Israelites
were exiled in Babylon (about 587-539 B.C.). There they were
not only governed by polytheists but also prohibited from
returning to the land which their God had promised them. Such a
situation could easily lead to a loss of faith and probably did
for many Israelites. But others kept the faith and reinforced
it by preserving and renewing the ideas and practices which
characterized the Israelite religion.

Among the latter were a group of priests (hereafter called P)
who carefully preserved the traditional stories, laws, and other
writings which the Israelites had developed over the centuries.
P put these writings together during the exile or shortly there-
after (about 550-500 B.C.) in order to insure that the Israelite
faith would not be forgotten.

To begin this collection of sacred writings which we now
call the Pentateuch (the first five books of the Bible), P chose
a hymn about God's creation of the world. Although we do not
know how much of the hymn is P's invention, we can see that it is
consistent with P's theology which envisions one God who is the

almighty ruler of the world and remains at a distance from his
creation. The Creation Hymn is also consistent with P's style
as seen in his works throughout the Pentateuch. P often emphasizes logic over imagery, avoids anthropomorphisms, and writes
in a dry theological style. In this, he differs from some
Israelite theologians, such as the Yahwist, who convey their
messages primarily through mythic conventions. (See Introduction
to Chapter 5.)

The Creation Hymn itself is a highly structured lyric poem
which enumerates the attributes and mighty deeds of P's God.
It presents a series of tableaus in which God creates one part
of the world at a time and fits each into his logically planned
world. This approach differs from such polytheistic narratives
as *Enuma Elish* in which the gods create various parts of the
world in response to their needs at any particular time. These
creator-gods, like human beings, act out of necessity or whim
but rarely have a grand design from which they work. The brevity
and logical structure of the Creation Hymn suggest that it was
probably used as a communal prayer like Psalms 33 and 104. Even
the few mythic conventions P employs are consistent with this
purpose. His description of the primordial world, for instance,
contains a mythic image of "the mighty wind that hovers over
the surface of the waters" (1:1). This brief but vivid image
depicts the awesome setting in which God will produce the new
world, but it is simply expressed so that it does not intrude on
the structured creations which follow.

Patterns in the Creation Hymn

Despite such occasional use of metaphor in the Creation Hymn,
P relies more on logic and structure to convey his message. The
complex structure of the hymn reveals the orderly process by
which P's God creates the world. It is apparent that this God
had a comprehensive plan for creation and that each part of the
world fits harmoniously into the whole. P's God moves from the
simple to the complex, from the general features of the earth to
the particular creatures which populate it. His creation begins
with a chaotic mass and progresses step by step from chaos to
the creation of working space, to inanimate objects, to organic
life, and finally to humanity.

Moreover, P's God is transcendent; in other words, he is
outside of and above his creation. He works at his own pace,
unhindered by the things he creates. He schedules his work in

six well-ordered days and takes the seventh to rest because his
work is complete. Even within this simple six-day structure,
God organizes his work in his own logical way. On each of the
first three days, he creates a basic feature of the cosmos:
first the sky, then the waters, and then the dry land. On the
fourth, fifth, and sixth days, he creates the inhabitants of
these regions: first the sun and moon, then the fish and birds,
and finally the animals and human beings. After each creation,
he is able to stand back and assess it as good.

His methods also indicate that P's God has total control over
his creation. He creates primarily by word, a method which
suggests his overwhelming power. No other being in the world
could bring a whole world into existence merely by speaking a
word. But P's God also manifests his power by separating the
light from the darkness, heavenly from earthly waters, species
from species, and day of rest from days of activity. God's
ability to separate so many different parts of the world emphasizes that he has total mastery over the created cosmos. Although
the gods in polytheistic creation accounts also use these methods
of creating, they do so with less frequency and in more limited
ways because they do not have the all-encompassing power of P's
God.

Finally, P emphasizes the logical consistency of God's method
by repetition of seven phrases which describe the process God
uses: 1) "God said"; 2) "Let there be"; 3) "and so it was";
4) the particular work of creation; 5) God's naming or blessing
of the creature; 6) God saying that it was good; and 7) "there
was evening and morning" (Bruce Vawter, *On Genesis*, p. 51). Only
for the most important creations, the first and the last, is the
pattern given in full. But for the other creations, P uses
enough of these phrases to suggest that the pattern is followed
each time God creates.

Theological Argument in the Creation Hymn

Within this intricate structure of repetitive phrases, P
concisely argues for his theological position. P's arguments can
best be understood in the context of the religious atmosphere
which surrounded the Israelites during the exile. The polytheism
of the Near East was antithetical to Israelite monotheism. It
stressed theogony (origin of the gods) in creation accounts, and
the world it envisioned differed radically from that of P.

For example, in the Babylonian *Enuma Elish*, Marduk makes a
new, orderly world out of the pieces of the old, chaotic one. He
uses the body of one god to form the surface of the earth,
another to make the human race. But there is no indication that
the world cannot be refashioned in an entirely different way.
New gods may still be born, new leaders arise, and a new order
established. Over such events, Marduk has little, if any,
control. In P, however, the finality of creation is stressed
when God rests on the seventh day. The world which he created
is a finished product, and there is no more to be done.

Likewise, P differs with Near Eastern polytheism in his view
of humanity's place in the created world. The few verses he
uses to describe human creation (1:26-28) stress the dignity of
humanity. Human beings are pre-eminent among God's creatures.
Created to rule the world, they alone are made in the image of
God. Only after this creation does God survey his finished world
and emphatically pronounce it "very good." Such an idea clearly
contrasts with the typical Mesopotamian view of human creation.
In *Enuma Elish* and *Atrahasis*, for example, humans are created as
slaves to do the hard work which the gods no longer wish to do
themselves.

In his conception of the basic features of the cosmos, however, P does not differ significantly from traditional Near
Eastern ideas. He probably meant to depict a dynamic world
rather than a static one. But the completeness of his description allows his cosmos to be pictured somewhat as follows:

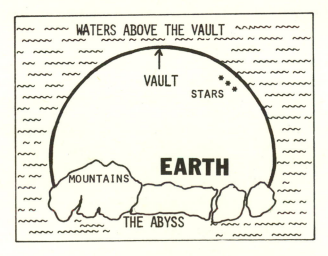

For P, the earth is a flat surface with a solid vault, or dome, covering it like a bowl. The vault prevents the waters above it from flooding down upon the earth. Below the earth is the abyss, a dark chaotic place which remains unformed.

Despite this agreement with Near Eastern cosmology, P opposes the religious significance of some features of the cosmos. For example, in Mesopotamian religion, the sun, moon, stars, and some animals were often considered cult objects closely identified with the gods. But in the Creation Hymn, P depicts these objects as totally separate from God. In particular, P subordinates the sun and moon in a series of steps. On the first day, God creates light rather than the sun. When God creates the sun and moon on the fourth day, P calls them the "greater" and "lesser" lights (1:16). In this way, he avoids giving them any stature by naming them. Here and in similar passages, P may well be criticizing specific Mesopotamian religious practices which the Israelites witnessed frequently during the exile.

Finally, P's cosmos differs from others in the ancient Near East because it is harmonious. In other creation accounts, conflict often provides the reason for gods to create new portions of the world. In *Enuma Elish*, for example, Tiamat creates seven monsters to fight a war while Marduk creates the earth and the stars to prevent further fighting. At times, conflict is even caused by creation as in *Atrahasis*. But in P's vision, the whole world is "very good." Living beings receive God's blessing. Humanity is made in the image of God and given dominion over the rest of creation. There is no conflict among these creatures. All have their respective places in a world designed for them.

P, then, is using the Creation Hymn to argue against some fundamental conceptions of creation which were prevalent in the ancient Near East. But the hymn still belongs in the same tradition as many polytheistic creation accounts. Like *Enuma Elish* and Hesiod's *Theogony*, for example, it is propagandistic since it advocates the supremacy of the Israelite God. It glorifies this God and argues that he is total master of the world.

P's arguments have indeed been persuasive. Even today, his precision and thoroughness, his intricate patterns and concise descriptions have convinced many people, despite the great differences between his cosmology and modern science. But most of all, P's vision of an almighty creator and harmonious creation have made his hymn one of the most important works in the Bible.

THE CREATION HYMN (GENESIS 1:1-2:4a)

The First Day

In the beginning of creation, when God made heaven and earth, 1:1
The earth was without form and void, with darkness over the 2
face of the abyss, and a mighty wind that swept over the
surface of the waters.
God said, 'Let there be light', and there was light; 3
and God saw that the light was good, and he separated light 4
from darkness.
He called the light day, and the darkness night. So evening 5
came, and morning came, the first day.

The Second Day

God said, 'Let there be a vault between the waters, to 6
separate water from water.'
So God made the vault, and separated the water under the 7
vault from the water above it, and so it was;
and God called the vault heaven. Evening came, and morning 8
came, a second day.

The Third Day

God said, 'Let the waters under heaven be gathered into one 9
place, so that dry land may appear'; and so it was.
God called the dry land earth, and the gathering of the 10
waters he called seas; and God saw that it was good.
Then God said, 'Let the earth produce fresh growth, let there 11
be on the earth plants bearing seed, fruit-trees bearing
fruit each with seed according to its kind.' So it was;

the earth yielded fresh growth, plants bearing seed according 12
to their kind and trees bearing fruit each with seed
according to its kind; and God saw that it was good.
Evening came, and morning came, a third day. 13

The Fourth Day

God said, 'Let there be lights in the vault of heaven to 14
separate day from night, and let them serve as signs both
for festivals and for seasons and years.
Let them also shine in the vault of heaven to give light 15
on earth.' So it was;
God made the two great lights, the greater to govern the day 16
and the lesser to govern the night; and with them he made
the stars.
God put these lights in the vault of heaven to give light 17
on earth,
to govern day and night, and to separate light from darkness; 18
and God saw that it was good.
Evening came, and morning came, a fourth day. 19

The Fifth Day

God said, 'Let the waters teem with countless living 20
creatures, and let birds fly above the earth across the
vault of heaven.'
God then created the great sea-monsters and all living 21
creatures that move and swarm in the waters, according to
their kind, and every kind of bird; and God saw that it
was good.
So he blessed them and said, 'Be fruitful and increase, fill 22
the waters of the seas;
and let the birds increase on land.' Evening came, and 23
morning came, a fifth day.

The Sixth Day

God said, 'Let the earth bring forth living creatures, 24
according to their kind: cattle, reptiles, and wild
animals, all according to their kind.'
So it was; God made wild animals, cattle, and all reptiles, 25
each according to its kind; and he saw that it was good.
Then God said, 'Let us make man in our image and likeness 26
to rule the fish in the sea, the birds of heaven, the cattle,
all wild animals on earth, and all reptiles that crawl upon

the earth.'

So God created man in his own image; in the image of God he   27
created him; male and female he created them.

God blessed them and said to them, 'Be fruitful and increase,   28
fill the earth and subdue it, rule over the fish in the sea,
the birds of heaven, and every living thing that moves
upon the earth.'

God also said, 'I give you all plants that bear seed every-   29
where on earth, and every tree bearing fruit which yields
seed: they shall be yours for food.

All green plants I give for food to the wild animals, to all   30
the birds of heaven, and to all reptiles on earth,
every living creature.'

So it was; and God saw all that he had made, and it was   31
very good. Evening came, and morning came, a sixth day.

The Seventh Day

Thus heaven and earth were completed with all their mighty   2:1
throng.

On the sixth day God completed all the work he had been   2
doing, and on the seventh day he ceased from all his work.

God blessed the seventh day and made it holy, because on that   3
day he ceased from all the work he had set himself to do.

This is the story of the making of heaven and earth when   4
they were created.

NOTES TO THE CREATION HYMN

1:1. When God made heaven and earth. This opening line
seems to contain a "when" clause similar to the first line of
Enuma Elish and other creation stories. (See note on *Enuma
Elish* I:1-9 and Conclusion on comparing myths.) But the Hebrew
word which begins the hymn is ambiguous. It is variously
translated, "In the beginning of creation, God created heaven
and earth"; or "In the beginning of creation, when God created
heaven and earth." The difference is important since a "when"
clause would suggest that God began creating after matter had
first come into existence. The other translation suggests
that God began to create out of nothing. The ambiguity, however,
cannot be resolved by reference to the text.

Made. The Hebrew word *bara* in the Old Testament is used
exclusively of God's activity. (See Isaiah 40-45.) *Bara*
describes God's creation of the world, work in history, and
founding of the Israelite nation. Its meaning has less to do
with physical creation than with God's saving action and
imposition of order where there was chaos. Since P had just
come out of the chaos of exile, he stressed God's role as a
restorer of order.

1:2. Without form and void. Hebrew *tobu wa-bohu* is an
onomatopoetic phrase meaning a formless waste.

With darkness over the face of the abyss. "Abyss," Hebrew
tehom, is etymologically related to Tiamat, the Mesopotamian
goddess who is one of the original forces in the world (*Enuma
Elish* I:1-9). But here the abyss is simply the background for
creation and is not divine.

Mighty wind. Hebrew *ruah* means "wind," "breath," and
"spirit." It is used in the Hebrew scriptures as a figure for
the creative power of God in action. *Elohim* can mean either
"mighty, awesome, divine" or "of God." Thus, the phrase is
variously translated "the mighty wind" or "the spirit of God."
Earlier, it may have been used to describe a storm god.

1:6. Vault. "Firmament," the traditional translation,
means approximately the same thing. It comes from the Latin
word *firmamentum* which means "something made solid." The
original Hebrew word means "a plate beaten out." P thought of
the sky as a thin sheet of metal stretched out to form the
dome of the sky.

1:16. P purposely avoids the words *sun* and *moon* since the common Semitic words for sun and moon were also divine names. In the ancient Near East, P's stance was quite revolutionary. See Introduction to the Creation Hymn.

1:22. So he blessed them and said, "Be fruitful and increase." With the creation of animals and later of humanity, a new element, the blessing, is introduced. The Hebrew word for "blessing" means giving the power to be fertile. Since both receive God's blessing, P is stressing the kinship of humanity and the animal kingdom.

1:26. Let us make man. The impersonal phrase, "Let there be" is changed here to "let us." There is no thoroughly satisfactory explanation of the plural here. One explanation, that the plural refers to the Trinity, can be discounted on historical grounds: the Trinity is a much later Christian doctrine which would be completely foreign to P. Other possible explanations include 1) a grammatical plural, 2) a royal or rhetorical plural, or 3) a reference to a heavenly council:

1) Speiser (*The Anchor Bible: Genesis*) contends that the plural is used here simply because P used *elohim*, a plural noun, for his God. He therefore translates the phrase, "I will make man in my image."

2) If a royal plural is used for God, there are no convincing uses of it elsewhere.

3) The idea of God being with his heavenly court is quite common throughout the Old Testament. For example, there are references to the host of heaven (1 Kings 22:19-22) and the council of the holy ones (Psalms 89:6-8). Some scholars see a momentary lapse into polytheism here in which God, like the Mesopotamian Anu, is conferring with a council of gods. But P is a very careful theologian who is quite precise in his language. So it may be that this phrase simply preserves an archaic expression.

Man. The Hebrew word for "man," *adam*, is a collective noun for the human race and is never used in the plural. It means humanity, encompassing both male and female. The other two meanings of *adam*, the male of the species and the proper name, Adam, do not apply here. These uses can be found in the story of Adam and Eve.

In our image and likeness. This phrase gives important insight into P's view of human nature. Hebrew *selem*, "image," means a duplicate and is often used to designate an idol of a god. This was a bold word for P to use, given his opposition to idols (Exodus 20:4). P seems to be saying that human beings are the only allowable images of God since they partake in divine life. "Likeness," Hebrew *demuth*, may have been added to tone down the bold *selem* since *demuth* often suggests only a vague similarity.

To rule. Hebrew *radah* is often translated "have dominion" to bring out its royal connotations since the word was frequently used of kings. The human race, then, is to assume a king's responsibility to the rest of creation. "To rule" and "to subdue," Hebrew *kabas*, in the next verse have often been taken as a license for humanity to abuse and deplete the earth. The literal meanings of *radah*, "to tread" or "to trample," and *kabas*, "to stamp," substantiate this reading. But recently, some theologians, such as Claus Westermann (*Creation*), have challenged this idea. They stress that a king has responsibility to care for his realm, not abuse it.

1:27. So God created man. The Hebrew word *bara*, "created," is the same word used in 1:1 for the creation of the world. The triple use of *bara* in this line emphasizes P's point that the creation of humanity is the climax of all creation.

Male and female he created them. Only of human creation does P make a point of noting the difference in sex. Obviously, he presumes male and female in the creation of animals. P wants to make a point of the creation of sexuality in order to emphasize that God is beyond sexuality. Unlike the Mesopotamians for whom deities were male and female, P neither deifies nor abhors sex. It is one of the good things in creation.

The structure of this line is also meaningful. Semitic hymns often use parallel structures in which the second half of the verse explains the first. Thus, P seems to be saying that "male and female" both existed from the beginning; he does not picture human creation in two separate acts as in the story of Adam and Eve (2:7 and 2:22).

But this structure has been interpreted in many ways. Rabbi Jeremiah B. Eleazar, for instance, thought that it signified the creation of a single individual, an androgyne. Another rabbi thought it meant that a two-faced person was created and subsequently severed in two. Augustine and other Christian writers called the latter idea a "Jewish fable." The Neo-platonist Philo inferred that the original human was androgynous. The division into male and female, then, belonged to a later and lower state of creation, and the divisions would be reunited when all creation returns to its maker. But many other scholars believe that such a precise theologian as P would be more explicit if he meant to indicate androgyny.

1:31. And it was very good. The refrain, "and it was good," is put in the superlative here. As God finishes his work, he revels in it. Joy in the created world distinguishes P from his polytheistic neighbors. The Hebrew word for "good," *tob*, has a broader range than our English word. It encompasses both good and beautiful and is seen in experience and encounters rather than in things.

2:2-3. P arranges God's works in six days so that God rests on the seventh. P may be giving an etiological explanation for the Sabbath since the Hebrew word for "rested," *shabath*, resembles Sabbath. Sabbath and circumcision were trademarks of the Hebrews in the exilic period. See Chapter 8.

STUDY QUESTIONS ON THE CREATION HYMN

1. The First Five Days (1:1-23)

   What does the original earth look like? Of what material is it composed? Note the sequence of events during the first three days. What plan do they reveal? What methods of creation does God use? How is the pattern changed during the third, fourth, and fifth days? Why does God create the sun, moon, and stars? Compare to *Enuma Elish* and Hesiod's *Theogony*. How do the sea monsters fit into the scheme of creation?

2. The Sixth and Seventh Days (1:24-2:4)

   What does God create on the sixth day? Why does he create the human race? What does he use as a model? What does he give them to eat? How are humans and animals treated in similar ways by God? Why is the seventh day holy?

3. General Questions

   Describe God as he is depicted in this hymn. How powerful is he? How much control does he have over the world? Is he good? Compare to the gods who create the world in *Enuma Elish* and Hesiod's *Theogony*.

   Is the world God created a logical one? How does it differ from the world depicted in *Enuma Elish*? In Hesiod's *Theogony*? How do human beings fit into the scheme of creation?

Chapter 3

From Greece: Hesiod's *Theogony*

INTRODUCTION p. 48
OUTLINE p. 53
SELECTIONS p. 54
NOTES p. 63
STUDY QUESTIONS p. 66

INTRODUCTION TO HESIOD'S *THEOGONY*

Hesiod set a difficult task for himself when he began to compose the *Theogony*. Early in the poem he invokes the Muses:

> Celebrate the sacred race of everlasting gods
> who were born from Gaia and starry Ouranos,
> from dark Night and the salty sea.
> Tell about the gods and earth at the very beginning,
> about the rivers and the limitless sea
> with stormy waves,
> the brilliant stars and the broad sky above.
> Tell how the gods divided their wealth
> and distributed their honors among themselves
> and how they first came to possess
> the peaks and vales of Olympos.
>
> (*Theogony* 105-13)

The poem covers all these topics and several more. It contains long genealogical lists of the Greek gods and stories of succession which culminate in Zeus' reign. It also includes tales of such minor deities as Hekate and Styx and of such monsters as Medusa and the hydra. Although it does not account for the origin of the human race, it does tell the story of the first woman. It even includes a detailed description of Tartaros, the underworld where the defeated Titans are imprisoned. Despite all of this, however, the poem as we have it is not complete. It breaks off just as Hesiod is about to begin a catalogue of mortal women who bore children of gods.

Such a mixture of genealogies and stories makes Hesiod's purpose difficult to define. In general, it is clear that the divine genealogies at least provide a framework for the stories. When Prometheus' name occurs in the list, for example, Hesiod digresses to tell how Prometheus outwitted Zeus and how his trickery led to the creation of the first woman. In a similar way, he tells stories about Hekate, Styx, and many other gods. Some scholars have attempted to find some thematic unity in this sprawling poem. M. L. West, for example, has tried to explain the link between the genealogies and the stories in terms of an overall plan. (See M. L. West's edition of Hesiod, *Theogony*, p. 16ff.) Unfortunately, so little is known about Hesiod's life, historical background, and literary sources that such explanations cannot be conclusive. (See Chapter 9.)

Creation in Hesiod's *Theogony*

For our purposes, however, it is not necessary to find a unified theme for the entire poem. Instead, we can concentrate only on those parts which are relevant to the three main themes of creation accounts: theogony, cosmogony, and succession. Much of Hesiod's poem is centered on these topics. The genealogical lists dominate the poem, and the stories of Ouranos, Kronos, and Zeus are more closely linked to the genealogies than Hesiod's other digressions.

Yet, Hesiod himself states that he had other themes in mind as well. The *Theogony* is not just an account of the origins of the world. It is, at least in part, a poem in praise of Zeus. The invocation reveals this purpose indirectly when Hesiod asks the Muses to sing to him. He wants them to sing the same song which "delights [Zeus'] great soul." Surely, Zeus would have been pleased to hear Hesiod's song. It tells how he has come to rule the gods, how he populates the world with his own offspring, and how he establishes a lasting, civilized order where before there was savagery. Such a propagandistic purpose is common in creation stories. Both *Enuma Elish* and the Israelite Creation Hymn use accounts of creation to praise their respective gods. Like Hesiod's *Theogony*, they glorify the mighty deeds of their creator-gods to prove that these gods rightly rule the world.

Hesiod's nearly comprehensive lists of the gods, however, overshadow the theme of Zeus' glory. The genealogies account for such non-Olympian deities as the fifty daughters of Nereus and the children of Night, making the poem predominantly a theogony (birth of the gods). Moreover, Hesiod attempts to make his poem a definitive catalogue of the Greek pantheon. Minor deities, monsters, and demi-gods are included as well as the major gods.

It is not known how original Hesiod's classification is since most of his possible sources are now lost. But it is clear that cataloguing has a long tradition both in Greek culture and in others. For example, Homer's *Iliad* lists the ships of the various Greek tribes who fought at Troy. Likewise, the

Israelites include many genealogical lists of their ancestors in their sacred writings. The Mesopotamians also had a penchant for listing. At various times they made comprehensive lists of their gods as well as other things. (See Part Three on cultural background.)

In Hesiod's *Theogony*, however, the genealogies also provide a complete cosmogony (origin of the world). Unlike the Mesopotamian and Israelite creation myths, it depicts a world which is developed almost completely through sexual generation. There is no Marduk who forms the world out of the body of a defeated goddess nor any Yahweh who plans a logical structure culminating in the creation of the human race. Instead, the world grows as each new generation of gods is born. Gaia (the earth) comes into existence on her own. But the Sky, the Ocean (a river which encircles the earth), the seas, the forests, and all the rest are born, not made. The natural laws which govern the universe--Night, Day, and the Hours--are born of goddesses. Finally, concepts of social interaction such as Justice, Strife, the Graces, the Fates, and even Death are all products of sexual generation. It is not surprising, then, that Hesiod places Eros (sexual desire) with the primeval forces. Like Chaos, Tartaros, and Gaia, Eros shows his influence continually from the very beginning.

Within this structure of a living, reproducing, and con-stantly changing world, Hesiod develops the theme of succession. In particular, he explains the rise to power of Ouranos, Kronos, and finally Zeus. Each story enhances the image of a world generating itself as the gods produce more offspring. Taken together, the three stories show an evolution toward a more civilized world. Cosmic order replaces chaos, political stabil-ity replaces violence, and male rule replaces female. In the first generation, Gaia originally dominates with her unlimited capacity to produce new features of the world. But soon Ouranos, her own offspring, attempts to hold her in check and maintain supremacy over her. While in power, each succeeding male ruler is reluctant to give way to progress and so precipitates his own downfall. First Ouranos, with brute savagery, tries to prevent Gaia from giving birth to the next generation of gods. Filled to the bursting point with her unborn children, Gaia then plots Ouranos' demise. Next, Kronos, only slightly less savage, gobbles down his children but is eventually forced to vomit them up. Finally, Zeus, more clever than the others, swallows his first wife before she can conceive his heir-apparent.

Zeus also maintains his power by less violent means. His political skill makes the Cyclopes and Hundred-Arms his allies although the previous rulers imprisoned them. Furthermore, instead of trying to inhibit the growth of the world, Zeus is the most prolific sire of all the gods. His seven wives produce numerous offspring who personify an advance in culture and civilization. Law, Justice, the Graces, the Muses, and many others all help Zeus establish a new era of order and stability reminiscent of that which Marduk establishes in *Enuma Elish*.

Hesiod and the Mythological Tradition

Hesiod, then, works within a mythological tradition similar to that of the ancient Near East. He even uses some Near Eastern stories. For example, a Hurrian creation myth shows some similarity to Hesiod's succession story. In the Hurrian myth, the god Kumarbi castrates his father and swallows his phallus. Later Kumarbi is deposed by a storm god who establishes a long lasting rule. Although different in detail, this myth develops the same motifs of castration, ingestion, and hatred for the father which Hesiod later uses in his own stories. (See Peter Wolcot, *Hesiod and the Near East*.)

Despite these similarities to Near Eastern mythology, Hesiod's emphasis on conflict, reliance on Homer, faith in the Greek pantheon, and even his interest in origins are firmly rooted in Greek traditions. Greek writers, however, have shown very little agreement about the origins of the gods and the world. Homer, for example, alludes to Ocean as the "genesis of the gods" and "the genesis of all" without attempting to explain these origins (*Iliad* 14:201,246). A later writer, Pherecydes, also wrote a *Theogony* in which Zeus shares the responsibility for creating the world. In this story, Zeus, Earth, and Time have always existed. Zeus gives Earth a beautiful covering (her foliage), and Time produces fire, air, and water from which other things are made. Many other Greek writers, such as Sophocles, Aeschylus, and Aristophanes, also attempted their own explanations of the world's origin. (See West's "Prolegomena" to *Theogony*.)

Not long after Hesiod, some Greek thinkers attempted to break away from the mythological approach to origins. Starting in the sixth century, B.C., various "physical" cosmogonies were proposed. Thales, for example, thought that the world originated with water, Heraclitus with fire, and Empedocles with a combination of earth, water, air, and fire. Although these explanations have little in common with Hesiod's mythological approach, they do indicate the widespread interest in origins among the Greeks.

Another sixth century philosopher, Anaximander, proposed an idea which has some similarity to Hesiod's. He thought that a kind of unformed matter was the original substance. He called it *to apeiron*, the boundless, indeterminate, or indefinite. Although similar to Hesiod's Chaos, it is not a living god, cannot be found in one location, and produces an infinite number of worlds without the help of the gods. These worlds all separate from *to apeiron* and will eventually return to it. Anaximander, then, tried to explain scientifically the same things which Hesiod explained in a mostly mythological way.

These first Greek scientists, searching for the original substance, owed much to Hesiod. For his *Theogony* represents an earlier attempt to search for the origin of all things. Hesiod found most of his answers in the mythological tradition which surrounded him. In many ways, his conclusions were similar to those of the other two cultures which we are studying. He maintained that the world began in chaos, proceeded through a period of violence, and finally was ruled by a god who brought a new order and stability to the world.

OUTLINE OF HESIOD'S *THEOGONY*

A. Hymn and Invocation to the Muses (1-115)

B. First Generation and Succession (116-210)*
   1. First Beings: Chaos, Gaia, Eros, Tartaros (116-22)
   2. Children of Chaos and of Gaia (123-53)
   3. Castration of Ouranos and Birth of Aphrodite (154-210)

C. Second Generation and Succession (211-735)
   1. Descendents of Night and of Pontos (211-336)
   2. Children of Various Titans (337-452)
   3. Children of Kronos and Rheia (453-506)*
   4. Children of Iapetos and Story of First Woman (507-616)
   5. War in Heaven (617-735)*

D. Description of Tartaros and Fight with Typhon (736-880)

E. Third Generation and Succession (881-1019)
   1. Zeus' Kingship and Marriages (881-929)*
   2. Children of Other Gods and Mortals (930-1019)

Starred passages are included in the readings which follow.

HESIOD'S *THEOGONY*

First Beings (116-22)

First of all there was Chaos; and then broad-breasted Gaia,
always the secure home of all the immortals,
who live at the top of snowy Olympos;
and gloomy Tartaros in the innermost recess of wide-
pathed earth; and the most beautiful of the immortal gods,   120
Eros the knee-buckler, who seduces reason
and common sense in all gods and all mortals.

Children of Chaos and of Gaia (123-53)

Out of Chaos, black Erebos and Night were born.
Out of Night were born both Aither and Day,
whom she conceived after making love with Erebos.   125
Gaia first bore starry Ouranos, her equal,
so that he might cover her all over
and always be the secure home of the blessed gods.
Then she bore the high mountains, the beautiful dwellings
of the godly Nymphs, who live in the wooded heights.   130
She also bore Pontos, the restless sea with its raging
waves. All of these she conceived without love's embrace.
But then she slept with Ouranos and bore deep-eddying
Ocean and Koios, Kreion, Hyperion, Iapetos,
Theia, Rheia, Themis, Mnemosyne,   135
golden-crowned Phoibe and lovely Tethys. After these
her youngest and most terrible son Kronos was born,
the most insidious of children, who hated
his over-sexed father. Then she bore the arrogant Cyclopes,
Brontes, Steropes, and stormy Arges,   140
who later made thunder and the thunderbolt for Zeus.
They resembled the gods in every way except that
each had a single eye in the middle of his forehead;

54

they were aptly named Cyclopes (circle-eyed) because of
the one round eye in the middle of their foreheads;   145
there was strength, power, and skill in their works.
Then three more sons were born to Gaia and Ouranos;
they were large and mighty and should not be named,
Kottos, Briareos, and Gyges, arrogant children.
Each had fifty pairs of shoulders, with a hundred arms   150
shooting out in all directions; a head grew out of each pair,
above the massive body; no statue should be made of them!
Awesome was the monstrous strength in their huge forms.

Castration of Ouranos and Birth of Aphrodite (154–210)

All those born to Gaia and Ouranos were the most terrible
of children and were hated by their father   155
from the beginning. As soon as they were born,
he would hide them all away in the hollows of Gaia
    and would not let them out to the light;
Ouranos delighted in his evil work.
But huge Gaia groaned deep within from being overstuffed
and plotted a crafty evil trick.   160
Immediately she created grey flint, fashioned a great
scythe from it, and told her own children about it.
Although grieving in her own heart, she encouraged them:
"My children, your father has gone amok. If you believe me,
we can get revenge on your mean, spiteful father.   165
For he was the first to devise shameful deeds."
Thus she spoke. Fear seized them all, and none of them
said a word until the insidious hulk Kronos summoned up
the courage and accosted his dear mother:
"Mother, since I do not care for our infamous father,   170
I promise that I will do this.
For he was the first to devise shameful deeds."
Thus he spoke, and huge Gaia rejoiced greatly within.
Then, she hid him in ambush, placed in his hands the scythe
with saw-like teeth, and revealed the whole plot to him.   175
Soon immense Ouranos came, bringing on the night.
    Eager to make love,
he threw himself all around Gaia; instantly, his son Kronos
stuck out his left hand from his hiding place
and with his right hand snatched the great scythe with its long,
saw-like teeth. Furiously, he mowed down   180
his father's genitals and threw them back behind him.

They did not fly fruitlessly from his hand,
for Gaia accepted all the bloody drops that darted out.
As the years rolled by, she bore the powerful Furies
and the large Giants who glittered in their shiny armor   185
and carried long spears in their hands. She also bore
the Nymphs, whom people over the wide earth named Meliai
    after the ash trees.
As soon as Kronos ploughed off the genitals with the flint
and threw them from the land into the surging sea,
they drifted over the deep for a long time,   190
and white foam surrounded the immortal flesh. In it a maiden
was nurtured. First she approached holy Kythera;
from there she floated to the island of Cyprus,
where she emerged a lovely, innocent goddess.
Grass grew up under her slender feet. Both gods and men   195
call her Aphrodite because she was nurtured from the foam
and well-crowned Kytheria because she landed on Kythera.
They also called her Cyprus-born
because she was born on sea-washed Cyprus,
and laughter-loving because she sprang from the genitals.   200
Eros and handsome Desire joined her as soon as
she was born; immediately she entered the gods' ranks.
From the beginning, she has held this place of honor
among mortals and immortals, and she has been allotted
girlish small-talk, smiles, deceits,   205
sweet delight, sex, and tenderness.
The immense father Ouranos tauntingly called the children
whom he had fathered by the nickname "Titans,"
because he said that they, by tightening their muscles,
had done a violent deed, for which they would later be punished.

    211-452. This passage includes long genealogies listing
the descendants of Night, of the sea god, Pontos, and of Ouranos.
It also contains stories about the river Styx and about monsters
such as the Medusa, and the three-headed dog of the underworld.
The passage concludes with an elaborate tribute to the lasting
power of Hekate whom Zeus honors above all others.

Children of Kronos and Rheia (453-506)

Rheia, overpowered by Kronos, bore him glorious children:
Hestia, Demeter, gold-sandalled Hera,
strong, pitiless Hades who has his home   455
under the earth, the crashing Earthshaker Poseidon,
and Zeus the planner, father of gods and men,
whose thunder shakes the wide earth.

Hulking Kronos gulped them down as each one
dropped from Rheia's holy womb to her knees   460
so that no other noble descendant of Ouranos
should have the honors of a king among the immortals.
For he learned from Gaia and starry Ouranos
that he was fated to be overthrown by his own
more powerful son, through the plan of mighty Zeus.   465
For that reason he did not keep a blind man's watch.
Waiting without sleep, he gulped down his children.
Insufferable grief overwhelmed Rheia. But when she was
about to give birth to Zeus, father of gods and men,
she begged her own parents, Gaia and starry Ouranos,   470
to help her devise a plan. She wanted to bear her child
in secret and repay the insidious hulk Kronos
for injuring Ouranos and gulping down her children.
They listened to their daughter
and advised her of the fate awaiting   475
king Kronos and his strong-spirited son.
They sent her to Lyktos, in the fertile land of Crete,
when she was about to bear the youngest of her children,
mighty Zeus. Huge Gaia took him from his mother
to nourish him on wide Crete and raise him herself.   480
Carrying him through the fleeting black night, she
arrived first at Lyktos; there she took him in her arms
and hid him in a deep cave far under the holy earth
in the thickly wooded Mount Aigaion. But she wrapped up
a large stone in a blanket and handed it   485
to Kronos, the lord and king of the earlier gods.
Grabbing it, he stuffed it down into his belly,
the stupid fool. He did not know that his son was replaced
by the stone, that Zeus remained safe and sound,
that he would soon overpower his father with force,   490
expel him from honor, and become the ruler of the immortals.
As the years rolled by, the strength and glorious limbs
of the lord Zeus grew rapidly; and in time,
the insidious hulk, Kronos, was trapped by the intricate
scheme of Gaia and was beaten by the craft and strength   495
of his son. So he spit out his offspring again. But first
he vomited up the stone which was the last thing
he had gulped down; and Zeus set it down
on the wide-pathed earth, in holy Pytho
    below wooded Parnassos,
to be a sign henceforth, a wonder to mortals.   500

Then he freed the Cyclopes from the ruinous chains
with which their father Ouranos had irresponsibly bound them.
They gratefully remembered Zeus' good deed
and gave him thunder, the fiery thunderbolt,
and lightning, which huge Gaia had kept hidden before.   505
With these weapons, he rules mortals and immortals.

    507-616. This passage tells how Zeus afflicts the four sons
of the Titan Iapetos. Epimetheus foolishly accepts his gift of
the first woman. Menoitios is cast down into the underworld.
Atlas is fated to hold up the heavens on his head. Finally,
Prometheus is chained to a pillar for daring to match wits with
Zeus; each night an eagle eats his liver. Hesiod then digresses
to tell how Prometheus tries to trick Zeus and how Zeus retali-
ates with the creation of the first woman.

War in Heaven (617-735)

When father Ouranos was angered at Briareos, Kottos
and Gyges, he bound them with strong chains--
he was awed by their fighting spirit, their shape
and sheer size; he pounded them down   620
    into the wide-pathed earth.
Nursing their wounds, they sat underground
at the remotest edge of the immense earth. They fretted
for a very long time with sadness in their hearts.
But Zeus, son of Kronos, and the other immortal gods whom
fair-haired Rheia bore after love-making with Kronos   625
brought them back up to the light
    with the shrewd advice of Gaia;
for she told these gods the whole story of their fate
in order to fulfill her hopes and obtain victory with them.
For too long a time, the Titans and the gods
born of Kronos fought against one another   630
in powerful combat, a heart-rending task;
on one side the noble Titans from high Othrys;
on the other the gods from Olympos, givers of good fortune,
whom fair-haired Rheia bore after Kronos bedded her.
They fought each other continually   635
for ten full years in a heart-rending struggle.
There was no let-up in the harsh conflict; neither side
held an advantage; victory was balanced equally between them.
But when Zeus had furnished the Hundred-Arms everything
they needed, including nectar and ambrosia   640
which the gods themselves eat, their manly courage grew.
Then Zeus, father of gods and men, spoke to them:
"Hear me, glorious sons of Gaia and Ouranos,   643

so that I may speak as my heart urges me.   645
For too long a time now we have been fighting
for victory and power without a rest,
those of us born of Kronos against the Titan gods.
But come, show your great strength and unconquerable arms
against the Titans in this bleak battle. Remember   650
my friendly gesture toward you. You have suffered so much,
but, because of my plans, you have come back up to the light
from your hard bed of chains and murky darkness."
Thus Zeus spoke, and blameless Kottos shot back:
"Chief, what you say is no secret, but we also know   655
that your thinking and planning are the greatest,
and that by your plans you protect immortals
from the icy curse of evil.
Lord son of Kronos, our plight was hopeless,
but thanks to your clever planning, we have returned   660
     from cruel chains.
Now with unbending purpose and willing heart
we shall defend your power in terrible battle
and fight against the Titans in powerful combat."
Thus he spoke, and the gods, givers of good fortune,
applauded what they heard. Now their hearts craved war   665
even more than before, and on that day
both male and female gods began a horrible battle.
The Titans fought against those born of Kronos
and those Zeus brought to the light from dank Erebos.
They were terrible and powerful in their armor-clad force.   670
All were alike: each had fifty pairs of shoulders
with a hundred arms shooting out in all directions;
a head grew out of each pair above the massive body.
At that time, the Hundred-Arms stood against the Titans
in bleak battle, scooping up huge rocks   675
     in their massive hands;
On the other side, the Titans hurriedly strengthened
their flanks; both sides at once showed their might.
All around, the boundless sea resounded in horror,
the earth roared loudly, the wide heaven groaned
     in a violent
upheaval, and towering Olympos   680
     was rocked from its foundation,
all because of the explosion of immortal battle.
A rumbling quake ripped through the dark underworld,
caused by the gods' thundering feet and the deafening whirl

of swift spears flying in pursuit. They flung their painful
shafts at one another. The bellowing of both sides   685
reached the starry sky. They clashed with a loud battle cry.
Then Zeus no longer held himself back, but at once his fury
strengthened him. He unleashed his full force.
Flashing down, now from the sky, now from Olympos, he struck
continuously. The thunderbolts from his massive hand   690
smacked together with the thunder and lightning, emitting
a dense godly flame. All around, the life-giving earth
crackled with fire, and all around, the unspeakably immense
woods crashed down; everything on the earth boiled,
even the river of Ocean and the restless sea.   695
The stifling blast surrounded the earthly Titans,
and an indescribable flame hovered over the bright atmosphere.
The glaring brightness of the lightning and thunder bolts
robbed the Titans of their eyesight, despite their strength.
The extraordinary heat even choked Chaos. To any eyes   700
seeing it and any ears hearing the sounds,
it seemed to be the time when earth and wide sky collided.
So great a roar arose when the sky came crashing down
from above, and the earth collapsed underneath;
such a roar occurred when the gods met in battle.   705
The winds stirred up earthquakes, dust storms,
thunder, lightning, and burning thunderbolts, the shafts
of mighty Zeus; those winds carried the screams and warcries
into the midst of both armies; a deafening noise
arose as the troops showed their valor   710
    in the terrible struggle.
Each side fought unceasingly, holding off the other
in a stalemate until the battle turned.
Now Kottos, Briareos, and Gyges, ever bloodthirsty,
stirred up the sharp contest in the front lines. Easily
they flung three hundred rocks with their massive arms,   715
one after the other, and their missiles enveloped the Titans.
In spite of the Titans' high spirits,
the Hundred-Arms beat them soundly, sent them
under the wide-pathed earth and bound them in painful chains.
They relegated them to gloomy Tartaros, as far   720
beneath the earth as the sky is above it.
For a bronze anvil, falling down from the sky for nine
nights and days, would reach the earth on the tenth;
but again for nine nights and days a bronze anvil,
falling down from earth, would reach   725

Tartaros on the tenth.
Around Tartaros stands a bronze wall. Three layers
of cloudy night flow around its throat. Above it,
the roots of the earth and the restless sea spring up.
There under the misty darkness, the Titan gods are hidden,
according to the plan of Zeus the cloud-gatherer,   730
in a dank space at the ends of the huge earth.
For them there is no exit; Poseidon set up bronze
gates and a wall surrounds it on both sides.
There, too, dwell the stout-hearted Kottos, Briareos,
and Gyges, staunch guards of aegis-bearing Zeus.   735

736-880. This passage continues to describe the underworld
and tells the story of Zeus' battle with the ugly monster,
Typhon, the tornado-spirit.

Zeus' Kingship and Marriages (881-929)

After the blessed gods had completed their task
and forced the Titans to give up their prerogatives,
they urged far-seeing Zeus to be king and lord
over the immortals with the shrewd advice of Gaia.
He then dispensed offices among them.   885
Now that he was king of the gods, Zeus appointed Metis
his first wife; of all gods and mortals, she knew the most.
But when she was about to give birth to the goddess
owl-eyed Athena, Zeus deceived her with flattering words
and stuffed her down into his belly,   890
because of the shrewd advice of Gaia and starry Ouranos.
They gave him this advice so that no other eternal god
would have kingship instead of Zeus. For it was fated
that Metis would bear highly intelligent children:
first the owl-eyed girl Tritogeneia (Athena)   895
whose strength and wise planning would equal her father's,
then a child of arrogant heart who would become
king of gods and men. But before that could happen,
Zeus stuffed Metis down into his belly
so that she might plan good and evil together with him.   900
Second, he married sleek Themis who bore the Hours,
Eunomia (Law), Dike (Justice) and flourishing Eirene (Peace)
who watch over the deeds of mortals;
and the Fates, Klotho, Lakhesis, and Atropos, to whom
wise Zeus gave the greatest honor. They give to mortals   905
the ability to possess good or evil.
Next, Eurynome, the shapely daughter of Ocean,

bore to Zeus the three fair-cheeked Graces,
Aglaia, Euphrosyne and lovely Thalia.
Knee-buckling desire flows out from their gleaming eyes   910
as they peek alluringly from under their eyelids.
Then Zeus came to the bed of all-nourishing Demeter:
she bore white-armed Persephone whom Hades snatched away
from her mother, and wise Zeus let him have her.
Fifth, he loved beautiful-haired Mnemosyne (Memory),   915
from whom the nine golden-crowned Muses were born
who enjoy festivities and the pleasures of singing.
Then Leto mingled in love's embrace with aegis-bearing Zeus
and bore Apollo and arrow-firing Artemis,
the most charming of all the Olympians.   920
Last of all, he made Hera his fertile wife.
She bore Hebe, Ares, and Eileithyia after joining
in love-making with the king of gods and men.
But on his own Zeus bore from his head owl-eyed Athena,
the fearsome, tireless, rabble-rousing army commander,   925
a lady whom war, fighting, and pandemonium delight.
Without love's embrace, Hera bore famous Hephaistos
because she quarrelled and was angry with her husband.
Hephaistos surpassed all the Olympians in craftsmanship.

930-1020. This final passage catalogues the children of
Poseidon and other gods and ends with the marriages of ten
goddesses and ten mortals.

NOTES TO HESIOD'S *THEOGONY*

1-115. The opening passage, not included in the readings, is a hymn to the Muses, the nine goddesses of inspiration. It describes their birth, their activities on Mount Helikon and on Mount Olympos, their songs about Zeus' just reign, and the gift of poetic inspiration which they grant to Hesiod. Just before the main part of the poem begins, Hesiod begs the Muses to give him the ability to sing about the origins of the gods.

116. Chaos. The Greek word *chaos* suggests gaping, yawning, wide-openness that is often associated with darkness in the ancient Near East. It is Hesiod's word for what we would call primeval, undifferentiated matter. He seems to have had something of the modern meaning of *chaos* in mind since he describes a progression from chaos to order in the poem. See Plato's *Timaeus* 30 for a more advanced idea of this progression. Some translators mistakenly translate Hesiod's *chaos* as "chasm" or "gap," thinking that the poet meant to designate a space between the sky and the earth.

There was. Hesiod uses the verb *genet'*, "it occurred" or "there was," to indicate spontaneous generation of these original forces. Chaos, Gaia, Eros, and Tartaros came into existence without the help of any outside force. This concept is quite different from the one in the Israelite Creation Hymn. (See Note on Genesis 1:1.)

119. Tartaros. See 720ff. for Hesiod's description.

121. Eros. Hesiod may have originated the idea of Eros, "sexual desire," as a primeval cosmic force. His idea, however, is consistent with the ambivalence which Greek culture shows about the erotic. Eros is the most beautiful of the gods, but his effect on both gods and men can be debilitating. The Eros Hesiod depicts here should not be equated with the baby Eros, better known to us as Cupid, whose arrows make one swoon in love. This conception of Eros became prevalent in later antiquity.

Knee-buckler. The Greek word is *lusimelēs* which also can mean "limb-freeing" or "limb-relaxing." It is used in Greek to describe both sleep and love.

63

126-28. Gaia, Mother Earth, is the initiator here. Ouranos, Sky, is her pale complement. Although her influence gradually declines as new gods come to power, Gaia is the only deity who remains prominent from the beginning of the poem to the succession of Zeus. Ouranos is the sky which the Greeks pictured as a solid, flat roof covering the earth. The union of sky and earth in a cosmic marriage is seen frequently in mythologies worldwide. (See Mircea Eliade, "The Sky and Sky Gods," in *Patterns in Comparative Religion*.)

133-38. This is a list of the twelve Titans who are an older generation of gods no longer active in the world. Many peoples in the ancient Near East believed in such gods. For example, the Hittites had a group known as "the former gods."

134. *Ocean*. Ocean is a river which surrounds the earth. In Homer, the river Ocean is the origin of the gods. See *Iliad* 14:201,246.

139-46. *Cyclopes*. Since the Cyclopes make thunder for Zeus, Hesiod gives them names which suggest thunder; *Brontes*, for example, comes from the Greek word for thunder, and *Steropes* from the Greek word for lightning. Although they look like the Cyclopes in Homer's *Odyssey*, Hesiod's Cyclopes come from a different tradition. They are not related to the giant Polyphemus whom Odysseus blinded and who was a son of Poseidon.

152. *No statue should be made of them*. This phrase translates one Greek word which is parallel in meaning to the more familiar Hesiodic "should not be named." Just as it was dangerous to name a god since the god might then appear, it was also dangerous to make likenesses of the god for the same reason. This would be particularly true of the Hundred-Arm monsters.

182-87. Here Hesiod is following the tradition that every part of a god is fertile. Even the drops of blood from Ouranos produce offspring which include monsters and godlike figures. See also 133-53 for a similar combination of Ouranos' children.

191-92. This description of the formation of Aphrodite is the original source of many later literary and artistic works. Perhaps the most famous is Botticelli's painting of *The Birth of Venus* which pictures the goddess floating to the island on an oyster shell.

479. *Gaia*. Although Hesiod uses a pronoun here, we have inserted Gaia's name to clarify the story. The pronoun, however, might refer to Rheia. Either way there are inconsistencies in the story at this point which make interpretation difficult.

617-735. *War in Heaven*. This entire episode is confusing and repetitious. The Hundred-Arms (Kottos, Briareos, and Gyges) enter the battle several times (639ff. and 713ff.), and Zeus nearly wins the war singlehandedly at one point (687ff.). Apparently, Hesiod fused several older accounts of the war into one but did not iron out all of the inconsistencies. His main theme of Zeus' glorification, however, is emphasized throughout the episode.

636. For ten full years. Ten years was the conventional length of a great war. For example, the Trojan War lasted ten years. See Homer's *Iliad*.

735. Aegis-bearing Zeus. The aegis is Zeus' shield, a piece of armor so terrible that just the sight of it terrified his enemies. Athena is the only other deity allowed to use the aegis.

886-929. Zeus' Marriages. Zeus' family is a combination of personal deities and personifications of abstract qualities. Some like Athena, Ares, Apollo, and Artemis, are traditional Olympians. Others personify the civilization which Zeus establishes: Metis (Widsom), Dike (Justice), Eirene (Peace), Eunomia (Good Law), and the three Graces.

Most of these personifications are probably Hesiod's invention. But a few, such as Themis (Established Custom), Hebe (Youth), Moirai (the Fates), and Eileithyia (Birth), were used before Hesiod's time. In Hesiod's view, then, Zeus' family represents the positive virtues of civilization. Their opposites, Ignorance, Deceit, Lies, and the like, are all children of Night. See 211ff.

890. Stuffed her down into his belly. This action is reminiscent of the savagery of Ouranos and Kronos. But Zeus acts sooner than the other rulers when he swallows Metis before she conceives Zeus' heir-apparent. Some Near Eastern myths, such as the story of Kumarbi, have similar patterns. But Hesiod also uses this event to strengthen Zeus' claim to kingship. When he swallows Metis, Zeus acquires the wisdom she personifies (900.)

904. The Fates, Klotho, Lakhesis, and Atropos. Greek *Moirai*, "fates" or "portions," are here represented as daughters of Zeus. Klotho is the "spinner" of the thread of life, Lakhesis is the "distributor", and Atropos is the "inflexible one" against whom there was no appeal. Since Homer refers to Fate in the singular, Hesiod is our earliest source of this idea and the names of the three Fates. In later Greek literature, the fates were often pictured as independent of and above Zeus.

924. Athena. Here Zeus supposedly produces Athena on his own. But earlier (895) Hesiod has told us that Metis was pregnant with Athena when Zeus swallowed her. Hesiod may well have been using two different sources for these stories and wanted to make Zeus' action here parallel to Hera's (927).

927. Hephaistos. Hera produces Hephaistos on her own as Gaia produced so many offspring earlier without a male partner. But Hera's ability to do this is much diminished. She does so only when she is angry with Zeus, and her offspring is the ugliest of the gods.

STUDY QUESTIONS ON HESIOD'S *THEOGONY*

1. **The Beginnings (116-53)**

   Describe the original world. Why are Chaos, Gaia, Tartaros, and Eros the original beings? When Gaia produces
   children by herself, what does she produce? What does she
   produce when Ouranos is the father? What else is created by
   other gods and goddesses? How do they fit into the world?
   Compare to *Enuma Elish* and the Creation Hymn.

2. **Castration of Ouranos and Birth of Aphrodite (154-210)**

   What does Ouranos do to his children? Why? How does Gaia
   solve her problem? Why does Kronos help her? Compare Gaia
   to Tiamat. Describe the birth of Aphrodite and the origin
   of her name? What does the name Titan mean?

3. **Children of Kronos and Rheia and the War in Heaven (453-735)**

   Compare Rheia and Gaia. How have Ouranos and Kronos changed
   since the last episode? How does Gaia help Rheia? Is Kronos
   smarter than Ouranos? less savage?

   How does Zeus recruit the Hundred-Arms? In his handling of
   this situation, how is he different from Ouranos and Kronos?
   What part does he play in the war? Compare Zeus to Marduk.

4. **Accession of Zeus and His Marriages (881-929)**

   Who makes Zeus king? Since Metis is a personification of
   wisdom, why does Zeus swallow her? Compare to Kronos and
   Ouranos. What personified abstractions does Zeus beget?
   What do they suggest about his reign? What is special about
   Athena? What is Zeus' relationship with fate?

5. **General Questions**

   Characterize the world in Hesiod's *Theogony*. Is it complete?
   stable? orderly? civilized? Compare to the worlds depicted
   in *Enuma Elish* and the Creation Hymn. Characterize the gods
   in Hesiod's *Theogony*. How do they behave? How do they
   create? Compare to the gods in *Enuma Elish*.

PART TWO: CREATION OF THE HUMAN RACE

Chapter 4

From Mesopotamia: *Atrahasis*

INTRODUCTION p. 70
OUTLINE p. 77
SELECTIONS p. 78
NOTES p. 85
STUDY QUESTIONS p. 87

INTRODUCTION TO *ATRAHASIS*

Stories of human creation are often incorporated into larger mythic traditions. Some, for instance, are used in myths which describe the creation of the entire cosmos; and others are used to introduce histories of the human race. *Enuma Elish* exemplifies the former idea in which human creation helps put order into the cosmos. Marduk creates the human race in order to relieve the defeated gods of their onerous duties. After this creation, all the gods unite to celebrate Marduk's accomplishments since he has finally stabilized the divine world. (See *Enuma Elish* VI:1-44.) Likewise, the Israelite Creation Hymn uses a variation on this pattern. The human race is the final step in God's well-conceived plan of a complete cosmos. Human beings are the crowning glory of creation and are given dominion over the earth. (See Genesis 1:26-28.)

Both of these myths, then, place the human race in the scheme of cosmic creation. But another mythic tradition uses stories of human creation as a starting point rather than a conclusion and traces the earliest history of the human race. This tradition usually combines a number of previously independent stories into a continuous account although the sequence of stories may vary from one account to another. Such primeval histories begin, of course, with the creation of the human race. And they often continue with a utopian era in which human beings prosper and a degenerate era which brings divine displeasure. Finally, they end with the gods destroying the human race (frequently by a flood) and renewing it after the destruction.

Like the cosmic tradition, this pattern can be seen in several different cultures throughout the Mediterranean area. The early chapters of Genesis provide the best known example: the human race is created in the story of Adam and Eve (2:4-3:24); the utopian period is suggested by the genealogy of the early

patriarchs (5:1-32); the decline is found in various places
including the story of Cain and Abel (4:1-26); and finally the
destruction and renewal are contained in the story of Noah (6:1-
9:29). From the Greco-Roman culture, Ovid's *Metamorphoses* also
exemplifies this tradition. It begins with human creation,
continues through the easy life of the golden age and the degeneracy of the iron age, and ends with a flood and subsequent
repopulation of the world. (See Appendix).

The Mesopotamian poem *Atrahasis* is the oldest known example
of this mythic tradition. Probably written in the early second
millennium, the poem presents the same sequence of events as the
primeval histories in Genesis and Ovid's *Metamorphoses*. Since
it was discovered only a little over a hundred years ago, the
text of the poem causes many difficulties. Scholars are still
debating the significance of some lines and even the meanings of
some words. But perhaps the biggest problems are caused by the
many breaks in the clay tablets on which the poem was originally
written. They leave large gaps in the story and many incomplete
lines whose meanings can only be surmised.

It is fortunate, however, that several versions of the poem
have been discovered. The oldest, copied by a scribe a few
generations after Hammurabi, is also the most complete. Fragments
of other versions, dating as late as 600 B.C., are written in
various languages including Babylonian and Assyrian. Although
these versions often differ from the oldest copy in many details,
they help fill gaps in the general plot of the story. (See
Lambert and Millard, *Atrahasis*.) The summary which follows gives
a general indication of how the story as a whole fits together.

Summary of the Poem

Atrahasis begins before the human race existed, but the gods
are already organized in an orderly society. Anu, the father and
king of the gods, controls the sky; Enlil, second in command,
rules the surface of the earth; and Ea (also called Enki) is in
charge of the waters. Enlil has assigned many of the lesser gods
to do the heavy work of digging canals, and they have been working for forty long years under very oppressive conditions. So
they unionize and, late one night, form a picket line at Enlil's
house where they set fire to their tools. When Enlil is awakened
by the hubbub, he calls a council of the major powers, bursts into
tears, and wants to retreat to the sky with Anu. But the ever-
crafty Ea has a plan: the birth-goddess, Nintu (also called Mami),

is to create *lullu*, the aboriginal human being, so that this new
creature can take over the back-breaking work on the canals.

Next, the creative process is described in some detail.
Nintu mixes clay with the body and blood of a dead god, and the
other gods spit on the mixture. Then Nintu boasts of her accomplishments, and the worker-gods join her celebration by giving
her the new title "Mistress of all the gods." Finally, fourteen
birth-goddesses bring the mixture into the "house of destiny"
where Ea trods on the clay and Nintu shapes it into fourteen
statues, seven male and seven female. Ten months later, Nintu
eagerly plays the role of midwife as the new creatures emerge
from the womb. When the birth is completed, she happily exclaims,
"I have made it; my hands have made it."

After a large gap in the story, we discover that the situation has changed dramatically. Human beings have been multiply-
ing at an alarming rate for twelve hundred years. Because they
are constantly making noise, Enlil is unable to sleep and so
tries to cut back the human population by plague and drought.
But his attempts are thwarted by Ea who has befriended the human
race. Then Enlil conceives a plan which he thinks Ea will be
unable to stop; he decides to destroy the human race with a
massive flood which Ea himself must direct as ruler of the
waters. Ea, however, is too clever for Enlil and circumvents
the commands by warning his human friend, King Atrahasis, who
then survives the flood in a boat.

After the flood, all the other gods rejoice that the human
race has been saved, and they blame Enlil for trying to destroy
these creatures in the first place. While the gods are bickering,
Ea devises a plan to mollify Enlil and still allow human beings
to survive. He commands Nintu to create once again; but this
time she will create three new classes of creatures: women
unable to bear children, demons who "snatch the baby from the
lap of her who bore it," and priestesses who remain celibate.
Although it is likely that the poem ends soon after this, the
rest of the text is missing.

Interpretations of the Poem

There are many problems involved in attempting to interpret
Atrahasis. The summary above indicates that the plot follows
the traditional pattern of primeval history, but it does not
help us understand the significance of the events. In addition,
the missing parts of the main version may have contained

important clues to the meaning of the poem as a whole, and the fragments of other versions sometimes contradict the main version. These difficulties are increased by the lack of evidence on the date of the poem's composition. It was probably first written down during the early years of Babylon's rise to power in Mesopotamia (early in the second millennium B.C.), but this dating is not certain and at best provides only a general historical setting. (See Chapter 7.) Because of these difficulties, any interpretation of the poem must be tentative. But scholars have found several clues within the poem itself which may point to its main themes.

First, the poem concentrates on Enlil as the god who has most influence over the human world. No matter how much Ea may help human beings in the short run, Enlil's plans and decisions ultimately determine the fate of the human race. According to Thorkild Jacobsen, the poem displays an ambivalence about the character of Enlil. On the one hand, it shows a perverse fascination for the tremendous destruction which Enlil can unleash; on the other, it reveals an awareness that he is an adversary and that his motives are suspect (*Treasures of Darkness*, p. 223). If the poem is in effect a paean to Enlil, it belongs in the same tradition as *Enuma Elish* and Hesiod's *Theogony*, which exalt one god over all the others in their pantheons. But *Atrahasis* would be unique in this group because it glorifies a god who is an adversary of the human race.

Second, the poem frequently explains the origins of various Mesopotamian social practices. In its description of human creation, for example, the poem elaborates on the origin of rituals related to childbirth. But perhaps the most important of these etiologies occurs at the end of the poem when the problem of human overpopulation is resolved by the creation of female sterility, miscarriages, and religious celibacy. According to Tikva Frymer-Kensky, these new creatures are useful to Mesopotamian society because they limit the human population and thus avoid further divine attempts to destroy the entire human race ("The Babylonian Flood Stories," p. 36).

Finally, the pattern of primeval history also provides a clue to the poem's meaning. In the Mesopotamian worldview, the original human beings were apparently too wild and barbarous to begin any kind of organized life on their own and were thus dependent on the gods to provide it for them. In Babylonian tradition, seven sages received the gods' instruction on civilized behavior and passed it on to the rest of the human race. The

extent of these teachings can be seen in the Sumerian concept of
the *mes*. A *me* was any organized segment of human civilization,
including the institution of kingship, the building of cities,
all occupations and crafts, and even the low life of prostitutes,
thieves, and other criminals. It did not matter whether a *me*
was legal, helpful, or moral; if it existed in civilized life,
it must have come from the gods. (See Lambert and Millard,
pp. 18-21.) The gap in Tablet I of *Atrahasis*, which immediately
follows the creation of the human race, may have contained a
similar explanation of the development of human civilization.
In that case, the first part of the poem would have emphasized
not only the hard work which human beings had to perform but
also the sanctity and value of Mesopotamian institutions.

The Human Condition

   According to Mesopotamian tradition, then, human beings were
dependent on the gods for their creation and their way of life.
Atrahasis follows this traditional belief in the two processes
which the gods use to create the human race. In the first
process, the gods act as craftsmen as they shape a new creature
out of unformed clay mixed with divine flesh and blood. Nintu
and Ea cooperate in forming statues of the new creatures and in
reciting magic incantations. But even this elaborate procedure
is not enough to finish human creation. The creatures must still
stay in a womb for the normal period of human pregnancy before
being born. This second process indicates how the civilized
life of human beings follows divine patterns. The gods set a
precedent for later human behavior as they perform various
rituals connected with childbirth. These etiologies include
many details which are not clear to us such as the placing of
the brick and the beating of the drum. But each of these acts
shows how the gods give the human race their first lesson in
civilized living, the proper way to handle birth.
   The materials the gods use to create the human race also
show how human life reflects the divine pattern. Human beings
are a mixture of clay, divine spittle, and the flesh and blood
of a god "who has rationality." In general, this idea is similar
to that in other accounts of the creation of the human race.
Humanity is a combination of earthly and divine elements, for
example, in the story of Adam and Eve when God takes up some soil
and breathes life into it. But *Atrahasis* divides the divine
element into four parts. First, the blood of the slain god

provides human beings with life just as God's breath does in the
story of Adam and Eve. The divine blood gives movement and
growth to an otherwise unliving form. Second, the spittle of
the gods serves the practical purpose of wetting the clay to
make it malleable, but it also provides a further divine element
in human nature. Spittle, like breath and blood, is a symbol of
life and is often considered to have magical qualities. Third,
the flesh of the slain god introduces a spirit which will live
on after death. Although the use of a god's flesh to signify
this idea is not found elsewhere in Mesopotamian literature,
it is consistent with their belief in a spirit which survives
death and can haunt the living (Lambert and Millard, p. 22).
Finally, the slain god is characterized as one "who has rationality." Although the meaning of this phrase is not completely
understood, it is clear that this characteristic is also passed
on to the newly created human beings. Thus, *Atrahasis* attempts
to account for the complex nature of human life which shares so
much with the divine world.

Finally, the poem suggests that there is an interdependence
between the human and divine worlds which grows as human history
progresses. At the beginning of the poem, the gods have a
simple and clear reason for creating the human race. They find
that the hard work necessary for survival causes too much dissension among themselves, so they create a new class of creatures
to perform these duties. Human beings, then, are essentially
slaves who work so that their masters may enjoy freedom and
leisure. Later in the poem, it becomes apparent that the divine
plan has not worked, for human beings are making so much noise
that the gods cannot rest. Whether this condition is the result
of overpopulation or some other cause, the human race has
apparently lost many of the civilized values which the gods gave
them. Enlil, who rules over the earth, finds the problem
sufficiently serious to suggest complete destruction; and the
other gods agree that human beings are not worth the trouble
which they cause. After the attempted destruction has failed,
however, the gods turn against Enlil, for they realize that they
need the sacrifices and hard work which the human race has
performed for many generations. By the end of the poem, then,
the gods have realized that there is an interdependence between
the divine and human worlds which gives added stature to humanity.
Human beings are originally created as slaves, and their civilization is patterned after the divine world. But the gods are

ultimately dependent on the human race to provide them the means of maintaining their freedom and leisure.

This seemingly simple poem, then, contains some very complex ideas about creation and defines human nature in terms of its relationship to the divine world. The poem is in some respects traditional: it uses primeval history as its broad setting and it pictures human beings as a mixture of divine and human elements. But it is also unique in its complex conception of human creation and its great concern for explaining the origins of its native social practices. Its ideas and artistic conventions may appear alien to us, but they can also give us a fresh perspective on the meaning of human life and the idea of the divine.

OUTLINE OF *ATRAHASIS*

A. Creation of Human Race (I:1-304)*

  1. Worker gods rebel (I:1-73).

  2. Enlil is awakened (I:74-98).

  3. Chief gods hold council (I:99-177).

  4. Nintu and Enki plan creation (I:178-220).

  5. Human race is created (I:221-304).

B. Problems with the Human Race (I:352-II:iv)

  1. Noise of multiplied human race bothers Enlil.

  2. Atrahasis consults Enki about plague.

  3. Enki advises Atrahasis about plague.

  4. Famine is described.

C. Flood (II:v-III:iv)

  1. Enki is ordered to flood the earth.

  2. Atrahasis is ordered to build a boat.

  3. Atrahasis builds and stocks the boat.

  4. Earth is flooded.

D. Aftermath (III:v-viii)

  1. Gods suffer hunger and thirst when sacrifices cease.

  2. Atrahasis makes an offering.

  3. Gods descend upon offering.

  4. Enlil and Enki argue.

Starred passages are included in the readings which follow.

Worker Gods Rebel (I:1-73)

When the gods, like man,
bore the work, carried the labor-basket--
the labor-basket of the great gods--
the work was heavy, much was the distress.

The seven great Anunnaki   5
caused the Igigi to bear the work.
Anu their father was king.
Their counselor was hero-Enlil.
Their "throne-bearer" was Ninurta.
And their sheriff was Ennugi.   1 0
These are the ones who seized power.
The gods cast lots and divided (the Cosmos):
[Anu] went up to [heaven];
[Enlil had] the earth as his subject;
[the lock,] the snare of the sea,   1 5
[was given] to Enki the wise.
[After Anu] went up to heaven
[and Enki w]ent down [to the ap]su,
. . .
[they caused] the Igigi [to bear the work].   2 0

    21-36. These lines are fragmentary. Enough is left,
however, to reveal that the gods' work includes digging the
Tigris and Euphrates rivers.

. . . Forty more years
. . . they bore the labor night and day.
They [wearied], complained,
[grum]bled in the workpits.   4 0
"Let us confront the throne-bearer
that he may remove from us our [hea]vy labor.

. . .

come on, let us confuse him in his dwelling,
Enlil, the counselor of the gods, the 'hero,'   45
come on, let us confuse him in his dwelling."

  47-60. Most of these lines are lost, fragmentary, or
repetitious. But it is clear that one of the worker gods is
speaking to the others and exhorting them to rebel. His speech
ends with the following:

"Now, engage battle,
stir up war and hostilities."

The gods listened to his words.
They set fire to their implements,
to their spades (they set) fire,   65
their labor-baskets into the flames
they threw.
They held them (as torches); they went
to the gate of the shrine of hero Enlil.
It was night; at mid-watch   70
the house was surrounded; the god did not know.
It was night; at mid-watch
the Ekur was surrounded; Enlil did not know.

                 Enlil is Awakened (I:74-98)

Kalkal observed and was disturbed.
He slid the bolt and looked [outward].   75
Kalkal awakened [Nusku].
They listened to the noise of [the Igigi].

Nusku awakened [his] lord,
made [him] get out of bed.
"My lord, [your hou]se is surrounded;   80
battle has come up to your gate.
Enlil, your [house is surroun]ded;
battle has come up to your gate."

Enlil had [his servant] come down into his dwelling.
Enlil opened his mouth   85
and said to his vizier Nusku,
"Nusku, lock your gate,
take your weapon, stand before me."

Nusku locked his gate,
took his weapon and stood before Enlil.   90
Nusku opened his mouth

and said to hero Enlil:
"My lord, these children are your own;
they are your sons; why are you afraid?
Enlil, these children are your own;   95
they are your sons; why are you afraid?
Send (the order); let them bring Anu down (to earth);
let them bring Enki into your presence."

Chief Gods Hold Council (I:99-177)

He sent and they brought Anu down;
they brought Enki into his presence.   100
Anu, king of heaven, was seated.
The King of the Apsu, Enki, was in [attendance];
the great Anunnaki were seated.

Enlil arose . . .
Enlil opened his mouth   105
and said to the great [gods]:
"Against me [have they come]?
They have waged war . . .
Battle has come to my gate."   110

Anu opened his mouth
and said to hero Enlil,
"The matter of the Igigi--
has its reason been brought to you?
Let Nusku go out. . . ."   115

   116-17. These lines are too fragmentary for translation.

Enlil opened his mouth
and said to [his vizier Nusku],
"Nusku, open [your gate],   120
take your weapon.
In the assembly [of all the gods]
bow down, stand up, [say to them]:
'[Your father] Anu has sent me,
your counselor [hero Enlil],   125
your throne-bearer [Ninurta],
and your sheriff [Ennugi].
Who is the one [who instigated] battle?
Who is the one who [provoked] hostilities?
Who is the one [who started the] war?'"   130

131-58. Most of these lines are either fragmentary or repetitious. It seems that Nusku goes to the rebel gods and repeats Enlil's words as he was instructed. Then, he returns to Enlil with their reply which he repeats as follows:

"Every [single one of us g]ods
has started the war.   160
We . . . in the workpits.
Excessive [labor] has killed us;
our wo[rk was heavy], much was the distress;
[and every] single one of us gods
has spoken . . . with Enlil."   165

Enlil heard these words
and his tears flowed.
Enlil (heard) these words;
he said [to] hero Anu,
"Noble one, with you in heaven   170
carry your authority, take your power.
With the Anunnaki seated before you,
call one god, let him be thrown to the netherworld."

Anu opened his mouth
and said to the gods, his brothers,   175
"Why are we accusing them?
Their work is heavy, much is their distress."

Nintu and Enki Plan Creation (I:178-220)

178-88. There is a small gap in the text here. In later versions of the story, Enki, rather than Anu, is speaking at this time. In those versions Enki reveals his plan for creating the human race. In this version he is probably speaking when the story resumes:

"While [Nintu the birth-goddess] is present,
let the birth-goddess create the offspring,   190
let man bear the labor-basket of the gods."

They called the goddess and asked (her),
the midwife of the gods, wise Mami:
"You are the birthgoddess, creatress of man.
Create *lullu*-man, let him bear the yoke.   195
Let him bear the yoke, the work of Enlil;
let man carry the labor-basket of the gods."

Nintu opened her mouth
and said to the great gods,
"It is not properly mine to do these things.   200
This work belongs to Enki.

He is the one who purifies all;
let him give me the clay, and I will do (it)."

Enki opened his mouth
and said to the great gods: 205
"At the new moon, the seventh day, and the full moon,
I will set up a purifying bath. ~ enter ritual
Let them slaughter one god.   moment
Let the gods be purified by immersion.
With his flesh and blood   210
let Nintu mix the clay.
God and man--
let them be inseparably mixed in the clay;
till the end of time let us hear the 'drum.'
Let there be spirit from the god's flesh;   215
let her proclaim 'alive' as its sign;
for the sake of never-forgetting, let there be spirit."
In the assembly, "Aye," answered
the great gods,
the administrators of destiny.   220

Human Race is Created (I:221-304)

At the new moon, the seventh day, and the full moon,
he set up a purifying bath.
We-ila, who had rationality,
they slaughtered in their assembly.
With his flesh and blood — Hebrew Dam   225
Nintu mixed the clay.   ~ Jesus ?
Till the end [of days they heard the drum].
From the flesh of the god there was spirit.
She proclaimed "alive" as its sign.
For the sake of not-forgetting there was a spirit.   230

polytheistic After she had mixed the clay,
she called the Anunnaki, the great gods.
The Igigi, the great gods,
cast their spittle on the clay.
~Ninti
Mami opened her mouth   235
and said to the great gods,
"You commanded me a task--
I have completed it.
You slaughtered a god together with his rationality.
I have removed your heavy labor,   240

have placed your labor-basket on man.
You raised a cry for mankind;
I have loosened your yoke, have [established] freedom."

They heard this speech of hers;
they ran around and kissed her feet.   245
"Formerly we called you 'Mami.'
Now, may 'Mistress of all the gods' be your [na]me."

They entered the house of destiny,
Prince Ea and wise Mami.   250
With the birth goddesses assembled,
he trod the clay in her presence.
She recited the incantation again and again.
Ea, seated before her, prompted her.
When she finished her incantation,   255
she nipped off fourteen pieces of clay.
Seven pieces to the right,
seven to the left, she placed.
Between them she placed the brick.

   260-76. There is a gap in the text here. From an Assyrian
version we learn that fourteen birth goddesses shape the clay.
They make seven males and seven females and align them in pairs.

[The birth g]oddesses were assembled;
Nintu was seated.
She counted the months.
At the destined [moment], they called the tenth month.   280
The tenth month came.
The end of the period opened the womb.

Her face was beaming, joyful.
Her head covered,
she performed the midwifery.   285
She girded her loins;
she made the blessing.
She patterned the flour and laid down the brick.

"I have created, my hands have done it.
Let the midwife rejoice in the prostitute's house;   290
where the pregnant woman gives birth,
the mother of the baby
severs herself.
Let the brick be laid down for nine days
that Nintu the midwife be honored.   295
Let them continually call Mami their . . .

praise the birth goddess, praise Kesh.

When the bed is laid . . .

let husband and wife lie together.   300

When for wifehood and husbandhood

they heed Ishtar in the house of the father-in-law,

let there be rejoicing for nine days;

let them call Ishtar Ishara.

305-end. After a gap of approximately fifty lines, the story continues. Twelve hundred years later Enlil is trying to destroy the human race because it is making too much noise. See Introduction to this chapter for a summary of this part of the poem.

NOTES TO *ATRAHASIS*

Translator's note. This translation follows the edition of
the Atrahasis Epic by W. G. Lambert and A. R. Millard, *Atrahasis:
The Babylonian Story of the Flood* (Oxford, 1969) and uses the
line numbers of that edition. The only significant differences
between my translation and theirs are in the section relating to
the creation of man, lines 204-230, but there are various lesser
differences, and the reader might want to compare the translations. This translation also incorporates several unpublished
suggestions by the late J. J. Finkelstein although, of course,
the responsibility for the translation is mine.

Note to the text. The passages included here are taken from
the first tablet of a Babylonian version dated about 1700 B.C.
Although many versions and copies exist, this copy is the most
complete. Parts of the poem have been known to exist for over
a hundred years, but it was not until 1969 that Lambert and
Millard edited all the available versions in a bilingual edition.
Lambert and Millard's edition also includes "the Sumerian Flood
story," edited by M. Civil. The text of this story is even more
fragmentary than that of *Atrahasis*, but both apparently follow
the same plot from the creation to the aftermath of the flood.

5. *The seven great Anunnaki*. Anunnaki and Igigi are frequently synonymous collective names for the gods. Here the
seven great Anunnaki administer the destinies of all the gods;
in other words, they fix and can change the status quo. Thus,
they are the gods who impose the heavy work on the other gods.

16. *Enki the wise*. Enki is also named Ea (250) and is the
same god who rules the fresh waters in *Enuma Elish*.

18. *To the apsu*. The apsu is Ea's home in the subterranean
fresh waters. See *Enuma Elish* I:73-78 for an explanation of the
origin of the apsu.

73. *Ekur*. Ekur is the house of Enlil.

74. *Kalkal*. Kalkal is Enlil's door-keeper.

119. *Vizier*. A vizier is an adviser and second in command.

85

189. *Nintu the birth-goddess.* Nintu is also called Mami (193) and Mistress of all the gods (248). See Chapter 10 for the view that Nintu probably played a larger role in an earlier version of the story.

195. *Lullu-man.* *Lullu,* a general word for humanity, apparently referred to human beings in the remote past. Here it may indicate human beings in their original state.

210-17. See *Enuma Elish* VI:1-44, Genesis 2:7, and the Sumerian poem "Enki and Ninmah" for similar ideas about the materials used in the creation of the human race.

214. *Let us hear the "drum."* The drum may refer to a heart-beat here.

216. *Let her proclaim "alive" as its sign.* Although this line is difficult to interpret, it seems to mean that the spirit taken from the slain god is the distinguishing mark of human beings.

223. *We-ila, who had rationality.* The god We-ila is not mentioned elsewhere in Mesopotamian writings. His rationality is emphasized to indicate that it was the characteristic passed on to human beings. See also 239.

259. *Between them she placed the brick.* The brick was apparently a structure on which women would lie during labor. See also 288 and 294.

280. *They called the tenth month.* Since the Mesopotamians used a lunar calendar, the normal human gestation period would have been ten months.

STUDY QUESTIONS ON *ATRAHASIS*

1. Before Human Creation (1-177)

   What work are the lesser gods performing as the poem begins?
   How do they feel about their job? How long have they been
   toiling? What do they do in front of Enlil's house? What
   is Enlil's first response to the gods' strike? What advice
   does Nusku give Enlil? At the council, what does Enlil
   propose to do about the strike? What does Ea propose? Do
   their reasons differ?

2. Creation of the Human Race (178-304)

   How is the decision made to create the human race? Who
   makes it? Why? Why is the human race created? What does
   this tell us about the place of human beings in the world?
   What is the human race made out of? What parts of the
   slaughtered god are used? What does this tell us about
   human nature? What deities create the human race? What
   does Nintu do? What does Ea do? What rituals concerning
   child-birth are explained?

3. Important Names to Identify

   Anu, Ea, Enlil, Nintu, We-ila.

4. General Questions

   Compare this account of the creation of the human race to
   that in *Enuma Elish*. Are they similar enough to suggest
   that they both came from the same tradition? If so, what
   are the most important features of that tradition? If not,
   what features make the accounts so different?

   Compare this account to the creations in the Israelite
   Creation Hymn, the story of Adam and Eve, and the story of
   Pandora and the Five Ages in terms of the purpose of
   creation, the materials used, and the view of human nature.

   In *Atrahasis*, Nintu and the fourteen birth-goddesses play
   significant roles in the creation of the human race. Compare
   their roles to those of the female deities in the story of
   Pandora.

Chapter 5

From Israel: Adam and Eve (Genesis 2:4b-3:24)

INTRODUCTION p. 90
TEXT p. 97
NOTES p. 101
STUDY QUESTIONS p. 105

INTRODUCTION TO ADAM AND EVE

Although the story of Adam and Eve played a very minor role in the culture of the ancient Israelites, it is perhaps the best known story in the Bible today. Most of us remember how the man and woman are created, how they disobey, and how they are expelled from the Garden of Eden. Indeed, elements of the story have become so common that they are now part of our everyday language and thinking: Eden connotes a utopian existence and the snake an evil, tempting influence; we accept that we are made of dust and to dust we shall return. In addition, the story is still fraught with religious significance for countless people. Even in our science-oriented world, it survives as the religious explanation of our origin alongside of, if not in opposition to, the theory of evolution. Furthermore, theological interpretations of the text are so numerous that it is nearly impossible to say anything about it without contradicting someone's religious beliefs.

Despite all this familiarity and controversy, we usually pay little attention to the story itself and the context in which it is placed. The story of Adam and Eve opens the epic of Yahweh which relates the history of the Israelites from the call of Abraham to the arrival in the promised land. This epic incorporates the most famous stories of the period such as Abraham and Isaac, the flight into Egypt, Moses on Mount Sinai, and the wanderings in the wilderness. The story of Adam and Eve sets the pattern, as we shall see later, which prevails throughout this epic.

The Yahwist

The artist-theologian who composed this epic is known as the Yahwist because he used the name Yahweh for the Israelite God. Much about the Yahwist reminds us of Homer. Like Homer, he is

known to us only through his writings from which we can surmise
that he probably lived in the tenth century B.C., perhaps during
the reign of Solomon. He composed his epic long after the
formative period of the sagas: Abraham, for instance, lived
seven or eight centuries before the Yahwist's time. He put into
their classic form the sagas which gave the Israelites their
identity as a unique people. Finally, he was apparently the most
gifted story teller of his culture and left his distinctive stamp
on the legends and history which he recorded. In the story of
Joseph, for instance, he composed a dramatic, well-developed
novella. He tells how Joseph's brothers envy him and how their
plot to kill him results in his being sold into Egypt. There, in
adventures reminiscent of the popular stories of the day, he is
tempted by Potiphar's wife and is thrown into prison where he
remains until his interpretations of dreams win the Pharaoh's
acclaim. Finally, as "lord of the land" of Egypt, he saves his
brothers, tests them, and is reconciled to them. The Yahwist
develops each of these episodes with the same sensitivity for
character and situation which Homer shows in his epics.

Nevertheless, the Yahwist differs profoundly from Homer in
one important respect. He is one of the world's most creative
theologians, and his stories elucidate his theology. Whether he
was writing a short novel about Joseph, the history of the
wanderings through the desert, or the revelation to Moses on
Mount Sinai, his aim remained the same: to show the interaction
between Yahweh and his people as pivotal to universal history.
He cites Yahweh's promise to Abraham at the beginning of the
patriarchal history:

> Leave your country . . . and go to a country that I
> will show you. I will make you into a great nation
> I will bless you. . . . All the families on earth will
> pray to be blessed as you are blessed. . . . I give
> this land to your descendants.
>
> (Genesis 12:1-7)

The Yahwist sees the history of his people and indeed the subsequent history of "all the families on earth" as the unfolding of
Yahweh's promise to Abraham.

Such, then, is the nature and scope of the Yahwist's vast
plan. But we are concerned only with the prelude to the epic,
the so-called "primeval history" which accounts for the beginnings
of the human race in the stories of Adam and Eve, Cain and Abel,
Noah and the Flood, and the Tower of Babel. Because such myths
of creation, of family quarrels, and of floods were common in the

ancient Near East, the Yahwist had ample precedent for the
stories he chose to introduce his epic. He fashioned or adapted--
we do not know which--these stories to suit his theme of universal history. In the story of Adam and Eve, for instance, he
depicts not just the first Israelites but the parents of the
whole human race. His intent can be seen even in the names of
the first human beings: Adam is a collective name for all of
humanity and Eve means "the mother of all who live"
(Genesis 3:20). Similarly, the other myths of primeval history
account for the fragmentation of society after the first couple
is expelled from Eden. Not only does brother kill brother (Cain
and Abel) but whole nations fail to communicate with each other
(the Tower of Babel); even the flood covers the entire earth
rather than just a limited area. So the Yahwist prefaces his
history of the Israelite people with stories of universal
significance.

Patterns in the Story of Adam and Eve

Let us turn, then, to the story of Adam and Eve and see how
the Yahwist imposed the same pattern on it he used in the whole
epic. The pattern has four elements: the goodness of humanity,
the flawed nature of human beings, Yahweh's punishment, and
finally his promise. In Adam and Eve, the first three elements
of the pattern are clearly visible; the fourth is only suggested.

The first scene (2:4b-2:25) establishes the first element,
the harmony and goodness of human creation. The writer takes
advantage of an obvious Hebrew pun to suggest a harmony between
the human creature and the earth: Yahweh forms *adam*, the first
human being, from *adamah*, the ground. Yahweh breathes into this
"clod-creature" (Trible, p. 76) and produces a *nephesh*, a "living
creature" who has a harmonious personality. Everything about the
surroundings of the clod-creature reinforces this harmony: the
beautiful garden provides delightful working conditions (the
Hebrew word for Eden also suggests enjoyment); the woman is
created as the man's full, equal partner (see 2:18 note), and
the two become one flesh. In the final verse of the scene(2:25),
the couple's nakedness and lack of shame underscore their goodness and sexual openness. In addition, an intimacy and trust
between Yahweh and his creature underlies the whole scene:
Yahweh breathes into the creature, forms him like a potter, lets
him tend the garden, and surprises him with a fitting companion.
The tone throughout is happy, especially at the woman's birth.

Still, even within this first scene, there is a subtle foreshadowing of the disruption to come. When Yahweh warns the man that he will die if he eats the forbidden fruit (2:17), a new discordant element is introduced. In the second scene (3:1-3:13), this element predominates as the wily serpent entices, the woman disobeys, and the man passively follows suit. The writer artfully describes the steps of temptation and the resulting sin. There is the progression from doubt, to half-truth, to the sensual enticement of the fruit itself; there are the two different kinds of disobedience, hers by action and his by compliance; and there are the multiple effects of the disobedience: guilt, shame, and shifting of blame. The couple's new consciousness of guilt causes them to hide in fear from Yahweh, and it separates them from each other, from Yahweh, and from the animal world. The man tries to pass the buck back to Yahweh and to the woman (3:12); and the woman tries to pass it to the serpent (3:13). The harmony of the original creation has been shattered by the couple's acts of disobedience.

The third scene (3:14-24) contains the third element, Yahweh's punishment, and a hint of the fourth element, the promise. Yahweh's punishments account for the serpent's crawling on its belly, the woman's labor in childbirth and subordination to the man, and the man's toiling by the sweat of his brow. Beneath these somewhat naive etiologies, however, the author is grappling with the problem of evil and hints at its final resolution through Yahweh's promise. The serpent, who was earlier a cavalier, chatty tempter typical of folklore, becomes the venomous snake whose poison can and does wound:

> I will put enmity between you and the woman,
> between your brood and hers.
> They shall strike at your head,
> and you shall strike at their heel (3:15).

The snake's poison and the fear it engenders provide the Yahwist with the perfect symbol for evil and its effects. The gradual spreading of this venom over the whole world is the theme of the subsequent primeval history (3:16-11:32). Finally, the obscure reference to the woman's brood crushing the snake's head hints at ultimate human victory over the venomous evil, but otherwise the fourth element is not clarified until Yahweh promises Abraham a great nation (12:1-7 quoted above).

The Yahwist, then, is a highly accomplished artist and theologian who uses all the tricks of his trade--myth, symbol, etiology, suspense, paradox, excitement, an anthropomorphic god, and a talking serpent--to write a compelling, unforgettable story. Although he may be adapting older stories, he is careful to shape the materials to his theological themes: human goodness and evil, divine punishment and promise. The Yahwist's use of narrative illustrates the profound difference between him and the author of the Creation Hymn. Whereas the Priestly writer aims for theological precision, avoids myth, and depicts the majesty of a transcendent God, the Yahwist writes in bold, imaginative strokes about a God who is close at hand. Yahweh fashions the first human creature like a potter shaping his clay, mulls over a problem himself, plays the role of a marriage broker, asks questions like a judge unsure of the facts, and takes a walk in the cool of the evening.

Interpretations and Adaptations of the Story

The innumerable literary and theological works that this story has spawned demonstrate how uncannily it captures the human enigma. From the rabbis to Saints Paul and Augustine, from Milton and Alexander Pope to modern times, theologians have interpreted and poets have recast this myth. The idea of the fall originated in late Jewish tradition and the doctrine of original sin in Paul's epistles; Augustine elaborated on the sexual dimension of the story and Milton created an heroic, rebellious Satan very different from the original serpent; Pope made the first couple a combination of body and soul, a concept that owes more to Plato than to Genesis; finally, from Kierkegaard to Ernest Becker, there have been many psychological interpretations of the story. Over the centuries, then, practically every word of the story has been debated and reinterpreted.

These layers of interpretation cause us problems when we approach the Yahwist's story. We often presume that the text speaks directly of a fall and of original sin. It does not. We presume that the serpent was equivalent to Satan, but the idea of Satan is of much later origin. We look in vain for the apple which Adam and Eve ate. All these accretions, beliefs,and prejudices obstruct us from reading the story as it was originally written.

One of our traditional assumptions about the story, for instance, is that Eve is created inferior to Adam. This erroneous view has a long history, dating from late antiquity to our own time. The author of I Timothy connects woman's inferiority in his own society to Adam and Eve:

A woman must be a learner, listening quietly . . . .
For Adam was created first, and Eve afterwards; and it
was not Adam who was deceived; it was the woman who,
yielding to deception, fell into sin.

(I Timothy 2:11-14)

In fact, all the New Testament writers who explain woman's
subordination to man refer either directly or indirectly to Eve's
later creation. (See Krister Stendahl, *The Bible and the Role
of Woman*, p. 39.)

In subsequent ages, writers continued to use this same kind
of logic to explain their own social views. Gregory Nazianzus
(about 380 A.D.), for instance, called Eve "a deadly delight."
But perhaps the most influential shaper of the myth was John
Milton in the seventeenth century. Milton's massive and
majestic *Paradise Lost* has so overshadowed the simple biblical
story that even today we remember his portraits of Eve and Satan
when we think we are remembering the Yahwist's account. Milton's
view of Eve is more sympathetic than Gregory's, but it imposes
an inferiority on Eve which has had a profound influence on
later readings of the myth. Milton, of course, intended to
remain faithful to the Bible, but his hierarchical worldview led
him to assume that every creature had its proper place in an
elaborately descending order from God who is pure spirit, to
angels, men, women, animals, plants, and finally non-living
creatures. Even within human society, this hierarchy was
necessary. Rulers of the state were God's deputies on earth,
and husbands were his deputies in the family. (See Merritt
Hughes, *John Milton*, pp. 179-97 and Lawrence Stone, *Family, Sex,
and Marriage 1500-1800*.) Consequently, Eve is expected to follow
the "right reason" of Adam, her "head," and her duties consist
of studying "household good" and promoting "good works in her
Husband" (*Paradise Lost* 9.233). For Milton, then, Adam and Eve
are both created "in God's image" as in Genesis 1:27, but Eve is
less in God's image (8.540ff.) and Adam's "perfection far
excelled Hers in all real dignity" (10.150-51). Thus, despite
the redemptive role that Milton's Eve plays in the final books
of the epic, she is subordinated to Adam far more radically than
in the original story.

To examine the Yahwist's story, then, and to discover why it
inspired so many adaptations, we must peel off many layers of
interpretation and rediscover the original account. In doing
this, we may find a work of art that raises more questions than
it answers: questions about the origin of evil, the paradoxical

interaction between human freedom and divine power, and the relationship between men and women. Perhaps what we will most appreciate is its capacity to portray the mystery of human greatness and frailty.

ADAM AND EVE (GENESIS 2:4b-3:24)

Creation of the Man

When the Lord God made earth and heaven, $\qquad$ 2:4
there was neither shrub nor plant growing wild upon the $\qquad$ 5
earth, because the Lord God had sent no rain on the earth;
nor was there any man to till the ground.
A flood used to rise out of the earth and water all the $\qquad$ 6
surface of the ground.
Then the Lord God formed a man from the dust of the ground $\qquad$ 7
and breathed into his nostrils the breath of life. Thus
the man became a living creature.

The Garden of Eden

Then the Lord God planted a garden in Eden away to the $\qquad$ 8
east, and there he put the man whom he had formed.
The Lord God made trees spring from the ground, all trees $\qquad$ 9
pleasant to look at and good for food; and in the middle
of the garden he set the tree of life and the tree of the
knowledge of good and evil.
There was a river flowing from Eden to water the garden, $\qquad$ 10
and when it left the garden it branched into four streams.
The name of the first is Pishon; that is the river which $\qquad$ 11
encircles all the land of Havilah, where the gold is.
The gold of that land is good; bdellium and cornelians are $\qquad$ 12
also to be found there.
The name of the second river is Gihon; this is the one $\qquad$ 13
which encircles all the land of Cush.
The name of the third is Tigris; this is the river which $\qquad$ 14

runs east of Asshur. The fourth river is the Euphrates.

The Lord God took the man and put him in the garden of   15
Eden to till it and care for it.

He told the man, 'You may eat from every tree in the   16
garden,

but not from the tree of the knowledge of good and evil;   17
for on the day that you eat from it, you will certainly die.'

Creation of the Woman

Then the Lord God said, 'It is not good for the man to be   18
alone. I will provide a partner for him.'

So God formed out of the ground all the wild animals and   19
all the birds of heaven. He brought them to the man to
see what he would call them, and whatever the man called
each living creature, that was its name.

Thus the man gave names to all cattle, to the birds of   20
heaven, and to every wild animal; but for the man himself
no partner had yet been found.

And so the Lord God put the man into a trance, and while   21
he slept, he took one of his ribs and closed the flesh
over the place.

The Lord God then built up the rib, which he had taken   22
out of the man, into a woman.

He brought her to the man, and the man said: 23

> 'Now this, at last--
> bone from my bones,
> flesh from my flesh!--
> this shall be called woman,
> for from man was this taken.

That is why a man leaves his father and mother and is   24
united to his wife, and the two become one flesh.

Now they were both naked, the man and his wife, but they   25
had no feeling of shame towards one another.

Temptation and Disobedience

The serpent was more crafty than any wild creature that   3:1
the Lord God had made. He said to the woman, 'Is it true
that God has forbidden you to eat from any tree in the
garden?'

The woman answered the serpent, 'We may eat the fruit of   2
any tree in the garden,

except for the tree in the middle of the garden; God has   3
forbidden us either to eat or to touch the fruit of that;

if we do, we shall die.'

The serpent said, 'Of course you will not die.   4
God knows that as soon as you eat it, your eyes will be   5
opened and you will be like gods knowing both good and evil.'
When the woman saw that the fruit of the tree was good to   6
eat, and that it was pleasing to the eye and tempting to
contemplate, she took some and ate it. She also gave her
husband some and he ate it.
Then the eyes of both of them were opened and they   7
discovered that they were naked; so they stitched fig-
leaves together and made themselves loincloths.

Discovery and Judgment

The man and his wife heard the sound of the Lord God   8
walking in the garden at the time of the evening breeze
and hid from the Lord God among the trees of the garden.
But the Lord God called to the man and said to him,   9
'Where are you?'
He replied, 'I heard the sound as you were walking in the   10
garden, and I was afraid because I was naked, and I hid
myself.'
God answered, 'Who told you that you were naked? Have   11
you eaten from the tree which I forbade you?'
The man said, 'The woman you gave me for a companion, she   12
gave me the fruit from the tree and I ate it.'
Then the Lord God said to the woman, 'What is this that   13
you have done?' The woman said, 'The serpent tricked me,
and I ate.'
Then the Lord God said to the serpent: 14

  'Because you have done this you are accursed
   more than all cattle and all wild creatures.
   On your belly you shall crawl, and dust you shall eat
   all the days of your life.
   I will put enmity between you and the woman,   15
   between your brood and hers.
   They shall strike at your head,
   and you shall strike at their heel.'

To the woman he said: 16

  'I will increase your labour and your groaning,
   and in labour you shall bear children.
   You shall be eager for your husband,
   and he shall be your master.'

And to the man he said: 17

'Because you have listened to your wife
and have eaten from the tree which I forbade you,
accursed shall be the ground on your account.
With labour you shall win your food from it
all the days of your life.
It will grow thorns and thistles for you,   18
none but wild plants for you to eat.
You shall gain your bread by the sweat of your brow   19
until you return to the ground;
for from it you were taken.
Dust you are, to dust you shall return.'

The man called his wife Eve because she was the mother of   20
all who live.

The Lord God made tunics of skins for Adam and his wife   21
and clothed them.

He said, 'The man has become like one of us, knowing good   22
and evil; what if he now reaches out his hand and takes
fruit from the tree of life also, eats it and lives
forever?'

So the Lord God drove him out of the Garden of Eden to   23
till the ground from which he had been taken.

He cast him out, and to the east of the Garden of Eden   24
he stationed the cherubim and a sword whirling and
flashing to guard the way to the tree of life.

NOTES TO ADAM AND EVE

Editors' Note. The Yahwist's name is traditionally abbreviated J because German scholars first transliterated *Yahweh* as *Jahweh*. Throughout these notes, we refer to the Yahwist as J.

2:4b. Although this is the middle of verse 4, J's story of creation begins here. Chapter and verse numbers were added to the text of the Old Testament long after it was written. Verse numbers were inserted by the Masorites about 70 A.D., and the division into chapters was added later (about 1200 A.D.). The numbering was not always based on the content of the stories. Instead, various systems of numerology were often used in which the number of words, syllables, or even letters was the norm for division.

2:5. There was neither shrub nor plant growing wild upon the earth. Since J wrote from the perspective of a Palestinian farmer, he postulated that the world was originally dry, desolate, and uncultivated land. J's view is closer to Hesiod's than to *Enuma Elish* or the Creation Hymn, both of which view the world as originally water.

2:7. Lord God. "Lord" is the usual English translation for Yahweh, the name J uses for his God. "God," Hebrew *Elohim*, was probably added by the final editor (about 500 B.C.) who linked this story with the Creation Hymn (1:1-2:4) and the other accounts in Genesis which use *Elohim*. For this reason, the combination *Yahweh Elohim* is used only in this story and one other text.

Formed a man from the dust of the ground. J uses an old image from pottery to describe Yahweh's creative act. Yahweh forms the man out of the mud as a potter molds an earthen vessel. The same image is used when Yahweh creates the animals (2:19). See also *Atrahasis* I:221-259 for a similar idea and the Creation Hymn (Genesis 1:27) for a different view.

Hebrew *adam*, "man," has three possible meanings: humanity as a whole, the male of the species, and a proper name. There is no general agreement about which meaning applies in this context. The New English Bible translates *adam* "a man"; the Revised Standard Version uses "man." Phyllis Trible suggests that the "earth creature" created here is asexual (*God and the Rhetoric of Sexuality*, p. 80).

2:8. Eden. Hebrew *Edin* is related to the Sumerian word for plain or steppe. Ezekiel 28:11-19 also describes Eden but uses more mythological detail.

2:9. The trees springing from the ground suggest a motif similar to that in Hesiod's golden age when crops arise almost without tending. See Pandora and the Five Ages (*Works and Days* 115ff.). The tree of life is commonly connected with immortality. The tree of the knowledge of good and evil is connected with experience. The Hebrew word for knowledge emphasizes the process and result of experiencing rather than the accumulation of facts. For the Israelites, knowing suggested being in full possession of one's mental, physical, and sexual powers. See 3:5.

2:10-2:14. Many scholars think these verses are a later insertion. The Tigris and Euphrates rivers identify the location of Eden as in the vicinity of Mesopotamia. The location of the Pishon and Gihon is not known although their names probably mean the "Gusher" and the "Bubbler."

2:18. A partner for him. "Partner" translates the Hebrew phrase *hezer kenegdo* which indicates at least an equal partner. *Hezer* is often used in the Old Testament to describe God as the partner of the Israelites. See, for example, Exodus 18:4, Deuteronomy 33:7, and Psalms 33:20.

2:21. Into a trance. "Trance," Hebrew *tardemah*, is used in the Old Testament to describe a sleep in which God would do marvelous things such as the creation of woman in this passage. See also Genesis 15:12 and Job 4:13, 33:15.

He took one of his ribs. The Hebrew word for rib is related to the Sumerian word *ti* which means "rib" or "life." A similar creation takes place in the Sumerian poem "Enki and Ninhursag" when Enki gives birth to the goddess Ninti, "Lady of the Rib," after he has a pain in his side. Phyllis Trible argues against the belief that woman's creation from "Adam's rib" is a sign of female inferiority. She points out that Yahweh had to "build up" the rib before it was transformed into the woman ("Depatriarchalizing in Biblical Interpretation," p. 37.)

2:22. Out of the man, into a woman. J puns here with the Hebrew words *ish*, "man," and *ishshah*, "woman." *Ishshah* looks as if it is derived from *ish*, but the words are not etymologically related. See also 2:7 for the pun on *adam*, "man," and *adamah*, "ground"; and 2:25-3:1 for the pun on *arum*, "serpent," and *arummin*, "naked." J, like many ancient writers, loved word plays.

2:24. Some scholars have seen this verse as etiological. The man leaving his parents to live with his wife would then suggest that there was a matrilocal society in which woman was dominant. Others suggest that the verse indicates both man and woman left their parents to form a new family.

2:25. But they had no feeling of shame. In the Old Testament, the Hebrew word for shame means both a consciousness of adulthood and the feeling of having done wrong. Shame, therefore, is not sin but a by-product of sin. Its absence here implies the innocence of childhood.

At this point in the story, Yahweh has finished his creations. J has structured his story with a device called ring composition in which the main events of a story occur at the beginning and the end. Thus, J's sequence of creation--the man, the garden, the animals, the woman--puts equal emphasis on the importance of the first and last creations. Such a structure does not support the belief that woman is inferior to man because she was created last. See Trible, "Depatriarchalizing," p. 36.

3:1. The serpent was more crafty. J initially identifies the serpent as one of the creatures Yahweh made earlier (2:19). Its ability to talk is not necessarily an indication of super-natural powers since talking animals are common in myths. See, for example, Xanthos the talking horse who prophesies Akhilleus' death (*Iliad* 19:405). The serpent is not related to Satan who is a later development in Israelite religion. But since serpents were frequently used in Canaanite fertility cults, the Israelites identified them with their enemies and with forbidden religious practices. It is not surprising, then, that J would choose a serpent for the tempter. In other myths, animals, and even gods, are often used as external symbols of internal states of mind. See, for example, *Iliad* 1:193ff. where Athena embodies Akhilleus' struggle against his own anger.

3:6. The fruit of the tree was good to eat. J does not identify the fruit. The tradition that it was an apple is a later interpretation and may have resulted from the similarity of Latin *malum*, "apple," and *malus*, "bad."

She took some and ate it. Eve's disobedience has been inter-preted for thousands of years. The Christian doctrine of original sin stems from this act and its effects (3:7-24). The exact nature of original sin has been argued for centuries by Christian theologians. But the inescapable conflict between human freedom and human guilt lies at the core of most explanations. See Langdon Gilkey, *Maker of Heaven and Earth*. For the modern phil-osopher Kierkegaard, this passage illustrates the concept of dread, the alien power which both attracts and frightens. See *The Concept of Dread*. The prohibition against eating the fruit frightens Eve but also makes the fruit more attractive and awakens in her a new possibility of freedom.

3:7. Sexual awareness and wisdom in an earthly paradise are also combined in the *Epic of Gilgamesh* I:iv:16ff. See Speiser, *Genesis*, pp. 25-28, for other parallels between J and Mesopotamian literature.

3:16. You shall be eager for your husband, and he shall be your master. The first half of this line indicates the woman's erotic desire to possess. But the second half shows that her desire will be frustrated: she will not possess but be dominated by her "master." An interesting parallel occurs in the Song of Songs (7:11), "I belong to my beloved, and for me is his desire," where the mutual desire of the man and the woman for each other is fulfilled. According to some scholars, the Song of Songs

develops the idea of sexual equality seen in the story of Adam
and Eve before the disobedience. See Marvin Pope, *Song of Songs*,
p. 643 and Trible, *Sexuality*, pp. 144-65.

*3:20. The man called his wife Eve because she was the mother
of all who live.* J uses another pun here. Hebrew *Hawwah*, "Eve,"
resembles *hay*, "life." For an explanation of the epithet, see
Chapter 10.

3:22. The characterization of Yahweh in this verse is
difficult to reconcile with the rest of the story. It is not
clear to whom he is speaking or why he uses the plural "us."
In addition, he seeks to protect himself from the threat which
humanity has become instead of acting with the parental concern
he consistently showed in the earlier parts of the story. These
problems suggest that J may have based his story on an earlier
version which he had not fully adapted.

STUDY QUESTIONS ON ADAM AND EVE

1. Creation of the Man (2:4-2:7)

    What does the earth look like when it is first created?
    What is missing? What is its main substance? How does this
    differ from the original condition in the opening scene of
    the Creation Hymn? Of *Enuma Elish*? Of Hesiod's *Theogony*?
    How does God make the man? Out of what materials? What
    makes the man live? Compare to the creation in *Atrahasis*.

2. The Garden of Eden (2:8-2:17)

    Why does God make the garden? What is the man supposed to
    do in the garden? What is he to avoid? Compare to the
    purpose of human creation in *Atrahasis* and Hesiod's Five
    Ages. What is the attitude toward work in the story of
    Adam and Eve? Compare to the attitudes in *Atrahasis* and the
    Five Ages.

3. Creation of the Woman (2:18-2:25)

    What problem does God try to solve? How does he first try
    to solve it? How and why does he finally make the woman?
    How does the man react when he sees her? Compare her
    creation to the creation of Pandora in Hesiod's account in
    terms of the methods, purpose, and final product.

4. Temptation and Disobedience (3:1-3:7)

    Describe the serpent. What does he tell the woman? Is this
    temptation consistent with the character of the serpent?
    Why does the woman eat the fruit? Does the man or woman
    take the initiative in this scene? What does this reveal
    about the characters of the man and woman?

5. What is God doing when the man and woman hide from him?
    Why do they hide? How does the man's explanation implicate
    him? How does God know that they have eaten the forbidden
    fruit? How does each defend himself? What is the signifi-
    cance of the woman's name? Why does the man name her now
    instead of earlier? After the disobedience, how do Adam and
    Eve change in the following: 1) what they wear; 2) how they
    suffer; 3) where they live; and 4) what they know? What do
    these changes reveal about the author's idea of human nature?

6. General Questions

How does God compare with the creators in the Creation Hymn,
Atrahasis, *Enuma Elish*, and the story of Pandora? Does he
care about the human beings he created? How does he act
toward them after they eat the fruit? Compare to the other
accounts of human creation. Is God beyond sexuality like
the God in the Creation Hymn?

How are Adam and Eve portrayed as a couple and what distinctive characteristics does each have? Compare the author's
view of human nature to that in *Atrahasis* and the story of
Pandora and the Five Ages. What is the author's view of
sexuality? Is the woman portrayed as originally subordinate
to the man? Compare to the Creation Hymn. Is there a
change after the punishment? Compare to Hesiod's view of
woman in the story of Pandora.

Chapter 6

From Greece: Pandora and the Five Ages
(Hesiod's *Works and Days* 47-201)

INTRODUCTION p. 108
TEXT p. 114
NOTES p. 119
STUDY QUESTIONS p. 122

INTRODUCTION TO PANDORA AND THE FIVE AGES
(HESIOD'S *WORKS AND DAYS* 47-201)

Hesiod's *Works and Days* is a "farmer's almanac" permeated
with moral maxims. Hesiod addresses the poem to his brother,
Perses, whom he depicts as a lazy, aristocratic country squire.
He consistently describes Perses as the opposite of what he
should be. Perses has bribed the judges to gain Hesiod's share
of the family estate instead of doing an honest day's work on
his own portion. He indulges his champagne tastes in a world
too poor to sustain him. His delusions of grandeur make him
believe he lives in the long gone age of heroes rather than the
miserable age of iron. Hesiod sees himself, however, as a
simple hard working farmer. Dedication to work, he believes,
should lead to the good life. He preaches to Perses and his
fellow farmers a gospel of work in a world where "good is always
mixed with evil" (179). "Work!" he shouts to lazy Perses, "Pile
up work upon work" (382).

Hesiod weaves several antitheses into the intricate, sometimes confusing and inconsistent, design of the *Works and Days*.
He tirelessly points out that there are two ways to do anything.
He speaks of two roads: the steep, hard road to justice and the
easy, level road to evil. There are two contradictory laws and
two opposing cities. The fundamental antithesis, however,
involves the effects of work and idleness. *Ergon*, "work," is
the way to achieve the good life which will produce a new age of
Zeus' justice. Idleness leads away from this goal by fostering
all of this world's evils. Finally, there are two kinds of evil
which thrive when men shun hard work in favor of idleness.
Kakon, evil such as disease, pain, and hunger, besets one from
the outside; and *hybris*, internal moral evil, drives one to
violate the rights of others.

In the *Works and Days*, Hesiod also uses two myths to explain
how the present age, exemplified by Perses, has become degenerate.

The story of Pandora explains the emergence of external *kakon*
while the Five Ages accounts for the appearance of *hybris*, moral
evil. In both cases, Hesiod changes the traditional myths of
decline so that they describe the sudden emergence of evil and
backbreaking work. His versions of both myths have become
standard and have greatly influenced subsequent literature.

The Five Ages

   Since the rise of evil is more fully developed in the Five
Ages than in the story of Pandora, we will reverse Hesiod's order
and consider the Five Ages first. This myth narrates the creation of five successive, distinct human ages: golden, silver,
bronze, heroic, and iron. Similar myths existed long before
Hesiod and were popular throughout the Mediterranean area. Both
the Persians and the Indians had myths of decline in four ages,
which Hesiod may have known. (See Joseph Fontenrose, "Work,
Justice, and Hesiod.") The Sumerians and Babylonians, according
to William Hallo, had myths of decline from a former age of
peace and believed in the progressive shortening of human life.
Although Genesis 6:1-4 may reflect this idea, there are no known
myths of four ages from the ancient Near East. Finally, the
Greeks and Romans used the tradition of decline frequently. Such
writers as Aratus, Horace, and Ovid all had versions of the
decline in four ages.

   The pattern and purpose of the traditional myth are clearly
discernible in the version of the Roman poet, Ovid, even though
he lived some seven centuries later than Hesiod. (See Appendix
for Ovid's text.)   In Ovid's version, the growth of evil is
gradual over the course of the golden, silver, bronze, and iron
ages. The golden age is one of righteousness and fidelity in
which war, work, and crime are unknown; spring is eternal and
rivers run with milk. The silver age shows some decline from
the golden: spring is shortened, nature is not perfectly
benign, and human beings have to live indoors. The bronze age
is a savage, warlike age. Finally, the iron age of Ovid's own
Augustan Rome is characterized by every human crime: step-
mothers mix ghastly poisons and husbands long for their wive's
deaths. Ovid's version, then, shows decline from primitive
virtue and an earthly utopia to the degeneracy and decay of his
own time. Each successive age brings a more difficult natural
environment or a more degenerate human nature.

If Ovid's version is typical of the tradition, Hesiod changes
the pattern to show idleness as the begetter of *hybris*, the
cancer of the spirit. Instead of showing a decline, Hesiod moves
immediately from the utopian existence of the golden men to a
world of complete moral evil and destructive crime. (See
Friedrich Solmsen, *Hesiod and Aeschylus*, pp. 82-89.). The cancer
of the human spirit is already fully present in the second stage.
The silver men are a generation of reckless "big babies" who
criminally destroy one another. The wars of the bronze age and
the family feuds of the iron age only spread the area of the
same basic infection.

Hesiod interrupts the story of the metallic ages by inserting the age of heroes between the bronze and the iron ages. His
addition of this age is a problem for several reasons. The age
has no metallic name; it exhibits no *hybris* or laziness; even
the wars are the "glorious" struggles at Troy and Thebes. The
heroes are brave, just, and even godlike, and some of them
finally achieve a kind of "golden" immortality at the end of
the earth (170ff.). We may wonder why Hesiod would mar his
scheme of ages with this illogical intrusion. Such a reaction,
however, would never have occurred to Hesiod or his Greek audience. They traced their lineage back to this heroic "generation
previous to ours on the endless earth" (160). They could not
have imagined a scheme of ages without the heroes, no matter
how much it interrupted the thematic development of the poem.
It would have been as unthinkable for them to omit the heroes of
Thebes and Troy as it would be for us to omit the heroes of 1776
from an American chronicle.

The Story of Pandora

The other myth depicting the rise of evil concerns a woman
known to every feminist. She is Pandora, "the spine-chilling,
untouchable booby-trap" (83), who opens the jar containing all
the evil in the world. Hesiod makes no attempt to link this
story of Pandora to that of the Five Ages in a consistent time-
frame. The two stories are separate in origin, and each is used
independently to describe the appearance of distinct kinds of
evil. In the Five Ages, the basic antithesis is between work
and idleness. Work is healthy in the golden age, and idleness
brings on crime in the later ages. In the story of Pandora,
however, the poet introduces another antithesis, that between
male and female. The male is linked to the good, original,

happy, and natural state; the female is an unnatural copy whose
presence necessitates hard work and pain. (See Pietro Pucci,
Hesiod and the Language of Poetry.)

Hesiod, however, does not make Pandora responsible for *hybris*,
"internal evil." She and her jar account only for the spread of
kakon, "external evil." *Kakon*, as used by Hesiod and other early
Greek writers, is a cheap, plebeian word. No aristocrat was ever
guilty of it. Until the time of the tragedians, *kakon* was characterized not by insolent, tyrannical behavior but by docility
and the subservience suited to an inferior or slave. By analyz-
ing his version of the myth, we can see how Hesiod uses this idea
of external, inferior evil.

The story of Pandora is so condensed that some of the events
seem unrelated to each other. But the repetition of *kakon*, which
appears seven times, holds the poem together. The very occasion
of the woman's creation connects her to *kakon*. After Prometheus
steals fire, Zeus promises to send mortals "an evil [in] which
they will all delight" (57). Then Zeus gives the retaliatory
order for the production of a woman.

Everything about the new creation is second-hand; it is to
be given a human voice and human strength, the face of a goddess,
the mind of a bitch and the character of a thief (68). Whereas
humanity, like the gods, has arisen naturally from the earth
(108), the woman has an unnatural artificial quality and is
manufactured from earth and water. Various gods have a hand in
this cut-and-paste fabrication: the master craftsman Hephaistos
is in charge; Athena, the goddess of weaving, is to teach it
woman's *ergon*, working the loom; Aphrodiate is to "pour graceful
charm, consuming desire, and knee-weakening anxiety around
its head" (65-6); Hermes, the trickster god, is to provide the
bitch's mind and the thief's character. This woman is the first
product of an assembly line, a gift that is the opposite of what
gifts are meant to be. Before the birth of Pandora, "a race of
mortals lived on the earth far removed from evils, from harsh
toils, and from consuming disease which spell doom to men"
(90-92).

Hesiod, then, relies heavily on the misogynist tradition in
which man is created first and the woman's creation explains the
origin of evil. Curiously, the name Pandora comes from another,
very complex tradition, probably obscure even by Hesiod's day.
In this tradition, both sexes are created simultaneously and the
woman is exalted for her connection with the fertile earth.
Pandora was originally a complimentary title applied to Mother

Earth. She was called *Ge Pandora*, "Earth the Giver of all Gifts,"
because human beings were thought to receive all blessings from
her. Although we do not have all the clues to trace the tradition, we can see the irony of Hesiod's turning the giver of all
gifts into an evil booby trap.

The few sentences about Pandora's jar are perhaps the most
enigmatic element in the episode (94-104). The jar seems to
appear out of nowhere. Pandora opens it; and every kind of
earthly woe flies out, free to afflict men at random. Then,
under Zeus' aegis, she slaps the lid down, trapping hope under
its rim. Why are hope and all these external evils together in
the jar? The answer is perhaps suggested by the change in the
human condition. Although there is no need for hope in a utopia,
hope is necessary once evils flood the world.

But why does hope not escape along with the woes? Hesiod
does not say. He only leaves us with the cryptic image of
sedentary hope. This purely mythic image teases the imagination
and encourages us to explain its meaning. Perhaps hope does not
escape because it is not an external reality which can go to and
fro, like the woes that strike at will (102). Perhaps it remains
inside because it is an internal possession, a gift which one
must suggest that hope is the secret weapon capable of defeating
external woes. (See Note to line 94.)

A question about the story still remains: if Hesiod thinks
of woman in negative terms, why does he not blame her for moral
evil? The poet's attitude towards women, gleaned from the rest
of the *Works and Days*, suggests an answer. The poem is full of
advice for Hesiod's male audience. Men should be thirty years
old when they marry, and they should carefully pick very young
girls whom they can "teach sober ways." There is "no better
booty" than a good wife who will tend the farm, give birth to
an heir, and bring solace in old age. Woman, therefore,
is seen as a piece of man's property, a prize won in the battle
of life. As such, she lacks the stature to bear *hybris*, moral
evil. For *hybris* is the Greek word for any excessive human
behavior whereby one proudly asserts one's rights at the expense
of a god or a fellow human being. In Hesiod's society, no one
could be hybristic without equality, and no woman had the stature
for *hybris*.

In the Five Ages and Pandora, then, Hesiod shapes traditional
stories to reflect his own pessimistic outlook on life in his
own day. What was traditionally a gradual decline over four
ages becomes one drastic fall from the euphoria of the golden

age to the *hybris* of later times. And Pandora who once was the
bountiful earth bestowing blessings on all emerges in Hesiod's
version as the bearer of the world's woes. Although Hesiod's
Pandora is only responsible for *kakon* and men commit *hybris* on
their own, the popularity of the story of Pandora has thoroughly
obscured that point. We will probably never know whether Hesiod
can claim credit for this popularity or whether the image of
Pandora simply reinforced existing prejudices.

PANDORA AND THE FIVE AGES (HESIOD'S *WORKS AND DAYS* 47-201)

Pandora (47-105)

Zeus was angry and hid away the means of life
because subtle Prometheus tricked him.
So Zeus planned dismal troubles for mortals and hid fire.
But Prometheus, the good son of Iapetos, eluded   50
wise Zeus, lover of thunder. To help mortals,
Prometheus sneaked the fire away from Zeus in a hollow reed.
Angered at this, Zeus the cloud-gatherer spoke:
"Son of Iapetos, you know more tricks than anyone else,
and you are happy that you stole fire and cheated me.   55
But in return, great pain will afflict you and all men.
As a price for the fire, I will give men evil which
they will all delight in and embrace in their evil hearts."
Speaking thus, the father of men and gods laughed out loud.
Then he quickly ordered famous Hephaistos to mix   60
water with earth, put in it the voice and strength
of a mortal, the looks of an immortal goddess, and
the pleasing shape of a luscious maiden; he ordered Athena
to teach the thing to weave on the intricate loom;
he ordered Golden Aphrodite to pour graceful charm,   65
consuming desire, and knee-weakening anxiety around its head.
Finally, he ordered the Guide Hermes, Slayer of Argos,
to give it the mind of a bitch and the temper of a thief.
Zeus had spoken. They all followed the orders of Zeus,
    son of Kronos. Immediately,
according to Zeus' plan, Hephaistos, the famous Lame One,   70
molded from the earth the likeness of a blushing maiden.
Athena, goddess with gleaming eyes, dressed
and decked her out. The divine Graces and Lady Persuasion
encircled her neck with strings of gold.
The fair-haired Hours added a crown of spring flowers.   75

114

Then Pallas Athena arranged everything on her body.
Next the Guide Hermes, Slayer of Argos, planted
in her breast false, flattering words and the temper
of a thief, according to the plan of Zeus the loud-thunderer;
Hermes, herald of the gods, endowed her with a voice   80
and named this woman Pandora because every Olympian
gave her a gift, which meant pain for struggling men.
When he finished this spine-chilling, untouchable booby trap,
Father Zeus told Hermes, the swift messenger of the gods
and Slayer of Argos, to take this gift to Epimetheus.   85
Epimetheus did not recall that Prometheus had told him
never to accept a gift from Olympian Zeus but to return it
so that nothing evil could ever happen to mortals.
But he remembered only after accepting this evil.
Before this, a race of mortals lived on the earth   90
far removed from evils, from harsh toils,
and from consuming disease which spell doom to men.   92
But when the woman opened the great lid of the jar,
    everything scattered.   94
Zeus planned the release of these dismal troubles   95
for mortals. There alone, Hope remained within,
    in the unbroken chamber
under the lip of the jar. It did not fly outside.
Before that could happen, she slammed down the lid
of the jar, according to the plan of aegis-bearing Zeus,
    the cloud-gatherer.
But countless other gloomy things wander around   100
    in search of men.
Full is the earth, full is the sea of evil.
During the day, afflictions come to mortals; and at night
they go to and fro wherever they will, inflicting evils.
Noiselessly they come since wise Zeus snatched away
their voices. Thus, there is no way to escape Zeus' plan.   105

The Five Ages (106-201)

If you wish, I shall outline another tale
well and artfully. Store it in your mind and know
how gods and mortal people were born from the same place.

Golden Age

The golden age was the very first generation of mortals
which the gods dwelling on Olympos made.   110
They lived during the time when Kronos reigned in the sky.
Like the gods, they lived without care and breathed freely,
a race apart; for them there was no hard labor or misery;
wretched old age did not come upon them; but always
in the bloom of youth, they enjoyed life far from all evils. 115
They died as if overcome by sleep; all noble things
were theirs: their farms bore plentiful crops almost
without tending; they willingly accepted their share
of the light work and peacefully lived off the harvest.
When the earth covered up this generation,   120
they became spirits through the plan of mighty Zeus;
noble guardians of humanity, they live on the earth's surface
and watch over lawsuits and cruel deeds.
Clothed in mist, they roam everywhere on earth,
for they are kings who grant rich harvests.   125

Silver Age

Then the silver age was the second generation which
the gods dwelling on Olympos made. It was much worse,
not as noble in body or mind as the golden generation.
These men remained children for a hundred years,
feeding off their dear mamas and romping around   130
in the house like grown-up babies.
When they reached manhood and were on their own,
they lived only a brief time because they were sick
from their own foolishness. In their reckless violence,
they kept lashing out at one another. They refused   135
to obey the divine mandates: to worship the immortals
    and to sacrifice on their altars
as human beings always have. Zeus, son of Kronos,
removed them because he was angry that they did not give
respect to the gods who live on Olympos.
But when the earth covered up even that generation,   140
they were known as a second class of blessed mortals
and lived under the ground. Nevertheless, they have honor.

Bronze Age

Then father Zeus made the bronze age, the third generation
of mortal people; unlike the silver generation,
they were terrible and strong, and born from ash trees.   145
Ares' sad works and violence were their occupations.
They did not eat grain but had by their very nature
unbending hearts of steel. They had great power.
Invincible arms grew from shoulders attached
    to their massive bodies.
Their weapons and tools were bronze.   150
Even their houses were bronze since there was not yet
any black iron. Conquered by their own hands, they went
to the dank house of icy Hades, a nameless generation.
Yet black Death took away these men, fearsome though they were.
They had to give up the bright light of the sun.   155

Heroic Age

And when the earth also covered up that generation,
Zeus, son of Kronos, made another, the fourth
on the all-nourishing earth, a godlike age of heroic men
lawful and better behaved, who were called demi-gods,
the generation previous to ours on the endless earth.   160
Many of them were destroyed by evil war with its dire
battle cries: some under seven-gated Thebes, Kadmos' land,
died fighting for the possessions of Oedipus;
some went in ships over the great deep sea
to Troy for the sake of fair-haired Helen.   165
Death brought an end to some of these, covering them up;
for the others, father Zeus, son of Kronos, established
a house at the end of the earth, apart from living mortals.
These heroes dwell there carefree,
on the islands of the blessed, by deep-eddying Ocean.   170
Happy are the heroes, for three times a year
the fruitful land bears honey-sweet wheat for them!

Iron Age

Far-seeing Zeus put yet another generation of mortals,
    the fifth, on the all-nourishing earth.
I wish that I no longer were among the fifth generation,
but either died before them or were to be born afterward.   175
For now this is the generation of iron. By day,
they will find no end to toil and pain; and by night

they will have no relief; instead the gods will give them
harsh anxieties. For them, good is always mixed with evil.
Still, Zeus will destroy this generation of mortals   180
when their newborn babies have graying hair,
when fathers differ with their children and children
    with their fathers,
when guests differ with their hosts and friends with friends,
and when brothers no longer love one another as they
    did in the past.
Suddenly these men will dishonor their aging parents   185
and ruthlessly blame them with bitter words.
Stupid fools! They will not recognize that the gods
    punish them.
They will not compensate their old parents for raising them.
With power as their law, they will destroy each other's
cities. They will not extend good will toward   190
the trustworthy, the just, or the noble.
The evil-doer and the insolent will receive honor.
Might will make right, and there will be no restraint.
The evil men will deceive the better with twisted words
    and sworn oaths.
Malicious Envy, with her screeching cry and eyes flashing   195
with hate, will walk beside miserable mortals.
Nemesis and Aidos, robed in bright garments,
will return to Olympos and rejoin the gods,
leaving humanity behind on the wide-pathed earth.
Miserable pain will be all that is left for mortals.   200
There will be no strength to fight off evil.

NOTES TO PANDORA AND THE FIVE AGES

48. Because subtle Prometheus tricked him. Apparently this phrase refers to the account of Prometheus' trick in Hesiod's *Theogony* 534-62. In that passage, Hesiod tells a similar story of the first woman although he leaves her nameless. In many other myths, Prometheus is regarded as the creator of the human race, but Hesiod does not mention this. See F. Carter Phillips, "Narrative Compressions and the Myths of Prometheus in Hesiod," *Classical Journal* 68 (1973), 289-305.

49. For mortals. Here Hesiod uses the Greek word for all humanity, *anthrōpos*. Although this word normally includes women as well as men, Hesiod clearly thinks of humanity in male terms throughout both of these stories. He uses *anthrōpos* and *anēr*, "male," fairly interchangeably, but he never uses *andres kai gynaikes*, "men and women." *Gynaikes* is rarely part of his vocabulary.

57. I will give men evil. *Kakon* is Hesiod's word for external evils caused by woman's creation. It occurs also in lines 58, 88, 89, 91, 93, 101, and 103. See Introduction to this chapter.

68. The mind of a bitch. Other ancient writers also characterize women as dogs or bitches; for instance, Helen calls herself a bitch twice in one short passage (*Iliad* 6.344ff.).

81. And named this woman Pandora. Hesiod's explanation for the name "Pandora," literally "All Gifts," is ambiguous. The text can mean the gods all "gave her a gift which meant pain for struggling men" or "gave her as a gift." In either case, she embodies the gods' painful gift. (See Introduction to this chapter for the earlier use of "All Gifts" as a name for the Earth goddess.) Pain, Greek *pēma*, is closely linked to woman's creation in this story. At 56 woman's creation is a great pain. The same phrase is used of Helen's abduction in the *Iliad* 3.50 and in Hesiod's other account of woman's creation (*Theogony* 592).

We assume that Hesiod is making Pandora the first woman. For a different view, see Frederick Brenk, "Hesiod: How much a Male Chauvinist?" *The Classical Bulletin* 49.5 (1973), pp. 73-76. Brenk concludes that Pandora is the prototype not of all women but of lazy women.

119

85. Epimetheus. Epimetheus means "after-thought" which fits his mistake in this episode. In contrast, Prometheus means "fore-thought."

94. The jar. Although popularly known as Pandora's box, the Greek word is actually "jar." West traces the mistranslation to Erasmus, who perhaps confused the Pandora story with that of Psyche and the box she had been warned against opening. (See West, *Works and Days*, p. 68.)

The story of the jar may be modeled on the scene described in *Iliad* 24.527-33 where there are two jars on Zeus' doorstep, one containing good and the other evil. Zeus could then distribute good and evil to mortals in varying amounts.

There are many interpretations of the jar. For instance, if the jar is originally identified with the woman, as some suggest, the myth may imply that woman is paradoxically the source of woes and of hope. For various other interpretations, see Dora and Erwin Panofsky, *Pandora's Box: The Changing Aspects of a Mythical Symbol.*

96. Hope remained within. The Greek word for "hope," *elpis*, also means expectation or anxiety.

108. From the same place. Greek *homothen* may also mean "on the same terms." Thus, its use here may suggest that gods like mortals were born from Earth and Sky. Hesiod's main point, however, may be that mortals originally shared the gods' carefree state (112). See also West's *Works and Days*, p. 178.

134. Reckless violence. Hybris is Hesiod's word for internal violence. Forms of this word occur also at 146 and 192.

145. Born from ash trees. Trees are also used for human creation in Norse mythology. The victorious Odin found two trees on the shore, an ash and an elm; and the first man and woman, Askr and Embla, were created from them.

147. They did not eat grain. They were warriors rather than farmers.

159. Who were called demi-gods. A demi-god was a child of a god; that is, he had a divine parent but was not himself immortal.

173-74. The first line contains the pattern the poet uses to introduce the other ages, but the second line may be a later addition; 174 departs from the pattern with an emotional outburst.

188. Stupid fools! This phrase translates Hesiod's phrase for fatal ignorance. Compare *Theogony* where Kronos is fatally stupid.

197. Nemesis and Aidos.   These goddesses personify two
aspects of moral restraint.   Aidos is a sense of reverence or
shame that keeps a person from an immoral act.   (See 193.)
Nemesis (the daughter of Night, *Theogony* 223) is the moral
indignation society feels at offenses against justice or decency.
Thus, the departure of these spirits signals the end of moral
consciousness on earth.

STUDY QUESTIONS ON PANDORA AND THE FIVE AGES

1. Pandora (47-105)

    Why does Zeus want to punish human beings? How is Pandora
    made? What deities help to make Pandora? According to
    Hesiod, what is the significance of Pandora's name? Why
    does Hermes bring her to Epimetheus? What happens when
    Epimetheus accepts her? What is in her jar? What happens
    when she opens it? Why does hope remain inside?

2. The Five Ages (106-201)

    What is Hesiod's view of the human condition in each of the
    five ages? How are the human beings of each age created?
    Who creates them? Why? Compare these creations to the
    creation of Pandora. What is the difference between the
    evil depicted in this story and the evil in the story of
    Pandora? How does the heroic age upset the general pattern
    of the story? Who are the heroes Hesiod refers to in the
    heroic age?

3. General Questions

    Compare the creations in Pandora and the Five Ages to the
    creations in *Atrahasis* and the story of Adam and Eve in
    terms of the materials used, the methods used, and the
    motives of the creator-gods. How is Pandora different from
    the human beings created in the other accounts? How are
    the human beings in the Five Ages different?

    Compare the creator-gods in Hesiod's stories to those in
    the other accounts. Which gods are most similar to those
    depicted in Hesiod's stories? Why? Compare Hesiod's views
    of human nature to the views in *Atrahasis* and the story of
    Adam and Eve. Which account has the most complex view of
    human nature? Why? Which has the simplest? Why? Compare
    Eve and Pandora. Which one is more responsible for the
    introduction of evil into the world? Why?

PART THREE: THE CULTURAL BACKGROUND

CHAPTER 7

MESOPOTAMIA: A CULTURE BASED ON WRITING

The year 539 B.C. is not very memorable for most of us. The
great events which were to shape Western Civilization had not
yet occurred. The Greek victory over Persia which ushered in
the golden age of Athenian culture would not take place until
some fifty years later. Rome was nothing more than a collection
of small villages ruled by an Etruscan king. And the Israelites,
about to be freed from their exile in Babylon, had not yet
collected their sacred writings into the form we now know as
the Old Testament. But 539 B.C. marked the end of political
independence for a civilization which had lasted for more than
twenty-five hundred years.

That end came swiftly and all too easily for Mesopotamia.
Assyria, the northern portion of the area, was already under
foreign control when Cyrus the Great of Persia marched into
Babylon in 539 B.C.; and the Babylonian king, Nabonidus, gave
him the city without a fight. Called a weakling, a babbler,
and a tormentor, Nabonidus was not the most respected of rulers.
His abdication was only the last in a series of suspicious
actions. He worshipped the moon god, Sin, in preference to
Marduk, the patron god of Babylon; he interfered in religious
matters which were rightfully the province of the temple priests;
and he took up residence for a time in an Arabian city. Several
accounts from this time contrast Nabonidus' unkingly practices
with the actions of Cyrus who was praised as a liberator and
messiah. Nabonidus had surrendered, and apparently the
Babylonians acquiesced in his decision.

Such a finale was indeed ironic for Mesopotamia. The people
who built this "cradle of civilization" were not used to giving
up so easily. The land on which they lived was harsh, and yet
they developed successful agriculture. They were constantly
threatened by invasions from hostile peoples, so they built

large cities which were not only defensive fortresses but also centers for trade and culture. And they developed a system of writing which was the most durable the world has known. Indeed, writing was one of the most outstanding features of Mesopotamian culture. The Mesopotamians used a complex system of writing on clay tablets which they impressed with a reed to make wedge-shaped marks called cuneiform. Various groups of people who settled in Mesopotamia adapted this system to their own language and used it extensively to record their activities.

Proud of their ability to write, the Mesopotamians loved to draw up lists. They made lists, for example, of their kings from the beginning of time to the present; of their gods who numbered as many as three thousand; of medicines, laws, animals, and even unusual events. They used lists to express abstract ideas such as geometric relationships. Pythagoras, a Greek who lived about 500 B.C., first expressed the general theorem on the relationship between the sides of a right triangle; but long before Pythagoras, the Mesopotamians were aware of this relationship. Typically, they did not use a general formula to express the idea. Instead they made a list of the various sizes of triangles and their corresponding sides.

Their writing system helped the Mesopotamians build a civilization which was far more advanced than those of their neighbors. Their cities, for example, were run by complex bureaucracies which maintained records of their daily business transactions. They kept inventories of their crops and farm animals, carried on extensive trade, and even had a welfare system for their poor. They were also able to preserve their cultural tradition in writing instead of relying on oral transmission. They copied their prayers, myths, rituals, omens, and literary efforts for future generations to study. Writing even influenced their view of themselves and their world. They believed, for example, that a scribe lived in the underworld who kept a list of those who were to die each day. He was not originally a personification of fate, as later belief would have him; rather, he was understood to be the ideal bureaucrat, a divine bookkeeper, who carefully kept track of his clients and dependents. Writing, then, was virtually a national obsession with the Mesopotamians, and their ability to write enabled them to develop a highly sophisticated civilization. At the same time, however, they were constantly struggling for their survival because of the natural conditions of the area in which they lived.

Mesopotamia lies in the vicinity of the Tigris and Euphrates
Rivers and is now part of modern Iraq. The rivers and their many
tributaries provide the main water supply to the area without
which parts of Mesopotamia would be desert since there is very
little rainfall (about six inches per year) and the temperature
during the summer averages in the nineties. The rivers, fed by
streams and melted snow from the mountains, overflow regularly
in the spring and flood the southern portion of the valley, thus
fertilizing the land. This flooding which often proved disastrous to ancient farmers is now controlled by modern dams. But
as recently as 1954, the city of Baghdad was devastated by a
flood. In ancient times, the peoples of Mesopotamia recognized
the vast potential of the rivers. They built an extensive
system of canals to irrigate their land for farming. This system
has been in use for thousands of years and is so vast and intricate that it is now often impossible to distinguish between the
naturally formed tributaries of the rivers and the man-made
canals. The system required constant maintenance and redigging
because silt deposits would quickly build up and fill the canals
if they were left unattended. Thus, a high degree of cooperation
among the farmers was necessary to insure that water would be
available to all.

Although it provided the means for agriculture in the area,
irrigation had many drawbacks. Frequent inundation of the fields
left salt deposits on the land and decreased fertility of the
soil. Ancient Mesopotamian farmers, therefore, had to work
harder and harder while getting gradually smaller yields of crops
from their farms. They often had to abandon fields completely
and search for more fertile land. In addition, there was the
ever-present threat of flooding which could wipe out not only
the season's crops but the city as well. The same rivers which
provided sustenance for the Mesopotamians were also taking it
away. It is not surprising, then, to find reference to the
rivers in Mesopotamian myths. In *Atrahasis*, for example, the
gods are depicted digging the Tigris and Euphrates Rivers just as
men dig canals. The gods find the work so difficult that they
go on strike and refuse to return to work. Then they create the
human race to take over the hard labor. This story tells us
much about the Mesopotamians' view of their place in the world.
They were not only servants of the gods, but they also had to
take on the back-breaking work which those much stronger than
themselves were unwilling to continue. Indeed, as highly

developed as their civilization was, the Mesopotamians were
always aware of the difficulty of maintaining their way of life.

The Mesopotamian City and Its Institutions

Although agriculture was vital to Mesopotamian civilization
as it was to many ancient peoples, the city was the political and
cultural center of Mesopotamian life. To the individual citizen,
the city was not only a safe haven from hostile nomads and
foreign invaders but also the source of his livelihood, the place
where his most sacred institutions were located, and the link
between himself and the gods who dwelt high in the heavens. Like
the modern city, it was run by large bureaucracies, was the
center of commerce, and dominated the landscape on which it was
built. Even farmers, unlike their modern counterparts, frequently lived in the city and grew crops on land which was under
the protection of the urban kings. In fact, the city was so
prominent in the lives of the people that one Mesopotamian
cosmology describes the world as a vast sea which was empty
except for an occasional island city.

Each city was an independent political unit with its own
patron god, army, political structure, and characteristic
design; but many Mesopotamian cities were divided into three
parts. First, the "inner city" was surrounded by a wall for
protection against invaders and contained the two principal
institutions of Mesopotamian life--the temple of the patron god
and the palace of the king. It also contained the houses of the
citizens and the shops of the tradesmen and craftsmen. Wealthy
citizens who owned land in the area usually lived there and
elected their mayor to run the day-to-day affairs of the city.
Second, the "outer city" consisted primarily of farmlands which
provided food and other necessary raw materials for the citizens.
The farmers who tilled the soil and harvested the crops usually
did not own the land but were sharecroppers working for the
temple or the palace. Third, a "harbor" often served as the
commercial center of the city. Merchants from foreign lands
resided there and carried on international trade with the temple
and palace. (See Oppenheim, *Ancient Mesopotamia*, pp. 95ff.)

The walls of the inner cities usually had one or more large
gates. The open areas near these gates may have served as
market places for the populace and assembly places for the
mayors who ran the business of the cities. But the temple and
palace complexes were the dominant architectural features of

many inner cities. Each complex had a large number of buildings including residences, chapels, storehouses for grain, and courts. The ziggurats, or temple towers, rose high above the rest of the buildings. These mountain-like structures, some almost two hundred feet high, were sources of great pride to the cities which had them. The ziggurats which could be seen from many miles away were the main symbols of the culture and wealth of the individual cities. Temples were built at the top of the ziggurats to symbolize the cities' dedication to their gods. Since they were sacred mountains, the ziggurats were also considered the city's link to the divine world. Even the names given to these structures reflected this idea; the famous ziggurat of Babylon, for example, was named *Etemenanki*, "the house of the foundations of heaven and earth." Indeed, cities rivaled each other to build bigger and more elaborate ziggurats in much the same way as our modern cities build skyscrapers.

Unlike modern cities, however, the Mesopotamian city had two principal institutions, the temple of the patron god and the palace of the king. In both these institutions, complex bureaucracies controlled large shares of farmland which surrounded the city, collected grain in their storehouses, and distributed it to the members of their household or traded with other cities and foreign lands. In other respects, however, these two institutions had very different responsibilities. The temple existed primarily for the care and feeding of the patron god while the palace provided the king with the means to defend the city and to conquer other lands.

The temple provided the link between the patron god and his city. As long as the god's house was maintained, the city was assured of prosperity and happiness. But fulfilling the god's needs was not an easy task. The temple statue which symbolized the god was carved out of the most expensive wood, was overlaid with gold, and had staring eyes made out of precious stones. The temple priests dressed the statue in the costliest clothing, prepared meals for the god thought to be present in the statue, sang to him; bathed the statue as if it were the god, escorted it to bed, and held special feasts in its honor. This complex and expensive routine indicates the high value which the city put on the statue of its patron god. Its presence was a sign that the god was bestowing his blessings on the citizens.

As well as being the religious center of the city, the temple was also one of its financial centers. It often owned the largest amount of farm land in the area, hired many workers for the cultivation and harvesting of its crop, and stored the grain for the city's use or for trade. With this financial power, the temple also assumed social responsibilities. It standardized weights and measures, lent money (without interest to those in need), and even adopted the children of poor families during times of financial hardship. Finally, the temple provided the palace with essential cultic services such as divination and exorcism.

To perform all these services, the temple needed a large bureaucracy whose members had to be highly trained in the difficult art of writing. These scribes, as they were called, were members of the most prestigious profession in Mesopotamia. They drew up contracts, recorded legal transactions, kept records of business deals, and copied religious texts for the priests, diviners, physicians, and others. Their services were always in great demand. The temple hired many scribes who were considered the family of the patron god. The king's palace also needed a family of scribes to run its bureaucracy, and even the ordinary citizen at times needed to hire a scribe whose functions were similar to those of a modern lawyer. But the Mesopotamian scribe had much more prestige. Even Mesopotamian kings who were educated as scribes advertised their ability to write. As early as 2000 B.C., Shulgi, the king of Ur, boasted of his scribal skills. Later Assurbanipal, the last great Assyrian king, claimed to have copied the documents which stocked his enormous library at Nineveh.

Anyone wanting to become a scribe in ancient Mesopotamia had to undergo a rigorous education. Usually, only rich families could afford to send their children to a scribal school since schooling began when the child was small and ended when he was an adult. Most of this time was spent learning the complex system of cuneiform writing. Students copied religious and legal texts to learn the proper technique; but they also studied science, mathematics, and literature since a scribe had to know something of these fields to carry on his work effectively. The scribal school was organized in much the same way as ours. It had a principal, called the "Father of the School," and teachers who were known as "Big Brothers." But the school day was much longer and the discipline more severe. Even for young children, school began at sunrise and continued until sunset with only a break for lunch. The morning hours were filled with writing practice in which the students would copy texts given to them for the purpose. During the afternoon, the students would

study and memorize the texts to be written out the following day.
If their work was unsatisfactory, they would be whipped for
their trouble.

A Sumerian short story gives us a glimpse of student life
during the third millennium. It tells the story of an average
student who begins his day in typical fashion: he rises in the
morning, tells his mother to hurry with his lunch, and runs off
to school. Having arrived late, he is beaten and then settles
down to his assignment. When he gives his finished tablet to
his Big Brother, he is beaten again for being a dunce. The
student then decides drastic action is necessary if he is to
pass the course. So he invites the teacher to dinner, and his
parents prepare a sumptuous feast. The teacher then announces
to the student's parents that he is a fine scholar. There was
apparently more than one way to earn good grades in ancient
Mesopotamia. (See Kramer, *History Begins at Sumer*, pp. 8-11.)

The king's palace was run in much the same way as the temple.
The king also controlled large amounts of land and engaged in
foreign trade, but his primary responsibility was the defense of
the city and the conquest of new lands. The latter role was
especially important in Assyria where successful military
expeditions were necessary for the cities to prosper, for
Assyrian cities often functioned near the subsistence level
unless the king was able to subjugate other areas and bring
back spoils and tribute. These conditions explain at least in
part the aggressive imperial policies which the Assyrian kings
employed throughout most of their history.

The king was also responsible for the building and maintenance of the temple. When victorious in war, he was expected
to share the booty with the temple priests in order to thank the
patron god for his success and guarantee future successes. But
the king often had a religious stature of his own. The
Mesopotamians believed that the monarchy as well as other
civilized institutions had a divine origin. This belief is
expressed, for example, in the *Sumerian King List* which uses the
recurring phrase, "When the kingship was brought down from
heaven . . ." In addition, statues of kings were often erected
in the temple to indicate that the kings were divine, and the
kings were described with such epithets as "awe-inspiring
luminosity" which were normally associated with the gods.

Despite his divine stature, the king was still dependent on
the temple. Before undertaking any military expedition or other
important endeavor, he needed to discover the will of the gods

through divination. This art, practiced by specially trained temple scribes, was based on the belief that the gods wrote their will in everything on earth. They made their intentions known through the configurations of stars, animal organs, and even common everyday events. Theoretically, the diviners believed, it would be possible to determine what the gods had in mind for the future of the human race if everything on earth were known and classified properly. The problem for the diviners was to read the signs successfully. If they determined that the signs were favorable, the king could go ahead with his plans. If the signs were unfavorable, however, the priests could still offer special sacrifices to ask the gods to change their minds.

The diviners took their art very seriously. They dutifully recorded the signs which they found, their predictions, and the actual results of the king's campaigns, all for future reference. This practice led to the compiling of a huge body of "omen literature" which included analysis of the signs, predictions, results, and prayers. Each generation of diviners had to study these materials carefully in order to make proper predictions. Modern scholars have unearthed large numbers of these omens which have helped them piece together Mesopotamian history since the diviners were usually honest in recording the actual results of their predictions even when they were proven wrong.

Divination was only one indication of the complex relationship between the temple and the palace. The king often sought the permission of the gods to rule newly conquered territories and generally recognized the authority of the temple in religious matters. He usually took great pride in his role as lawgiver to the city but acknowledged that his power came ultimately from the gods rather than his own initiative. There are also instances in Mesopotamian history when the high priest of the temple became king and other instances when the high priest had at least equal status with the king even though he did not maintain an army.

A Brief History of Mesopotamia

Since their cities were in effect sovereign states, the peoples of Mesopotamia were not a politically unified group. These cities frequently fought each other for supremacy, and the defeated cities could not be kept under political domination for long. Empires were established several times within Mesopotamia, but they rarely lasted more than a few generations before the individual cities reasserted their political independence. In

addition, frequent migration of new groups into Mesopotamia kept
the political situation unstable. Many groups invaded the area,
took over one or more cities, and eventually were assimilated
into the culture. But some groups did not settle in the cities.
They led a semi-nomadic life in the countryside and posed a
constant threat to the population centers which maintained a
more settled existence. The cities often attempted to assimilate
these groups by taxing them, forcing them to work on the canals,
or drafting them into military service. Because these efforts
were not always successful, however, the tension between city
and open country remained an unstable part of Mesopotamian life.

The history of Mesopotamia, then, is characterized by frequent shifts in power from one city to another, invasion from
nearby or distant places, and sporadic attempts to unify the
area and extend its influence beyond Mesopotamian borders. It
is a complex story of many groups of people, some of whom modern
scholars are barely able to identify. Of all these groups, four
stand out as particularly important because of their contributions to the culture of Mesopotamia--the Sumerians, Akkadians,
Babylonians, and Assyrians.

Although some groups lived in Mesopotamia before them, the
Sumerians were the first settlers to have a history because they
developed the first known writing system to be used in the area.
Their history began about 2900 B.C. after they had already built
many cities which rivaled each other for political dominance.
The *Sumerian King List* names eleven cities which tried to rule
all of Sumer during the first six hundred years of its history.
Historians usually call this era the Early Dynastic Period and
subdivide it into three parts. (See, for example, William Hallo,
The Ancient Near East, pp. 27-54.)

A primitive democracy characterized the city governments of
the first part (about 2900-2700 B.C.). During times of peace,
the men of a city would assemble and make decisions about the
city's affairs. When a crisis arose, however, the assembly
would elect one of its members to solve the problem. He would
be granted only temporary powers to repel an invasion, settle a
land dispute, or fight rampant crime in the city. After solving
the problem, he would be expected to give up his special powers
and return to equal membership in the assembly. Likewise, many
of the cities in Sumer formed a league for mutual protection and
the settling of disputes. The *Sumerian King List* indicates that
Kish was the dominant city in this league for twenty-two generations, starting just after the Great Flood which Mesopotamians

reckoned as the beginning of their history. Since the prestige
of Kish continued long after the city itself lost its political
power, kings of other cities later adopted the title "King of
Kish."

The second part of the Early Dynastic Period (about 2700-2500
B.C.) was a much more unstable and threatening time. Invasions
from outside of Sumer were frequent enough so that many temporary
leaders maintained their positions for long periods of time.
Eventually, they were elected as permanent rulers and established
themselves as elected kings. During this time, a number of
different cities rose to political leadership in Sumer. But
Nippur became the most important city although it never did
attain political dominance. It was instead Sumer's religious
capital because it housed the temple of Enlil, the pre-eminent
Mesopotamian god. As part of their coronation ceremonies, the
kings of this time traveled to Nippur to receive Enlil's permission to rule over Sumer. This practice was continued even by
the powerful kings and emperors of the second and first
millennia.

The final part of the Early Dynastic Period (about 2500-2300
B.C.) produced some changes in the monarchy. The most important
change made the kingship a dynastic rather than elective office;
that is, the king chose his successor, if possible from his own
family. Through the end of this period, many Sumerian cities
continued to vie for supremacy in the area. Ultimately,
Lugalzagesi, the king of Umma, established himself as "lord of
Sumer," another title which would become a traditional indication
of power in Mesopotamia. In addition, Lugalzagesi claimed to
have "straightened the roads from the lower Sea [the Persian
Gulf] to the Upper Sea [the Mediterranean]," thus establishing
the first empire in Mesopotamia. Actually, he probably did not
establish a very powerful or lasting empire, nor did he reign
long enough for there to be much evidence of its strength since
increasing foreign invasions soon led to Lugalzagesi's downfall.
Eventually, various Semitic groups who originally settled in
cities to the north of Sumer dominated Mesopotamia for the rest
of its history.

The Akkadians were the first Semitic group to rule over large
portions of Mesopotamia. Their king Sargon, who built the city
of Akkad (about 2300 B.C.), defeated Lugalzagesi and established
himself as king of Sumer and Akkad. The vast empire he founded
eventually included not only Sumer and Akkad but also the shores
of the Mediterranean in the west, Assyria in the north, and the

mountainous regions in the east. Sargon ruled in Akkad for
fifty-five years himself and established a dynasty in which his
family continued to rule for three generations after his death,
a total of nearly two hundred years. He also began a number of
practices which his successors followed. He created the office
of high priestess of the cities of Ur and Uruk and named his
daughter to the post. He appointed governors to run the cities
under his power, even choosing Lugalzagesi as governor of Umma.
And he claimed the titles of king of Kish, Ur, and Uruk as well
as of Sumer and Akkad to indicate his vast sphere of influence.
Sargon's greatest achievement, however, was the unification of
Mesopotamia under a stable and long-lasting rule. Later empire
builders from Ur, Babylon, and Assyria looked to Sargon as the
example of how it could be done. For he was the first king to
successfully hold together the independent and constantly
bickering cities which characterized Mesopotamia through most of
its history. It is indicative of the fame of Sargon that fifteen
hundred years later, an Assyrian king, who usurped the throne,
adopted the same name, perhaps in the hope of accomplishing as
much as Sargon had.

Surely, then, Sargon was the stuff legends are made of, and
legends about his early life and rise to power were preserved and
recopied by later generations. As seen through these stories,
Sargon was the Moses of Mesopotamia. Born of a priestess who
was illicitly married to a man of humble origins, the baby Sargon
was set afloat on the Euphrates River in a basket. He was
rescued and raised by a water-drawer and gained the attention and
love of the goddess Ishtar. In his youth, he was cup-bearer to
the king of Kish who incurred the wrath of Enlil and was deposed.
Sargon usurped the throne and gained the permission of the god
Enlil to be the legal ruler of Sumer. He thus fulfilled the
destiny indicated by his name which means "the king is
legitimate."

Although Sargon's empire fell because of internal and external pressure, it was not without its lasting importance. During
its time, the Akkadians preserved and continued the Sumerian
culture which remained important to the Mesopotamian people
throughout their history. The Akkadians learned to write from
the Sumerians, first by copying Sumerian documents, then by
keeping their own records in the Sumerian language, and finally
by adapting the cuneiform script to their own language. Scribal
schools thrived throughout Sumer and Akkad during this time, and
their influence even extended beyond Mesopotamia. The distant

Syrian city of Ebla, for example, instituted scribal schools
where even Sumerians went to learn their own writing system.

Attempts to unify Sumer continued for hundreds of years after
the fall of Akkad. The Third Dynasty of Ur and the city of Isin
made the most successful attempts, but even they fell almost as
rapidly as they rose to their positions of power and influence.
About 1900 B.C., while these other cities were fighting for
supremacy in the area, a dynasty of long-lived kings ruled almost
unnoticed over the smaller city of Babylon. Destined to become
Mesopotamia's most famous city, Babylon gradually grew in power
and influence during this time; but the height of its power came
during the reign of Hammurabi (1792-1750 B.C.). Hammurabi built
an empire which covered almost as much territory as Sargon and
his descendents had controlled partly because of the failure of
Sumerian cities to develop a stable alliance among themselves
and partly because of Hammurabi's personality.

Hammurabi left his personal stamp on everything that he did.
His best known accomplishment was certainly his famous law code
which was studied in Mesopotamian schools and became famous
throughout the world. Even today it is the best known document
from ancient Mesopotamia, but its actual purpose is often
misunderstood. It was not really a code of laws in the strict
sense of the term; rather, it was a collection of laws of
different kinds which Hammurabi thought characterized his role
as the chief magistrate of Babylon. Nor is there any evidence
that these laws were ever used in the daily life of the city.
They were carved on a stone to serve as an advertisement of the
accomplishments of Hammurabi's reign, first to Babylon's god and
then to its people.   Their great fame suggests that Hammurabi's
advertisement was far more successful than even he could have
imagined.

Nor were the laws contained on this stone necessarily
original. Many of them were based on earlier collections of laws
made by Lipit-Ishtar of Isin and Ur-Nammu of Ur. But if
Hammurabi's laws are any indication of the general tenor of
Mesopotamian law, we can distinguish a few important features.
First, the laws were written almost exclusively in casuistic
form; that is, they list the conditions under which a given
sanction may apply. Sometimes the number of conditions listed
indicate that these laws could only be applied in very specific
or extreme circumstances. Laws of this kind imply a legal system
based on precedent in which previous decisions form the basis
for a judge's decision in a given case. Second, Hammurabi's

laws seem to emphasize property rights rather than human rights.
His laws provide, for example, sanctions for theft and damage to
property, property settlements in inheritance disputes, and the
obligations involved in the use of the irrigation system.
Unlike the Israelite system of laws, there is no mention of human
obligations to the gods. Finally, Hammurabi's laws stress the
role of the king and the city's patron god in making the laws.
In his introductory statement, he says that his role is to pass
the laws on from the gods to the people. In theory, then, the
laws were divine in origin and the king's status as law-giver
was sanctioned by the gods.

Hammurabi's empire did not grow after his death because it
was built and held together largely through his political shrewd-
ness. His complex maneuverings in building alliances with
Sumerian cities and eventually taking control over them was
beyond the ability of his successors. But Hammurabi's reign is
very important to us because he preserved and extended Sumerian
culture like his predecessors. In fact, most of what we now know
about Mesopotamian culture was preserved during the reign of
Hammurabi, for the Babylonians also learned the Sumerian language
and adapted the cuneiform writing system to their own language
by translating Sumerian literature.

By 1300 B.C., the Assyrians began to rival the power of
Babylon and of the many groups who migrated into Mesopotamia
since the time of Hammurabi. The Assyrians, named after their
patron god and capital city Assur, pursued the idea of a vast
empire more aggressively than either the Babylonians or the
Akkadians. Assyrian kings traditionally went on annual military
campaigns to conquer new territories and to collect tribute from
those already under their power. These kings were well-known in
the Near East for their severity in dealing with those cities
which would not readily surrender, for they even exiled the
entire population of some cities which they defeated. Such
policies were particularly effective in the west where the
Assyrians controlled not only the Mediterranean coast but also
large segments of Egypt and the Nile delta by 650 B.C.

Yet, the expansion of the Assyrian empire was not the
result of steadily increasing gains over this seven hundred year
period. Rather, with the end of each king's reign, territories
were lost which the new king had to reconquer before expanding
the empire in new directions. This situation was the result of
constant dissension and frequent revolts within Assyria's home
territory. The Assyrian king Tukulti-Ninurta I, for example,

captured Babylon about 1200 B.C. and carried off the Babylonian
statue of their patron god Marduk, thus signifying the complete
subjugation of Babylon to the Assyrian king. But his son led a
revolt against the king, imprisoned him in the newly-built capital city, and burned the whole city to the ground. As a result,
the first attempt to build an Assyrian empire collapsed. Likewise, Sennacherib (about 700 B.C.) expanded the empire through
frequent campaigns in the west, but his expansion ended when he
was killed by his son. Even the last great Assyrian king,
Assurbanipal, who died in 627 B.C., had to fight off his
brother's repeated attempts to destroy his power. Although
Assurbanipal held onto the vast domain which included parts of
Egypt, the Assyrian empire lasted less than twenty years after
his death. In 609 B.C., Assyria lost its political independence,
and one of the largest empires of ancient times came to an end.

Babylon again filled the void by assuming power over the
western portion of the Assyrian empire, and for a brief period
the city regained its imperial might. Nebuchadnezzar II best
exemplifies this final period of Mesopotamian history. He kept
the empire intact by following the Assyrian practice of collect-
ing tribute from the imperial provinces himself. His yearly
campaigns brought him to war with the Israelites whom he
eventually defeated and brought to exile in Babylon. He also
completely rebuilt the city of Babylon and made it the prime
example of luxury in the ancient world. But after his long rule
of forty-seven years, his successors could not hold the empire
together; and the Persians eventually took Babylon itself in
539 B.C.

Thus, Mesopotamia's political independence ended when the
Persians took control of Babylon, but the fame of the city lived
on long after it was subjugated. The "Hanging Gardens" which
Nebuchadnezzar II built were later called one of the Seven
Wonders of the World; the name *Chaldean*, taken from the last
group of Mesopotamians to rule Babylon, became synonymous with
astrologer since the Mesopotamians had developed this science
to a higher degree than any other civilization; and Babylon
itself was best remembered as the luxurious city it became during
this last era of political independence.

Mesopotamian Religion

We have already seen the complexity of religious pract[]
which revolved around the patron gods of Mesopotamian cities.
Each city in Mesopotamia had its own special patron; Babylon,
for example, claimed Marduk; Nippur claimed Enlil; and Uruk
claimed Anu. But Mesopotamia's religion was far from monotheistic since all of these gods were recognized as legitimate
deities throughout the area. The power and influence of these
gods waxed and waned with the political fortunes of their
respective cities, but they always remained members of the
Mesopotamian pantheon. In addition, the Mesopotamians recognized
many other deities since they tended to consider any power as
divine, including the powers of all natural phenomena and many
human institutions. This pantheistic outlook and the huge
number of deities which it recognized make Mesopotamian religion
difficult to define. Modern scholars hesitate to attempt such
an analysis because the evidence in many instances is very
slight. But Thorkild Jacobsen has offered a general framework
for understanding the development of this complicated religion.
He breaks down Mesopotamian ideas of the divine into three
historical stages which help explain the complexity of
Mesopotamian religion. (See *Treasures of Darkness*.)

According to Jacobsen, Mesopotamian religion evolved as the
expression of the people's most vital needs at various stages
of their history. The first stage, initially found in the fourth
millennium, stressed the need for food because the Mesopotamians
developed their agriculture and other systems of food production
at this time. Characteristic of this religious stage were the
stories centering on Dumuzi and Inanna, deities of grain and the
storehouse. They first manifested the powers within the phenomena they were identified with: Dumuzi, the growing power of
the grain; and Inanna, the stocking of food in the storehouse and
the idea of plenty. Later, as people wanted a closer relationship with these deities, they gave these gods human form and
developed stories about them. The stories of Dumuzi and Inanna,
for example, center on death and rebirth in a continuing cycle
suggestive of the seasons and the constant worry about the
yearly crop. Each area in Mesopotamia had its deities who
characterized the type of food production which was available to
it. In some areas of the south, gods of fishing and hunting were
pre-eminent; in other areas, gods of grain, orchards, or animal
and vegetable life were more important. All, however, were

originally understood as the power within these natural phenomena
and the difference between wealth and starvation for the people
of the area.

The second stage involved a shift from gods of fertility to
ruler and hero gods. This shift occurred in the third millennium
when the Mesopotamians' most vital concern was invasion and war
rather than the earlier concern for food production and famine.
During this period, the gods became successively more humanized,
and the myths and epics about them were first written down.
These stories pictured the gods in quite human terms; they were
born, grew, lived in the mountains of the sky or the earth,
received daily offerings of food from human priests, and traveled
in human conveyances like boats and chariots. In general, these
gods were organized in a society which echoed that of Mesopotamia
in the third millennium. They ruled over the human cities as an
all-powerful gentry and conducted their business in assemblies
like a primitive democracy.

All these human attributes made the gods more accessible to
human requests and understanding, but there was still a difference between the human and divine worlds. The gods ruled over
the human world like kings who were aloof from their subjects.
This distance was reflected in the "splendor" or "luminosity"
which the Mesopotamians attributed to their gods. "Luminosity"
was a constant image of beauty, joy, vigor, or power; so its
primary application to the gods signified their pre-eminence
and distance from the human world. Although human beings seemed
to lack the ability to achieve happiness or control in an
unpredictable universe, the gods had the power and splendor to
bestow it. During this second stage, then, an important deity
like Enlil became the lord of the wind rather than the wind
itself. Likewise, Anu became the ruler of the sky, and Ea the
ruler of the fresh waters. These more human figures could be
prayed to and petitioned for those human needs necessary for
survival which at that time depended on the kings and heroes
who fought to protect the city.

The third stage which developed during the second millennium
brought the gods to an even closer relationship with their human
subjects. During this period, individuals began to single out
personal gods to whom they could unburden their own particular
problems and ask forgiveness for their own transgressions. The
gods, in effect, became parents who not only had power over their
individual subjects but also cared about their welfare. This
relationship originally developed with lesser deities who could

intercede with the ruler gods on behalf of their human children.
But it later extended to the more powerful gods, including
Ishtar, Enlil, and Ea.   In *Atrahasis*, for example, Ea befriends
King Atrahasis and saves him from the flood despite Enlil's
warnings.

This development of ideas about the divine was a slow process
in which the earlier stages were sometimes mixed with later
ideas. By the second millennium, therefore, the gods were
understood as a complex mixture of many traits. Older deities
often showed characteristics of the natural phenomena with which
they were originally identified (first stage) as well as traits
of rulers (second stage) and parents (third stage). In *Enuma
Elish*, Tiamat exemplifies this combination. At the beginning of
the poem, she is identified with the salt water ocean. But
later she acts like a parent when she does not want to kill her
children; and finally, she assumes the role of a warrior-queen
when she fights Marduk. Such a fusion of concepts made the
individual Mesopotamian deities complex personalities.

But the Mesopotamian pantheon was even more complex because
it included nearly three thousand deities although many of these
were only of minor significance. Such a huge number resulted in
part from the influx of so many different peoples into
Mesopotamia, in part from each locality having its own gods, and
in part from the pantheism of their early religion. In addition,
some of these gods formed a national pantheon which was recognized throughout the area. With their pride in their ability
to write and their penchant for classifying, the Mesopotamians
did not leave this chaotic condition alone. Rather, they
attempted to make organized lists of the gods worshipped in
Mesopotamia. These god-lists often accounted for all the
Mesopotamian deities according to their origins. In these
genealogies, a major deity, such as Anu, Enlil, or Ea, would be
listed first and followed by a list of his wives, children, and
servants. It was indeed a formidable task to put such a huge
pantheon into some kind of order. A short list identifying some
of the major deities will give an indication of the complex
relationships which existed in the Mesopotamian pantheon.

ANU, or An, whose name like the Greek Ouranos means Sky, was
the leader and father of all the gods because his age gave him
the greatest authority. From the human viewpoint, however, he
was a distant god. A member of the older generation, he was
more passive than the younger gods and thus only infrequently

interfered in human affairs. Instead, his sons Enlil and Ea
ruled the human world with his authority.

ENLIL, or Ellil, whose name meant "Lord Air," was Anu's first
son and god of the atmosphere and surface of the earth. He was
the patron god of Nippur, the sacred city to which kings traveled
to receive permission to rule Sumer. Because he controlled the
winds and storms, he was the most important god for the human
race. He caused the rains which were necessary for human existence but were also destructive. Thus, despite his close links
to human survival, Enlil was often pictured as hostile to
humanity. In *Atrahasis*, for example, he plans the destruction
of the entire human race because their noise does not allow him
to sleep. He was second in authority after Anu although his
plans were often thwarted by his brother Ea.

EA, or Enki, whose name meant "Lord Earth," was also a son
of Anu and third in importance and authority. He ruled over the
subterranean waters from his home called the Apsu. He was the
cleverest of the gods who used his practical wisdom to solve
problems which the other gods found too perplexing. In *Enuma
Elish*, for example, when the god Apsu plots against the other
gods, Ea cleverly kills him while the others are unable to decide
on a plan of action. In *Atrahasis*, he must determine how to
create the human race, and the birth-goddess, Nintu, follows his
directions. Like the Greek god Prometheus, Ea was also a
trickster. He circumvented Enlil's commands to destroy the
human race and avoided Enlil's wrath with hair-splitting arguments. His usually benevolent powers over the human race came
from his position as ruler of the fresh water.

ISHTAR, or Inanna, was the most important goddess in the
pantheon. In her original form, she was goddess of the storehouse and consort of Dumuzi, a fertility god. But she was also
a goddess of rain, war, the morning and evening stars, and
protector of prostitutes. In the *Epic of Gilgamesh*, she even
claims to have created the human race. A versatile goddess, she
was also in charge of lighting and putting out fire, of sorrow
and happiness, and other contradictory traits. But Ishtar was
usually portrayed with a unified personality—a young, beautiful,
willful aristocrat. The epithet "Lady of myriad offices" seems
to summarize her best. (See Chapter 10.)

MARDUK was the patron god of Babylon, and his power in the
pantheon rose and fell with the political fortunes of the city.
In *Enuma Elish*, he assumes kingship over the other gods, supplanting Enlil who is only briefly mentioned in the poem. In

earlier times, however, he was a minor deity of thunder and
rainstorms. Originally depicted in the form of a bull, Marduk
could bellow as loud as a clap of thunder. In later times, he
was depicted in human form carrying his main weapon, the bow and
arrow. He was sometimes shown with two or even four faces,
symbolic of his greater power, and he was often accompanied by a
dragon which was perhaps the conquered goddess of chaos, Tiamat.

As we can see from this brief list, the Mesopotamian gods
had many functions and were not easily classifiable. This
condition was made even more complex by the substitution of one
god for another. Major deities often took over the functions of
lesser gods and supplanted them in the pantheon. Likewise,
older gods receded in importance as newer ones took their places.
The Mesopotamians sometimes showed these changes in their temples
by placing the statue of the new, more powerful god in front of
the god whom he was supplanting. We can also see this process
taking place in *Enuma Elish*. At the end of the poem, the gods
honor Marduk by giving him fifty names which indicate his
supremacy over the world. Even Enlil calls Marduk "Lord of the
Lands," a position which Enlil himself previously held, and Ea
gives Marduk total control over his domain by giving up his own
name.

We have seen, then, something of the complexity of the
Mesopotamian pantheon and the difficulty of defining Mesopotamian
religion. It developed after all through a period of twenty-five
hundred years from a time when civilization was barely getting
started to a time when Mesopotamian culture was very complex and
sophisticated. This religious growth is also indicative of the
complex changes in their other institutions and in their whole
culture. Their way of life changed greatly from its beginning
to its end. In such a vast period of time, very few things
remain constant, but surely two of them surface again and again.
First the Mesopotamians not only survived under difficult conditions but also built cities and a civilization which was the
envy of all its neighbors. Second, they learned to write and
never forgot the significance of that achievement. They used
this tool without ceasing to make list upon list, to classify
and to organize their property, their gods, and even themselves.
This was perhaps their greatest achievement and their greatest
limitation.

CHAPTER 8

ISRAEL: A CULTURE BASED ON MONOTHEISM

The ancient people whom we know as Israelites, or Hebrews,
or Jews saw themselves primarily as the people of Yahweh. They
were the people with whom the God Yahweh established his covenant. Yahweh, they believed, founded their nation with his
promise to Abraham, led them out of Egyptian bondage, and gave
them the land of Canaan to live in. The Israelites' national
identity sprang from the conviction that they owed their
allegiance to Yahweh and that he promised them his special
protection. Thus, when they recorded their history in the Old
Testament, they described it as the story of Yahweh's interven-
tion in the affairs of his people.

This covenant with Yahweh affected not only their existence
as a nation but also their daily lives. They followed numerous
laws which restricted their normal activities but which also
helped distinguish them from other peoples. They rested every
seventh day, practiced circumcision, did not charge interest on
loans, and refrained from eating certain foods, all in the name
of Yahweh. These practices were not necessarily unique in the
ancient Near East, but the Israelite devotion to one God who
required these practices gave them a special identity to which
they clung tenaciously. Such total devotion to a single God
was indeed unique. It separated the Israelites from the
neighboring tribes who worshipped all manner of gods, and it
distinguished them from the more highly developed civilizations
of Egypt and Mesopotamia which constantly threatened their
freedom. These other peoples often worshipped one god as their
particular benefactor and protector. The Assyrians, for example,
recognized Assur as their patron, the Canaanites were devoted to
Baal, and the Babylonians to Marduk; but none of them dared
ignore the many other gods who controlled their worlds. The
Israelites, however, prescribed in their law that only Yahweh was

worthy of such recognition. Although they often lapsed from this
faith, they never failed to return to the one God they thought
was worthy of their worship.

This devotion to Yahweh explains a great deal about the
historical writings in the Old Testament. The Israelites saw
their history not simply as a narration of human events but also
as the story of Yahweh guiding his chosen people. Every event
from the calling of Abraham to the arrival in the land of Canaan
was a vital part of this divinely centered history. Even the
long migration into Egypt and the enslavement by the pharaohs
were important steps in the process which made sense only in
light of Yahweh's promise.

The Exodus was the pivotal event in this story of Yahweh's
people. During the Exodus (about 1300-1250 B.C.), a band of
Israelite slaves left Egypt to settle in a new land where they
would be free. The narration of this event, as it is preserved
in the Book of Exodus, continually stresses the power of Yahweh.
He selects the Israelite leader, Moses, from the ranks of the
Egyptians, performs a large number of miracles to secure their
freedom, and gives them the Ten Commandments at Mount Sinai to
form the basis of their laws. Finally, he guides them to Canaan,
the land he promised them many generations before.

Yahweh's role in these events also provided the Israelites
with a link to their legendary past. The patriarchs, Abraham,
Isaac, Jacob, and Joseph, all guided by Yahweh, gave the
Israelites a common ancestry which was vital to their tribal
society. The Israelites defined their tribal membership by
tracing their family trees back to such important ancestors.
The patriarchs also served as models for their people since they
showed exemplary obedience to Yahweh, kept striving for their
goals even against enormous odds, and prepared for a future that
they would not see themselves. Furthermore, many episodes in
the patriarchs' lives contained brief moral lessons. In the
story of Sodom and Gomorrah, for example, Abraham displays his
ability to bargain shrewdly, even with Yahweh. When Yahweh is
intent on destroying Sodom, Abraham asks him to spare the city
if fifty "righteous" people live there. Eventually, Abraham
bargains the number down to ten before Yahweh walks away, apparently unwilling to bargain further (Genesis 18:16-33). Although
Abraham's efforts did not save Sodom, his persistence in bargain-
ing for a good cause was an example which later Israelites could
look to as a model for their own behavior.

The Israelites, then, viewed their early history as illustrative of their varied relationships with Yahweh. What they recorded as their past history taught them what they expected of themselves and their God in the present and the future. With this perspective, we can more easily understand why the early books of the Bible are such a strange mixture of legends, myths, genealogies, and laws. All had a common purpose. They were the Torah, or teachings, which told the Israelites who they were, where they came from, and how best to live their lives.

The Twelve Tribes of Israel (1250-1050 B.C.)

The history of the Israelite nation really began with their arrival in the promised land of Canaan. Before this time, they were scattered groups of people who lived throughout the Near East. Some were enslaved in Egypt, some were nomadic tribes who raised goats in the desert, and others lived in cities controlled by Egypt or Mesopotamia. Whatever their origins were, however, the Israelites who settled in Canaan shared a common belief in Yahweh and a tradition of tribal organization. All of them recognized themselves as the chosen people of Yahweh and worshipped at a common shrine. But these same people were divided into twelve autonomous tribes, each of which had its own share of the newly conquered land. Each tribe governed itself, administered its own laws, and raised its own army for protection. The tribes even fought among themselves as much as they did against the foreign peoples who surrounded them. The two fundamental elements of Israelite society, therefore, pulled in two different directions. Their Yahwism gave them common ground which differentiated them from the pagan cultures in the area while their tribalism kept them divided.

A tribe was essentially a loosely formed group of families bound together by common traditions and practices. The most important of these traditions was acceptance of a common ancestry although it was not necessarily an indication of biological descent. An outsider could become a full member of a tribe by accepting its ancestors, living on its lands, and agreeing to obey its laws. Also, the tribes themselves were not necessarily permanent units. Smaller tribes were sometimes absorbed by larger ones, and large tribes sometimes split into two or more independent groups.

This fluid political structure did not prevent the tribes from maintaining a fairly consistent social structure which was based on the family. The Israelite family was a much larger group than our modern nuclear family since it often included several generations of children and even hired workers who lived with the family. In effect, the family was the entire household which lived and worked on its own plot of land. Each family was nearly self-sufficient, owning its own land, growing its own crops, producing its own clothing and tools, and regulating the behavior of its own members. But the family did have certain obligations to the tribe: family members were expected to marry within the tribe, sell their land only to other tribal members, and provide manpower for the army which defended tribal property.

Although subject to the laws which governed all the tribes, the Israelite family was essentially patriarchal. The father had nearly absolute control over the entire household, including his wives, children, and his sons' wives. He enforced the laws in his household and even had the authority to put family members to death if they disobeyed. The status of women in Israelite society gives us some idea of how the patriarchal family func-tioned. In general, a woman had the same legal status as a child. Even the wife of a patriarch could not own property, divorce her husband (although he could divorce her), inherit anything from her husband, take any legal action, or be a party to a contract. Although these prohibitions were not strictly adhered to in practice, a woman's only real source of influence was bearing children. Only in this way could she gain the favor of her husband and the respect of the society as a whole. (See Chapter 10.)

The Israelites, however, granted special rights to widows who would otherwise be helpless. A childless widow was con-sidered part of her dead husband's property; so the nearest male relative of the deceased was required to marry her, have children with her, and raise these children as the dead husband's family. When her sons were old enough to manage the family property them-selves, they would provide for her needs. We can see these customs at work in the Book of Ruth when Ruth has to seek out a willing kinsman to care for her after her husband died.

In other respects, Israelite tribal society valued equality and autonomy. Some families may have been larger than others, some more successful or prosperous; but all had equal rights and responsibilities within the tribe. Likewise, the twelve tribes were usually autonomous. They formed a confederation only for the mutual convenience of maintaining the central shrine to

Yahweh, and each tribe was required to care for this shrine one month of the year. In addition, the confederation could mediate disputes between tribes and provide for a common defense when an enemy seriously threatened more than one tribe. But these important functions were performed only infrequently since it was rare for the tribes to agree on giving up their autonomy even when threatened with invasion.

During this early period of their history, then, the Israelites had no centralized government. Instead, elected "judges" settled disputes between tribes, and temporary military leaders led them against any foreign intruders who threatened a large number of tribes. These military leaders usually appeared in times of crisis by displaying a special "charisma" which indicated that Yahweh had chosen them to lead the Israelites. After the crisis ended, they were usually expected to retire again to private life. Gideon typifies this kind of charismatic leader. When the Midianites attack the Israelites, Gideon displays the necessary charisma by boldly destroying a pagan altar. He is then elected to lead the Israelites and quickly succeeds in defeating the Midianite armies. After his victory, some Israelite leaders offer him permanent rule over them, including the establishment of a dynasty. But Gideon refuses, saying, "I will not rule over you, nor shall my son; the Lord will rule over you" (Judges 8:23-24). Gideon's attitude, indeed typical of the time, expressed the highest political wisdom of the tribes. A human king, they thought, would only enslave the people and force them to do his bidding as the Pharaoh of Egypt once did. Yahweh was their only rightful king since he had brought them to the promised land and had chosen their leaders when any crisis arose.

Although the twelve tribes remained politically independent, they shared many practices, traditions, and beliefs. All of the tribes traced their ancestry back to the patriarchs Abraham, Isaac, and Jacob; and all considered themselves the chosen people of Yahweh who freed them from Egypt. The covenant with Yahweh formed the center of this tradition. Expressed in the Ten Commandments, it required exclusive worship of Yahweh, prohibited the making of statues, and included a moral code which made murder, stealing, and adultery religious as well as civil crimes. These ideas, formed during the early years of the tribal confederation, remained the basis of Israelite unity throughout the rest of their history.

The United Kingdom (1050-921 B.C.)

This loose confederation of tribes lasted about two hundred years, until the disastrous war with the Philistines. When the Philistines invaded Israelite lands and destroyed the central shrine at Shiloh (about 1050 B.C.), many Israelites saw the need for a stronger central government. So they broke their ancient tradition and elected Saul their first king. Although not accepted by some Israelites who considered a monarchy inconsistent with Yahwism, Saul's election was probably a compromise between those who favored a monarchy and those who wanted to keep the traditional tribal structure. Saul was a member of the smallest and weakest Israelite tribe, and his election was similar to that of the judges in the past. He was discovered by Samuel (the last of the Israelite judges) with the guidance of Yahweh, and he was accepted by the tribes because of his charismatic qualities. It was this charisma which enabled him to lead the Israelites in battle. He was successful militarily because he inspired the Israelite armies to fight as they had in earlier times, and as a result he gained several significant victories over the Philistines.

As head of the newly organized government, however, Saul was less successful. Constantly leading his armies against the enemy, he had little time to establish a central government or to maintain his personal relationships with other prominent Israelites. He quarreled with Samuel who was still an influential figure and lost his friendship. Even worse was his treatment of David. A popular young man, David had gained fame by defeating the Philistine giant, Goliath, and was a close friend of Saul's own son. But Saul feared David's popularity and apparent charisma, for he knew that these qualities made him a potential rival. Hoping to eliminate this threat to his power, Saul tried to kill David who escaped and found shelter with some Israelite friends. But Saul pursued him relentlessly and even slaughtered a group of priests who had helped him escape and seek the protection of the Philistines.

Obsessed with his hatred for David, Saul spent more and more of his time pursuing him. Meanwhile, with David's help, the Philistines began to recoup many of their losses in Israelite land. As a last resort, Saul led a final charge against them. Outnumbered and wounded, he was easily defeated; and three of his sons were killed in the battle. Saul then took his own life, thus ending the first Israelite experiment with permanent

rule. But after Saul's death, the Israelites did not revert to
the practices of the old tribal confederation. Instead, the two
largest divisions of Israelites each chose a new king. Soon,
however, David who was chosen king of Judah defeated the armies
of the northern tribes and became king of all the Israelites
(about 1000 B.C.).

David was a far more successful ruler than Saul had been.
He brought peace to the kingdom for the first time by driving
the Philistines out of Israelite territory. In fact, his triumph
was so decisive that Philistine soldiers served as members of
his royal body guard. David then conquered the rest of Palestine
and established an empire which controlled most of the region
between Egypt and Mesopotamia. With this territory under his
control, David made the kingdom a rich trading center.

David's greatest achievement, however, was his formation of
a strong centralized government despite the jealousies and fears
of the Israelite tribes. He made Jerusalem the capital of his
new kingdom because of its central location and neutral status.
Called the "City of David," Jerusalem soon became the political
center of the kingdom, similar to Washington, D.C., since it
belonged to the central state rather than to any one tribe.
David brought the Ark of the Covenant, the principal symbol of
the Israelites' relationship with Yahweh, to the city. He even
gave his rule a religious sanction by appointing the high
priest to his cabinet. As a result, a new theology developed
during his reign which made David the mediator between Yahweh
and the Israelite people. David became known as the "son" and
"anointed one" of Yahweh, and eventually the monarchy itself was
considered both the fulfillment of Yahweh's covenant and the
end of the long struggle to attain the promised land.

Although David's reign was a high point in the Israelites'
history, it was not without its problems. David successfully
suppressed tribal rivalries for a time but was troubled with
intrigues within his own court. Disputes over succession to his
throne were frequent even after he named Solomon his heir. He
even had to flee Jerusalem during his son Absalom's attempt to
usurp the throne. Nevertheless, by the time of his death
(about 960 B.C.), David had transformed Israel from a loose
confederation of tribes into a powerful centralized state with a
large empire.

Solomon, David's son and successor, represented the final
break with the customs of the old tribal confederation since he
was not a charismatic leader and his succession to the throne

was not necessitated by threats from any foreign power. In fact,
Solomon spent very little time on military matters. Instead, he
consolidated the Israelite state and fulfilled the potential of
David's empire. He made it the center of trade routes across
the Red Sea and overland to Mesopotamia because he shrewdly
formed political alliances which capitalized on Israel's strate-
gic location. Even the Egyptian pharaoh recognized Israel's new
importance by giving Solomon one of his daughters in marriage.
Her dowry included a Canaanite city which the pharaoh presented
to Solomon on their wedding day. Not even the powerful rulers
of Mesopotamia were given such lavish gifts as the pharaoh
presented to Israel's new king.

Under Solomon's policies, the Israelite economy flourished
because of the increase in foreign trade. But Solomon himself
benefited most because he was in control of the trade agreements.
Legends of his great wealth arose as a result of the money which
he accumulated through this control, but Solomon used the wealth
for a massive building program in Israelite cities. The temple
dedicated to Yahweh in Jerusalem was his most famous architectural achievement. This temple was the first permanent building
to house the Ark of the Covenant since the tribal confederation
had kept the Ark in a tent as a reminder of their nomadic
origins; even David had decided against building a temple in
deference to this ancient tradition. But Solomon's temple broke
the custom and eventually became the primary visual symbol of
Yahweh's presence among the Israelites. Since the temple was
under royal control, it further strengthened the link between the
religious and political institutions of the Israelite state.

Solomon's temple was also a monument to the many foreign
influences which world trade brought to the Israelites. Solomon
hired a Syrian architect who modeled the new temple after pagan
shrines which he had seen in Palestine and Syria. Such a structure, however, was viewed with great suspicion by those
Israelites who preferred the purer form of Yahwism practiced
during the time of the tribal confederation. Yet, the temple was
not the only pagan influence which Solomon brought to the
Israelite religion. Many rituals and sacrifices which the older
form of Yahwism avoided became part of the official state
religion.

The reigns of David and Solomon represented a high point in
the development of Israelite culture. The prosperity which
these kings brought to the Israelites fostered artistic develop-
ments of many kinds. In addition to the temple at Jerusalem,

for example, Solomon built many cities throughout Israelite territory and constructed a large palace for himself which took thirteen years to build (almost twice what it took to build the temple). Likewise, the Israelites developed the fine arts, including music and literature, to a high level. For instance, many songs in the Book of Psalms were traditionally attributed to David, and Solomon was credited with the Song of Solomon, Proverbs, and Ecclesiastes. Although it is unlikely that either David or Solomon actually wrote these books, some of the material in them can be traced back to their reigns.

But economic progress during the reigns of David and Solomon also cost the Israelites some of their most cherished national traditions. Their God of the desert was then housed in a city temple; their covenant was less a personal commitment since it was mediated by the king; and their tribal autonomy had given way to a centralized government. Ultimately, Solomon's economic policies brought many other difficulties to the nation as well. His massive building program and lavish court required more funds than even this rich king had available, so he instituted taxation and forced labor to meet his economic demands. Such policies were not very popular with the lower classes in Israel or among the traditionalists who always distrusted kings. Thus, by the time of Solomon's death in 921 B.C., the difficulties as well as the advantages of economic expansion began to show themselves.

The many changes which the monarchy wrought in Israelite social life also produced changes in their view of Yahweh and his covenant. The Israelites were no longer a group of independent tribes who lived only on what their land could provide. They had become enmeshed in world politics and had grown rich from trade with foreign nations. They even had a strong central government which ensured their security and wealth. Their theology, then, began to reflect these new conditions as well. The covenant with Yahweh once singled out the Israelites as a specially chosen group; but under the monarchy, it also became a promise to all nations that Yahweh watched over them. At the same time, the covenant's obligations seemed more remote to the average Israelite. Formerly administered by the tribal leaders and even the family patriarchs, the covenant was now managed by the king since he was the anointed son of Yahweh.

But one of the most significant changes came in the personal relationships that the Israelite leaders had with their God. During the time of the tribal confederation, this relationship

was relatively clear-cut. Yahweh chose the leaders and guided
them step by step through whatever crises arose. He even
performed miracles to ensure that they would attain and keep the
promised land for his people. All the human leaders had to do
was await Yahweh's instructions and then follow them to the
letter; Yahweh would take care of the rest.

With the establishment of an independent monarchy, however,
this theological outlook began to change. During his reign,
David did not rely on a God who would miraculously save him in
times of crisis. Instead, he took the initiative himself and
expected Yahweh to judge his deeds as he saw fit. When he is
forced to leave Jerusalem during Absalom's rebellion, for
example, David refuses to take the Ark of the Covenant with him.
In the older theology, such an action would have been considered
at best foolish, at worst a grave sin. Since the Ark was the
symbol of Yahweh's presence among his people, it had nearly
magical powers: whoever had the Ark in his possession had Yahweh
on his side. David, however, viewed his relationship with Yahweh
differently. In explaining his refusal to take the Ark, he
says:

> If I find favor with the Lord, he will let me see the Ark
> again. But if he says he does not want me, then here I
> am; let him do what he pleases with me.
>
> (2 Samuel 15:25-26)

Here David rejected the magical relationship between God and his
symbol (the Ark), and he acknowledged that Yahweh had the freedom
to judge his actions according to the divine will. Likewise,
David was free to choose his own course of action and was not
bound by the magical formula of the old view.

All of these new ideas about Yahweh can be seen in the Epic
of Yahweh, an extended history of the early Israelites from the
call of Abraham to the arrival in the promised land. This epic,
which is now part of the Pentateuch, was probably written during
Solomon's reign by an artist-theologian known to us as the
Yahwist. (See Chapter 5.) The Yahwist used the theology of his
time but tempered its optimism with a more balanced view of the
flaws in human nature. Perhaps the best known example is found
in the story of Adam and Eve where the first human beings are
given the ability to make their own choices, even with regard to
the forbidden fruit. Their choice of disobeying Yahweh leads to
dire consequences of their own making and affects human life for
the rest of time. The Yahwist, then, used the free-will theology
of his time but also pointed out that such freedom had its risks.

However unpopular this reminder may have been during the affluent times of the monarchy, the Yahwist consistently emphasized that faithfulness to the covenant was not necessarily an easy task.

From the Divided Kingdom to Post-Exilic Times (922-500 B.C.)

Despite the generally optimistic climate during Solomon's reign, problems erupted after his death. Tribal differences which had been suppressed for several generations again reasserted themselves. The ten Northern tribes formed their own government with their own capital in Samaria, their own temple, and their own king. Meanwhile, the Southern tribe of Judah remained under the leadership of the Davidic line of kings. These separate kingdoms were too weak to hold onto the empire which David and Solomon had built. But each did maintain the powers of a centralized state, and each remained subject to continuing influence from its polytheistic neighbors. Even during times of economic prosperity, the Israelite kings continued policies of repression. Corrupt courts and oppressive laws sharpened class distinctions between rich and poor. Life in the palace remained lavish and wasteful while the less fortunate lost their lands and homes.

In these autocratic regimes, it was dangerous to criticize the king, the prevailing social conditions, or the state-sponsored religious practices. Yet, despite such difficulties, a group known as the Prophets had a long tradition of speaking out against injustice. They criticized the Israelite leaders even in the days when the tribes were struggling against the Philistine invasions. On the whole, the Prophets were believers in the religious practices of the old tribal confederation and distrusted the centralized state because it brought inequities to Israelite society and lost sight of the original covenant with Yahweh. The covenant, they believed, had nothing to do with class systems, forced labor, and economic inequality; and pagan influences had changed the Israelite religion from its original stress on a personal relationship with Yahweh to an emphasis on empty rituals.

The prophets represented an ecstatic, charismatic strain in Israelite religion. They believed that they were specially called by Yahweh to speak his word but recognized the dangers in speaking out against the kings. Some even felt unworthy of such a high calling. Nevertheless, they did speak out in the

strongest language. Amos, for example, not only criticized the
injustices of his time but also openly predicted the destruction
of the Northern kingdom of Israel. Likewise, when the Southern
kingdom of Judah was rebelling against Babylon, Jeremiah said
that Yahweh himself was fighting against the Israelites.
Jeremiah was so strident in his criticism that the Babylonians
thought he was their ally. After they put down the rebellion,
they let only Jeremiah choose whether to go into exile or to
remain in Judah. Showing his true patriotism, Jeremiah chose to
stay in his homeland.

Events proved that the Prophets were right. The Northern
kingdom was destroyed by the Assyrians in 721 B.C., and its
inhabitants were sent into exile, never again to come together
as a unified people. The Southern kingdom of Judah lasted over
a hundred years longer, but it eventually succumbed in 587 B.C.
to the Babylonians. This event marked the end of Israel's
political independence since the Babylonians completely destroyed
the city of Jerusalem, including the temple, and took a large
segment of the population into exile at Babylon. This exile
lasted about fifty years until 539 B.C. when the Persians, on
their way to complete domination of the Near East, conquered
Babylon and allowed the Israelites to return to their homeland.

The exile was not only a political disaster for the
Israelites but also threatened their most basic religious
beliefs. The temple at Jerusalem, which had become the main
symbol of Yahweh's presence, was destroyed. The Davidic line of
kings, to whom Yahweh had promised a perpetual dynasty, came to
an end. Even the promised land, which Yahweh had given them as
part of his covenant, was no longer under Israelite control.
Nevertheless, the Israelites' faith in Yahweh survived these
obstacles through re-interpretation of their basic religious
beliefs. Since they no longer had a temple as a symbol of their
religious faith, the Israelites re-emphasized a number of practices as signs of their identity. Circumcision, for example,
became the mark of an Israelite since the Babylonians did not
practice it. Strict observance of the Sabbath also became a
crucial test of obedience to the covenant. Finally, since the
Israelites lost their physical symbols of Yahweh's presence, they
turned to an intangible symbol, the word of Yahweh which could
not be destroyed by conquest; what Yahweh said always came to be.
A theologian from this period, the so-called Second Isaiah,
expresses the idea in this way:

as the rain and the snow come down from heaven
and do not return until they have watered the earth,
    making it blossom and bear fruit,
and give seed for sowing and bread to eat,
so shall the word which comes from my mouth prevail;
    it shall not return to me fruitless
without accomplishing my purpose
    or succeeding in the task I gave it.

(Isaiah 55:10-11)

Yahweh was pictured as a far more powerful God than any pagan deity who might help a nation conquer its enemies. Since his word always became reality, he was all-powerful and could control events throughout the world.

This new view of Yahweh was reinforced by the events which led to the end of the Israelites' exile. Unaware that events occurring in far-away lands would eventually lead to their release, the Israelites thought that their situation was hopeless. The rise of Persian power throughout the Near East, the defeat of Babylon, and the lenient policies of the Persian king who gave them their freedom all seemed to be miraculous occurrences which only a God of cosmic proportions could bring about. The Israelites, then, returned to their promised land convinced that Yahweh was such an all-powerful God that he could control many different nations and individuals. Thus, their belief that there was only one God far above the gods their neighbors worshipped was reinforced by their newly attained freedom, as the Second Isaiah says:

There is no god other than I, victorious and able to save.
    Look to me and be saved,
      you peoples from all corners of the earth;
for I am God, there is no other.
    By my life I have sworn,
I have given a promise of victory,
    a promise that will not be broken . . .
In the Lord alone, men shall say,
    are victory and might;
and all who defy him
shall stand ashamed in his presence,
but all the sons of Israel shall stand victorious
    and find their glory in the Lord.

(Isaiah 45:22-25)

During the exile and after, a group of Israelite priests tried to preserve the Israelites' traditions by saving genealogical lists, laws, and several versions of their myths and legends. Eventually, these priests put their documents into the form that we now recognize as the Pentateuch and added some of their own writings as well. Their most artistic achievement was the opening hymn in the Book of Genesis in which they stress the

power of Yahweh's word. Through the refrain, "God said, 'Let
there be . . .' and it was," they emphasized the majestic power
of Yahweh who merely commanded the whole world into existence.
This conception of Yahweh is similar to the one we have already
seen in Second Isaiah; he is the all-powerful God in whom the
Israelites believed during the exile and after. He differs
from the original Israelite God of the desert who personally
promised to protect and help his people and from the God whom the
Yahwist pictures as a concerned parent, allowing his new
creations to make their own choices. Both of these earlier
conceptions of Yahweh were anthropomorphic and suggested that
Yahweh's powers were more limited.

There is far more to the story of the Israelites and their
ideas about Yahweh than we have discussed here. We have limited
ourselves to those areas most pertinent to the two creation
accounts from Genesis included in this book: the Creation Hymn
(1:1-2:4) and the story of Adam and Eve (2:4-3:24). They were
written by different authors at different times and with
different theological purposes; even their conceptions of Yahweh
were very different. But both reveal a belief in Yahweh which
sustained the Israelites as a people throughout their history.

CHAPTER 9

GREECE: A CULTURE BASED ON CONFLICT

The ancient Greeks saw all human experience as an *agōn*, a battle of words and deeds. Their athletics, politics, and wars were agonistic as might be expected, but so were their philosophy, drama, and rhetoric. In fact, *agōn* was so basic to the Greeks that they even believed in gods who represented essential conflicts in human life. Apollo and Dionysos were two gods who particularly embodied *agōn* both in Greek society and within the individual. Apollo, the Olympian god *par excellence*, was linked with civilization and its ordered creativity. He was the god of self-knowledge and self-control, of reason and controlled emotion, of law and the creative arts, of the prophetic future and the religious status quo. Dionysos, on the other hand, was the god who violated the limits set by civilization. He transcended the normal limits of human life by being both male and female, foreign and Greek, creative and destructive; he was also a god of nature, fertility, and wine.

Together, Apollo and Dionysos encompassed the tensions in Greek life; but they also represented forces which were in conflict with each other. Apollonian worship stressed reason and self-control, honored an idealized male aristocratic god, and eventually became the most important religion of the Greek establishment. Dionysiac cults fostered irrational ecstacy and mysterious faith, had mostly women followers, and threatened the established religion. Yet, the Greeks installed Dionysos alongside Apollo at Delphi, their central religious shrine. There, well-born Greek males found their inspiration in Apollo while Dionysos offered a release to downtrodden peasants, revolutionaries, and women. Whenever and wherever Greeks managed to hold these two forces in balance, they soared to incredible heights. We can see that greatness in the epics of Homer and Hesiod in the eighth century, B.C. and in the development of the arts and

sciences in the fifth and fourth centuries, B.C. But the balance
between ordered reason and ecstatic passion was precarious, and
whenever it was lost, the results could be catastrophic, as much
of Greek political history shows.

The Greeks' agonistic outlook went beyond the ideas represented by Apollo and Dionysos, for Greek culture had been evolv-
ing over hundreds of years before these gods came to represent
their opposing views. Even the physical environment in which the
ancient Greeks established their culture suggested conflict.
Mainland Greece is a landscape which is never monotonous.
Massive mountains and hollow valleys present ever-changing
contours which fire the imagination. The peak of Mount Olympos,
for instance, is shrouded in mist against an otherwise clear sky
and easily suggests a mysterious, holy place. To the ancient
Greeks, it seemed the perfect home for Zeus and the other immortal gods. But the Mediterranean Sea dominates the geography of
the Greek imagination. Tiny islands dot the turbulent waters
which nearly surround the Greek peninsula. The changing moods
of this sea suggest such contraries as the one and the many,
mythos and *logos*, freedom and destiny, nature and law.

These same physical features contributed to political fragmentation, separating Athenian from Theban, Corinthian from
Spartan, Rhodian from Cretan. An independent city-state or *polis*
became the center of each of these areas, and each *polis* tended
to regard all the others as rivals, even separate nations. The
city-state was built around a central hill, called an acropolis,
and could be as small as a village or as large as an American
county. About two hundred of these self-sufficient *poleis* dotted
ancient Greece, encouraging local autonomy and fierce competition
between neighbors. Although rich and poor, citizen and alien
mingled in the *polis* without much distinction, the independent
polis rarely joined with its neighbor states for any common
purpose. Thus, geographic variety encouraged not only agonistic
thought but also forms of government which valued independence
more than unity.

The mutual independence of the city-states caused them to
develop many different political systems. In the seventh century,
B.C., for instance, the Spartans introduced a unique form of
militaristic government. After twenty years of warfare with
their own serfs, they formed a government which required complete
devotion to the state and which could mobilize its citizens whenever a threat might occur. Seven-year-old boys were taken from

their parents and raised in military camps which trained them as
soldiers. Sparta came to be known for its iron discipline,
strong sense of comradeship, disparagement of the arts and
sciences, and tight control of its serfs. In the fifth century,
Athens developed a democratic government which required all
adult male citizens to participate directly in political decisions. This early experiment in self-rule was short-lived,
lasting less than a century; and it was a limited democracy since
women, resident aliens and slaves were not allowed to participate.
It was, nevertheless, to become the model for subsequent democratic governments, and to this day remains both symbol and
prototype of western democracy.

Athens and Sparta remained bitter rivals throughout most of
their history. Only once did they unite to repel an outside
invader, and even then they did not attract many of the other
Greek city-states to their common defense. When the Persians,
who already dominated much of the Mediterranean area, attacked
the Greek mainland in 481 B.C., Sparta and Athens formed an
alliance to keep them out. Although outnumbered, the Spartan
army and Athenian navy struggled together for ten years and
finally defeated the invaders. After the threat was dispelled,
however, the old animosities reappeared. Soon a long war
between the two Greek city-states broke out and lasted till the
end of the century. Sparta's ultimate victory was indeed a
hollow one because it was unable to unify Greece for any
constructive purpose. By the mid-fourth century, Alexander the
Great, who came from Macedon, was able to impose his own rule on
the contentious Greek city-states. Thus, Greek political
independence came to an end because the Greeks themselves were
unable to unite even for political survival.

Cultural Achievements of Ancient Greece

Despite the geographic boundaries which kept them isolated
from each other and their lack of political unity, the Greeks
became the cultural leaders of the ancient world. Even the
Romans, who later conquered Greece and the rest of the
Mediterranean world, used Greek slaves to educate their children,
copied Greek statues to adorn their buildings, imitated Greek
literature, and even adopted the Greek gods as their own.
Because of the Romans, Greek culture spread throughout Europe,
a pervasive influence that lasted throughout the Middle Ages
and continues to the present day. Western literature begins with

Homer, Hesiod and Sappho; its philosophy with the pre-socratics
and Plato; its sculpture with Phidias; its tragedy with Aeschylus
and Sophocles; and its comedy with Aristophanes.

The Greeks were a people who shared the same language, the
same gods, the same morals and customs (Herodotus 2.53); but
within this cultural unity there existed distinct divisions. Two
in particular, the Ionians and the Dorians, showed that opposing,
often contradictory, outlooks were deeply embedded in the culture,
and the conflict between these two outlooks contributed so
importantly to the creative tension in Greek thought. The
Ionians dwelt in Asia Minor and in Athens while the Dorians
settled in much of the Greek mainland. These two groups spoke
different dialects and diverged in significant ways. Ionians
like Homer were individualistic, sensuous, graceful people who
followed their intuitions and probed into scientific and philosophical questions. Dorians like Hesiod were community-minded,
disciplined practitioners of the art of war, and moral traditionalists in their beliefs. Since Homer and Hesiod were to attain
for the Greeks an authority comparable to the Bible for the
Israelites, the Ionian-Dorian tension pervaded all of subsequent
Greek culture. The Spartans, however, by remaining narrowly
Dorian, developed a rigid military mentality which proved to be
impervious to the philosophical, artistic and scientific currents
that swept through other Greek city-states in the centuries that
separated Homer and Hesiod from the Athenian golden age.

Agon in Athens' Golden Age

Unlike Sparta, Athens was able to assimilate the different
strains in Greek culture. Descended from Ionian stock, the
Athenians inherited the inquisitive and artistic character of
their ancestors. But they also absorbed some of the disciplined,
conservative strength of their Dorian neighbors, achieving a rare
synthesis in the fifth and fourth centuries. Although Athens was
a relatively small city-state with perhaps 20,000 adult male
citizens plus women, children, resident-aliens and slaves, it
became the New York City of Greece, attracting talent from as far
away as Asia Minor, and thus becoming preeminent in cultural
achievements. It produced masterpieces in sculpture, vase
painting, and architecture; it advanced the sciences of mathematics and medicine; gave birth to democracy; developed new
theories of education; and virtually created the arts of tragedy,
rhetoric, philosophy, and history. All of these achievements

grew out of and reflected conflicts of Greek culture. The
dialectical form of philosophy and the confrontations of
antagonists in tragedy best illustrate the creative use of these
conflicts.

In the *Antigone*, for instance, Sophocles reflects conflicts
he saw in Athens around 440 B.C. The young Antigone is pitted
against her uncle, King Kreon, who has decreed that her brother's
body must not be buried since he was a traitor to the state. "I
shall bury him," she asserts defiantly (70-71). A king's decree,
she argues, cannot transcend the divine law which protects a
family's right to bury its dead (450-70). Kreon, on the other
hand, insists that both piety and political order demand the
punishment of those who disobey the law and, in his view, thereby
threaten the civil order. About the same time that the play
appeared, Perikles led sixty ships to quell the revolt of Samos,
a tiny island that had rebelled against Athenian rule. The drama
raises the question of individual rights against state's rights.
In the tyranny of Kreon, Sophocles suggests, the Athenians may
see a reflection of their own tyranny. Furthermore, when Kreon
cries in fury: "You must obey whomever the city appoints in
matters small and just and their opposites" (666-67), he epito-
mizes the kind of ruthless demagogue that was to lead Athens in
the years following Perikles' death. The play is not historical
commentary, but it depicts the growing indifference to individual
rights that would ultimately undermine Athenian democracy.

That Athens should give birth to western philosophy is an
understandable miracle since philosophy often investigates the
conflicts between appearances and reality, matter and form, good
and evil. Greek philosophy reached its zenith in the fifth and
fourth centuries with Socrates and Plato, whose names became
synonymous with philosophical dialogue. Socrates' method was to
debate with his fellow citizens, asking them what piety, truth or
knowledge was, trying to convince them that the "unexamined life
is not worth living" (Plato, *Apology* 38a). Plato internalized
this method, perceiving that the mind could best pursue truth by
debating opposite sides of an issue. At the same time that
Socrates was engaged in his search for truth through dialogue
(*Apology* 18a), other thinkers in Athens, the Sophists, used the
same debating method with a different goal in mind. Their goal
was not truth but success. Protagoras claimed to be able to
teach his students how to be successful citizens (Plato,
Protagoras 318a ff.). But for many of the lesser sophists, the

debate was a way to win an argument irrespective of questions of truth. Thus, tragedy and philosophy aptly illustrate the creative friction that flowered in many different forms in the Athenian golden age.

The World of Homer's Epics

If fifth century Athens was to become the brilliant, colorful garden in which every kind of flower grew, Homer and Hesiod were the sacred groves that nourished that intellectual and artistic growth. Three hundred years before the Athenian golden age, the agonistic spirit was already discernible in their poetry. These poets were revered not because they produced sacred books--the Greeks had no orthodoxy, no religious dogma, no canon of religious books--but because together they gave later Greeks their myths and ideals, a theological framework and a continuity with the heroic past (Herodotus 2.53.2). If together they embody the Greek spirit, they are nevertheless light years apart from each other in style, subject matter and world view. These differences are even more striking when one remembers that they probably lived within fifty years of each other, Homer in Ionian Asia Minor and Hesiod on the Dorian mainland.

Homer is as Ionian as Hesiod is Dorian. Homer sings of the romantic and tragic heroes of the glorious past while Hesiod makes poetry out of the impoverished present. Homer's gods are usually capricious while Hesiod's are righteous. Homer's interest is in the story, Hesiod's primarily in the moral. Since the Greek selections in this book are from Hesiod's works, we will study his world in more detail after first sketching in the Homeric world which is Hesiod's point of departure.

Homer is the name traditionally given to the poet, or poets, who created the *Iliad* and *Odyssey* out of the myth and legend, poetic formulae, and historical memories handed down by earlier bards. The world he portrays is an imaginary construct shaped out of the many elements he received from his cultural past. For instance, the heroes and some of the artifacts he describes are from the late Mycenaean Age (about 1200 B.C.), and most of the social institutions reflect the subsequent Dark Ages. But the poet's shaping intelligence so combines disparate elements that later Greeks came to view Homer's mythical world as historical reality. Homer's heroes inhabit a world full of the gold and silver of the mythical past. Odysseus meets goddesses with golden shuttles and enchantresses whose palaces glitter with

magnificence. He goes to a never-never land where the palace
walls are bronze and the doors golden. And heroes like Menelaos
live in luxurious surroundings suggestive of the wealthy
Mycenaean palaces discovered by archaeologists.

But Homer's is a warrior society, and luxury is only the
backdrop for tragic conflict. The *Iliad* tells the story of the
massive conflict between Greek and Trojan armies "for fair-haired
Helen's sake." Its hero, Akhilleus, faces many conflicts but
none more destructive than that within himself, which endangers
the whole Greek army, results in the death of his best friend,
and, for a short time, destroys his sense of human decency.
"There can be no agreements between lions and men," he cries
as he denies humane treatment to the dying Hektor, (*Iliad* 22.262).
In the final book, he controls his terrible wrath and returns
Hektor's dead body to his father, recognizing in the old man a
likeness to his own father. Although Homer has none of the
vocabulary of modern psychology, he is nevertheless able to
convey the tragic *agōn* which tears apart the youthful Akhilleus.

The characters of the other heroes are depicted with broad
strokes. There is "wily Odysseus," the patient, clever man
with a bag-of-tricks who can survive the war and all manner of
disasters at sea and at home; there are Nestor, the silver-
tongued orator and Agamemmon, "leader of men;" there is "the
tower," huge, ponderous Ajax, whose mighty defensive fighting
saves the Greeks from destruction (*Iliad* 14 and 23.842-43).
These characters all portray different facets of the Greek
psyche. Odysseus and Ajax, for instance, are both revered heroes
but each is abhorrent to the other. "Resourceful Odysseus" uses
his powers of wit and deceit to devise the strategem of the
wooden horse that ultimately topples Troy; "Mighty Ajax" hates
duplicity, says little, and pits his massive body against the
enemy. After Akhilleus' death, his arms are given not to Ajax,
but to Odysseus, illustrating the Greek tendency to trust brain
over brawn. But the poet's sympathetic portrayal of the loser
reveals the deep respect Greeks would always have for Dorian
virtues. For Ajax came to symbolize the laconic, straight
forward Dorian hero and Odysseus the resourceful, wily Ionian.
Their relative merits continued to fascinate Greeks for centuries. (See, for instance, Sophocles, *Ajax* and *Philoktetes*).

Even though Homer's primary focus is always on his heroes,
the gods are everywhere in his epics. His conception of divinity dominated subsequent Greek culture. But the Homeric epics

are not systematic treatments of the gods such as Hesiod's
Theogony aimed to be. Rather, Homer pictures the Olympians as
characters in his epics. Since his audience is already thoroughly familiar with the Olympian pantheon, we learn of the gods'
natures, powers, and complex family relationships through
inferences based on action and speech. The ruling Olympian
gods are immortal, often carefree personalities who live in a
male-dominated divine world. Zeus is recognized as the ruler of
this family, and although he is occasionally described in
majestic terms (*Iliad* 1.528-30), more often he is shown presiding
precariously over the others. In an established hierarchy,
status is determined by the amount of influence each deity has
with Zeus. Hera, for instance, despite her pre-Olympian
independence from Zeus as a mother goddess, is near the top as
Zeus' nagging wife, while her ungainly son Hephaistos is near
the bottom. Often, these Olympians ingeniously bypass Zeus'
decrees, or get their way through bribery, trickery, or seduction.

Such intrigue at times proves too much even for Zeus, who is
not above using similar tactics himself. When, for instance,
the other gods are threatening to alter the already fated outcome
by their constant interference in the Trojan War, Zeus explodes
in anger. He can fling any disobedient god into murky Tartaros,
he warns, proposing a test of his strength:

> All you gods, come try this, so you will see:
> hang a golden rope from the sky,
> and all of you, gods and goddesses, hold on tight.
> You could not drag me from the sky to the plain,
> not Zeus, your supreme ruler, even if you pulled 'til
>   exhausted.
> But whenever I felt like dislodging you,
> I could propel you and the very earth and sea as well.
> Then I would bind the rope around the peak of Olympos,
> and leave everything suspended in mid air.
> I am that much stronger than gods and mortals.
>
> (*Iliad* 8, 18-27)

As unruly as the Olympian gods may be, Zeus' claim to supremacy
is clear.

Not so clear, however, is the distinction between divinity
and humanity. Homer's treatment of the gods shows them to be
much like human beings. They laugh and cry, love and hate. They
protect their human favorites and harm their enemies. They fight
among themselves, have love affairs and feasts with plenty of
wine, take vengeance for petty jealousies, and punish those who
disobey them. They are often comical, as when Hera schemes
against Zeus (*Iliad* 13-15), or when Ares and Aphrodite are caught

in adultery (*Odyssey* 8). Sometimes they are menacing. When
Aphrodite wants to reunite Helen with her cowardly lover Paris
against Helen's wishes, Aphrodite's laughter turns to angry
threats (*Iliad* 3.390 ff.). But on some rare occasions, these
same gods also display the finest traits of human nature, such
as in the scene between Akhilleus and Thetis (*Iliad* 1), or in the
relationship of Athena and Odysseus throughout the *Odyssey*.
Their power far exceeds even the greatest of mortals. They can
often manipulate nature by causing storms, controlling winds, and
moving with supersonic speed. They can disguise themselves as
human beings or animals, and they can make their favorites
invisible when the occasion demands. Yet their powers are not
unlimited since they cannot alter the consequences of their own
decisions. For instance, when Zeus decides that Patroklos shall
kill all the Trojans he encounters, he paints himself into a
corner. For Patroklos soon encounters Sarpedon, Zeus' own
grandson. The god's "bloody tears fell to the ground" as he
wept for his dear offspring whom he cannot save (*Iliad* 16.460).
He knows that if he does not allow Sarpedon's death, he will not
be able to control other gods in similar circumstances. Such
political considerations limit the wielders of divine power.

Gods also differ from humans in being free from the limitations of human morality. The Homeric heroes are constantly
measured against a code of behavior but the gods are not. The
heroes of the *Iliad*, for example, are expected to live by the
heroic code: "to stand in the forefront of the battle," to be
honored with the spoils of victory, and to receive the glory of
praise from their compatriots (*Iliad* 12.310-28). The gods, however, have no such code. They can be selfish, capricious, or
cowardly without fear of tragic consequences. Their immortality
makes immorality a fact of Olympian life, for death is the
measurer of all human accomplishment.

Thus, Homer's world is an aristocratic world of powerful,
but mostly carefree gods and heroic but, finally, tragic warriors.
It is essentially a male world since women, divine or human, are
treated but peripherally (Chapter 10). The heroes live by the
heroic code; and the deathless gods need no morals. Acceptance
of human responsibility, so vital to the heroes, has no divine
counterpart. Like irresponsible adolescents, the gods need not
act with maturity, but their comedy is the background for human
tragedy.

Hesiod's Dorian World and the Late Dark Ages

The Late Dark Ages in which both Homer and Hesiod lived (about 750-700 B.C.) was a period of turmoil. Family estates were no longer the central economic unit; the emerging *polis* was fast replacing the large family farm as the dominant unit. Whereas previously the farm was economically independent, producing everything the owner and his peasant-laborers received, now various independent tradesmen were achieving a new independence in the *polis*. In addition to farmers, specialized groups of craftsmen, minstrels, and potters with no visible connection to the land were emerging; also, merchants and colonists were establishing Greek colonies and trading posts along the edges of the Mediterranean and Black Seas and as far away as the Near East and Italy.

These changes brought tensions between social groups: between the wealthy and the poor, between often impoverished land owners and unlanded wealthy merchants; between mother colonies and trading posts. None of these tensions is focal in Homer's poetry since his subject matter is the heroic past, but some of them appear first in Hesiod's poetry since he wrote of the plight of the peasant in his native Boeotia. Many of the new tensions did not concern him since Boeotia was too poor and rural for trading-posts or colonies and his fellow-farmers were too poor to face problems of diversification. The same farmer tilled and plowed when the weather was right and sailed and fished in the off-seasons. Nor was he concerned about revolutionary solutions to poverty as some of the poets of the next generation would be. Hesiod was a conservative Dorian who looked for moral solutions, not revolutionary ones.

Still, considered in terms of literary history, Hesiod did lead a poetic revolution: The *Works and Days* and *Theogony* repudiate Homer's leisurely, high heroic style and assert a poetic world of homely truth against Homer's "false" poetry of heroic deeds set in a world of royal luxury. We may view his revolution as a new poetics of realism or as more accurate sociology of the times than Homer provides, or as a moral revolution in which Zeus becomes, if not the champion of human rights, at least the symbol that human justice is attainable. Hesiod's new poetics is especially apparent in the *Theogony*; and though a sociological realism permeates the *Works and Days*, a moral fervor dominates both works, being especially evident in his modifications of the Olympian gods. (For our purposes, we assume that one poet composed both the *Works and Days* and the *Theogony* although there may have been two "Hesiods.")

The preface to the *Theogony* contains a description of Hesiod's encounter with the Muses on Mount Helikon, where these goddesses of poetic inspiration describe the difference between Homer's and Hesiod's poetry:

> We know how to tell many false stories that seem true;
> We also know how to speak the truth when we wish.
>
> *(Theogony* 27-28)

The first of these adages alludes to Homer's style and his wily hero Odysseus. The line even seems to mimic a line in the *Odyssey* where Homer proudly asserts: "Odysseus knew how to tell many false stories that seem true" (*Odyssey* 19.203). But deceptive story-telling is as inimical to Dorian Hesiod as it was to the hero Ajax. Truth and justice are Hesiod's concern, rather than the imaginative flights of the clever hero of a remote past. Like Arthur Miller in our day, Hesiod believes "attention must be paid" to the common man, the indigent farmer of his own day. So, the Muses' second adage describes the new poetics.

Hesiod's realism is not so much the result of personal poverty as of his Dorian environment and character. Financially, he seems to have been fairly well off by contemporary standards. He mentions owning a slave, indulging in an occasional glass of choice wine and traveling to Euboia to accept a prize for his poetry (*Works and Days* 654). His moral vision is observable in the reasons Hesiod gives us for composing the *Works and Days*. Ostensibly, he wants to disabuse a spendthrift brother from attempting to live an aristocratic life on the model of a bygone Homeric world; but really he wants to focus on peasants' conflict with an unjust world. These peasants struggle against bad weather and poor soil, against long hours and lazy wives, against society's drones and cheats. Hesiod is convinced that Zeus will reward the backbreaking work of the farmer in a future golden age. This conviction accounts for the didactic, moral tone of the epic and for his tendency to see things in terms of simple opposites. He thinks in terms of present degeneracy (*Works and Days* 174-201) and Zeus' future when all will enjoy peace and happiness. Thus he balances his somber pessimism about the present with a long-range optimism about the human race.

This dualistic mentality may explain, in part at least, Hesiod's ambivalence towards women: he alternates between a fear or hatred of contemporary women and a dream of beautiful

women in an ideal future (*Theogony* 9). Pessimistic about the
present situation, he views women as booby-traps and drones
(*Works and Days* 83 and *Theogony* 593ff.). His failure to acknowledge women as positive contributors in the work force
contrasts sharply with Homer's view (see Chapter 10). Economic
reasons may account for his calling woman a drone if the farm
could not profitably use a second hand, but Hesiod must have had
deeper reasons for the strident misogyny which the following
quotation reveals:

> Let not a wench with loose behind
> Cajole you with her laughter;
> Although she's charming, you will find
> Your barn is what she's after.
>
> Put your trust in womankind--
> She'll turn around and steal you blind.
>
>   (*Works and Days* 373-35, translated by Sandra Moffitt)

If Hesiod's attitude toward women leaves much to be desired,
his concern for the rights of the individual male peasant
represents an advance over the Homeric view. *Dikē*, "justice,"
becomes the cornerstone of Hesiod's whole edifice, although the
word is without ethical content in Homer. *Dikē* originally meant
"way" or "direction" and, in Homer's aristocratic world, the
"way" that the lord of the manor ran things was, generally
speaking, not to be questioned. Aggrieved nobles could engage
in duels, submit to arbitration or otherwise defend their rights,
but the rights of nameless peasants generally were not even
mentioned in the heroic world. In Hesiod's Boeotia, however,
the civil rights of the peasant were at least worth considera-
tion. Injured peasants got a hearing and were able to call
witnesses even though their chances of winning appear to have
been slight if they lacked the good will of the aristocratic
judge whose word was final (*Works and Days* 371). Hesiod himself
experienced "crooked" decisions when the "bribe-devouring kings"
judged against him. Nevertheless, his own experience seems to
have convinced him that the common man could find justice through
hard work. By making Justice Zeus' daughter, the poet signals
his belief that retributive justice is attainable in his society,
if only in the long run.

Nowhere is Hesiod's repudiation of Homer more obvious than
in his treatment of divinities. The changes he makes are of two
kinds: additions to fill out the divine framework of the
universe and modifications to make the divinities more moral.
The additions occur mostly in the *Theogony*, or *Birth of the Gods*,

where he attempts to give a systematic account of the universe
from its beginning until its culmination in the reign of Zeus;
the moral changes begin in the *Theogony* and develop, albeit
without total consistency, in the *Works and Days*. Whereas
Homer's interest in the Olympian gods is mostly as a super-
natural backdrop for human conflict, Hesiod is interested in the
gods themselves, the universe they inhabit, their number and
variety, their origins and conflicts. In addition to Homer's
Olympian gods, Hesiod's cast includes all the powers and monsters
that inhabited the universe in pre-Olympian times, which Homer
knew but usually chose to ignore. In an effort to classify all
divinities, Hesiod also includes many abstractions and personifications like Eros, Peace, Justice, Ignorance and Deceit, which
enabled Hesiod to allegorize the moral conflicts between good
and evil.

The greatest of his divine personifications, and the one
that may be his crowning invention, is Eros, whom he places at
the very beginning of the universe as one of the four primal
powers. Eros is an enigmatic cosmic force, the "knee-buckler,
who seduces reason and common sense in all gods and mortals"
(*Theogony* 121-22). In his conception of Eros Hesiod gives
mythical expression to the fundamental *agōn* between passion and
reason. By calling him the "knee-buckler," the poet suggests
the power of passion to frustrate the best laid plans of gods
and mortals. And by placing Eros at the very beginning of the
universe, he suggests that all subsequent creations are sexual.
Thus, the sexual union of powers like Earth and Sky give birth
to other powers which in turn beget the Titans and Olympians.
There are a few exceptions to this sexual rule, as when Sky is
born from Earth or Day from Night without sexual partners. But
Eros, the desire that needs fulfillment outside itself, is alle-
gorized as the primary creative force. In this way, Eros is
given a much more central role in the Greek tradition than in
the Israelite where God's love is described in terms of generosity
(*agapē*) rather than desire or need, and where sexuality is
limited to human beings.

Hesiod's divine scheme also assigns roles to various monsters,
for instance, to Medusa and the Gorgons and especially to the
Hundred-Arms and Typhon. As their name suggests, the Hundred-
Arms are misshapen hulks and Zeus employs their brute strength
to wrest power from the Titans, creating thereby a world in which
Reason and Violence are balanced. Zeus thus owes his victory

over the brutal, titanic world in part to his creative use of the
very forces he conquers. (See Chapter 3.) The dragon Typhon,
however, appears as a tornado-spirit at the end of the epic and
challenges Zeus' power. Like Marduk destroying Tiamat, Zeus
overcomes Typhon in single combat and secures his power forever.

The greatest threat to Zeus' enlightened rule, however, is his
own father Kronos who leads the Titans against the Olympians in
a ten year struggle reminiscent of the Trojan War. But the
differences between Hesiod's and Homer's wars are more instructive than the similarities. Hesiod's is a cosmic struggle
between gods and monsters rather than an earthly contest between
heroes. Its drama lies in its vast scope: Olympos, Earth, and
the lower world all crash in a tumult that threatens the whole
universe. Moreover, Hesiod's theology prevents him from portray-
ing Zeus' antagonist sympathetically. No Hector fights for his
family and native land as in Homer's *Iliad*. In fact, Zeus'
father is not even mentioned by name throughout the war. This
absence of a worthy antagonist lessens the dramatic tension but
allows Hesiod to depict Zeus as a god of Justice, embodying the
forces of Reason and Power within himself. With these contradictory forces internalized, effective challenge can no longer
come from without. When, for instance, Prometheus challenges
Zeus by stealing fire for mortals, Hesiod alters the received
myth to show Zeus outwitting the challenger (*Theogony* 535ff.).
Similarly, the bickering Olympians of Homer are reduced to an
exemplary middle class family. The *Theogony*, then, shows Zeus
producing a harmonious balance between Reason and Violence
within his own being, thus providing the foundation for a just
world. The *Works and Days* suggests that human beings can spread
this justice by engaging in agonistic work.

Agōn, then, took many forms in ancient Greece, from Olympian
frivolity to human tragedy, from Olympic games to contests
between playwrights, from struggles between tragic or philosophical antagonists to wars between city-states or to spoofs
between buffoons. Many of these forms we have barely mentioned
since our focus has been on the heroic passions of Homer's
world and the mixture of philosophical probing, mythic lore and
peasant struggles of Hesiod's world. Even from this admittedly
narrow view of the Greek experience, however, we can see the
debt that western culture owes to the Greek competitive spirit.

CHAPTER 10

WOMEN IN THE THREE CULTURES

Cultural anthropologist Bronislaw Malinowski sees myths as
providing a social charter, a code of norms for a society. "The
main object of sacred tradition," he writes, "is not to serve as
a chronicle of past events; it is to lay down the effective
precedent of a glorified past for repetitive actions in the
present."[1] As Malinowski has shown, myths not only reflect a
society's institutions and social roles but also its social
ideals. They form and preserve "the social organization,
religious practices and moral conduct of the living society."
Subsequent generations come to regard the social organization
depicted in myths as true, immutable, and natural, especially
when the myths become immortalized in works of art.[2] Malinowski
is concerned with the positive effects that myths have in preserving morality. But in the last decade feminists have pointed
to the negative impact that the sanctification of social organization has had on women. Naturally, the social organization
depicted in myths reflects the status quo in a given society,
favoring the upper classes, and since most ancient societies,
including the ones we are studying, had a patriarchal structure,
all authority in religious life, in politics, and in the family
generally belonged to men. This helps us understand both why
mythical women from Eve and Pandora to Cinderella have been
subordinated to men and why these portrayals have been a potent
force in maintaining that subordination. Because most of our
institutions and thought continue to reflect these received
ideas and inherited patterns, we tend to equate the social
organization in ancient societies with "God's will," or "human
nature," or "woman's natural limitations."

In light of our modern consciousness of changing sexual
roles, both scholars and readers of myth are questioning the
treatment of women in ancient myths. Do the female portraits in

ancient myths reflect woman's nature or merely the perception
of woman's nature as the patriarchal mind conceived it? If the
latter, do the portraits of women in these myths totally inval-
idate their relevance for today's world, as some argue, or do
myths transmit perennial truths along with such inevitable
cultural prejudices? (See Introduction to Creation Myths.)
Will new myths grow out of old ones, melding what our age
considers the perennially true elements from the old myths
together with new truths such as equality in sexual roles? or
will new myths break radically with the past? Most of these
questions are beyond the scope of this book, but the materials
in the book should suggest to the student how myths combine the
perennial and the time-bound, and this chapter should provide a
good example of the historical limitations present in all myth.

Woman's position in ancient history and myth has only
recently begun to receive scholarly attention, and so little has
survived of what women wrote that the evidence available to us
on the topic is sketchy, incomplete, and often unreliable.[3]
Since most ancient authors were male, women were in effect "a
'muted group' made inarticulate by the lack of a language in
which to communicate their particular sense of society and its
relationship to the totality of society."[4] So what we know of
women in antiquity we know almost without exception from the
perspective of men. Sometimes the mythmakers were well-disposed
towards women, sometimes antagonistic; but in either case,
women were depicted as auxiliary or peripheral rather than as
integral to their societies. Until recently, not much progress
had been made in understanding woman's role in the ancient world,
since studies tended to substantiate pre-conceived ideas of
modern (predominantly male) critics. Even now, there is still
a tendency to oversimplification and to view issues emotionally.
Nevertheless, as male and female scholars together seek to
understand the role that a 'muted sex' played in ancient cultures, there is a new awareness of built-in prejudices, a new
attention to the way that myths oscillate between the ideal and
the real. Above all, there is a new realization that our knowledge of the sociology, anthropology and religion of the ancient
world is terribly limited. Sociological studies are now examining such issues as women's contributions to the work force;
cultic studies are now examining attitudes towards gender,
female sexuality and the relation of gender to power (for
example, Ochshorn);[3a] and anthropological studies are

concentrating, for instance, on the "extreme social dimorphism" of fifth century Athenian society, where the world was divided into male and female spheres to such a degree, it is argued, that all opposites (for instance, public and private, outer space and inner space, rational and irrational) were subsumed under and expressed imaginatively in terms of male-female polarities. (See Arthur, "Classics.")[3c] This assumption, if valid, leads to another question: is the identification of the feminine with the private, the fearful, and the irrational a particularly Greek characteristic, resulting from their agonistic outlook, or were the Greeks simply articulating the binary opposition basic to all human thinking in terms that patriarchal societies made "logical"? (See Introduction to Creation Myths and Chapter 9.) Such questions are as yet unanswerable.

All we hope to do in this essay is to sketch some of the important stories and other written materials about women from the three cultures we are studying and to suggest how they may be interpreted. Our analysis is tentative, meant to provoke discussion rather than to make definitive statements. Some specialized studies are cited in the footnotes. Despite the limitations of our knowledge, we do know that the patriarchal nature of these three societies resulted in ordinary women's being dependent on men from the cradle to the grave, but that extraordinary women did attain important positions. We know too that these portraits of women seldom captured a woman's perspective; that the male authors tended to idealize and protect women, or to use them as scapegoats.

Matriarchy and Mother Goddesses

Scholars have been theorizing for years about ancient matriarchies, matrilineal descent of dynasties, goddesses who once surpassed gods in importance, and related issues. A century ago, Bachofen argued that matriarchy preceded patriarchy in the ancient Greek world. He based his theory on the importance of Mycenaean queens and heroines in the late Bronze Age and on evidence of matrilineal descent. Bachofen investigated a topic previously ignored by classical scholars, but his evidence was insufficient. The few references to female rule in ancient Greek literature do not allow the general conclusion that there was a period of women rulers in Greece. The powerful Homeric queens (*Odyssey* 7.54-55, and *Iliad* 6.425), for instance, need not signal a matriarchy any more than Elizabeth I did in England.

Nevertheless, a recent study by C. G. Thomas seemed to confirm Bachofen's idea. Thomas extended the definition of matriarchy to include not just women as rulers but also women as dominant forces in social, economic, and religious institutions. From archeological evidence, she concluded that women were dominant in all areas of Minoan life (about 3000-1500 B.C.). The various religious rituals and social gatherings depicted in Minoan palaces suggest that women had a freedom and stature at least equal to that of men. In the later societies of mainland Greece, however, the evidence shows that men were dominant and that women lacked the freedom of their earlier Minoan counterparts, even though they were an essential part of the labor force. By the end of the Dark Ages when Homer and Hesiod lived (750-700 B.C.), political, religious and social patriarchy was virtually complete.[5] Thomas does not assert that women were ever rulers, however, and does not really refute the predominant view of most classical scholars, that "the concept of matriarchy as a social reality should be abandoned" (Arthur, "Classics," p. 385). The decline of women's power from the Greek Bronze Age to Homer's day is not sufficient proof of a matriarchal period.

This historical decline in women's status is also reflected in the portraits of mother goddesses found in the early myths of all three cultures. Although their existence is used to support the idea of a pre-historic matriarchy, these goddesses may have been images of Mother Earth, Chaos Mother or Fertility, having little connection with female political power. People who lived in a world at the mercy of nature would probably have worshipped it in one form or another. The rulers, male or female, would be expected to propitiate the mother goddesses. In fact, the earliest written evidence from Mesopotamia suggests that political power belonged to men who considered themselves proteges of the mother goddesses.

Whatever the reasons for mother goddesses' stature in the earlier periods, their influence had declined by later times. Rosemary Ruether suggests that this decline may have been due to a change in men's relationship to nature. As men came to feel themselves "the masters rather than the children of organic nature", reverence for mother goddesses and consequently for women lessened.[6] This pattern of decline is echoed in the early literature of all three societies. In Greece, for instance, Hesiod shows Gaia (Mother Earth) in a dominant

position at the very beginning of the world (*Theogony*, 116ff.).
Later, however, Zeus takes power and she is relegated to an
advisory position. (See Chapter 3.) Similarly, Hera, Zeus'
shrewish wife in Homeric times, was originally independent of
Zeus and seems to have been worshipped "as an embodiment of the
fruitful earth."[7] Elsewhere the earth goddess, Ge Pandora,
suffered an even more humiliating fate. Her name originally
meant "Earth the Giver of All Gifts," but by Hesiod's time
(about 700 B.C.), Pandora becomes the "spine-chilling, untouchable booby-trap" which Zeus creates to punish the human race.
(See Chapter 5.)

In the Near East, Mesopotamia offers several examples of what
Samuel Noah Kramer calls the "victimization and resentment of
female deities." Nammu, the goddess of the primeval sea, was
the creator of the universe and mother of all the gods in
several early myths. "By all genealogical rights, therefore,
had the theologians played it fair, she should have had top
billing in the pantheon." But the god-lists rarely mention her
and instead Enki, in a "bit of priestly piracy," acquires her
vast powers.[8] Similarly, the mother goddess, Mami (also called
Ninhursaga and other names), was originally a goddess of
productivity whose main task was "to give birth to lords, to
place the crown on their heads."[9] Although she may have been
one of the most important deities in the third millennium, she
had become a secondary goddess by the second millennium. In
Atrahasis, for instance, every time Mami does a task, she has to
rely on the god Ea for instructions and help. She even says,
"It is not properly mine to do these things. This work belongs
to Enki [Ea]" (I:200-01). Her former glory is only suggested
by the epithet "mistress of all gods," a title she is given
after creating the human race.

Likewise, in the Israelite story of Adam and Eve, Adam gives
Eve her name "because she is the mother of all who live"
(Genesis 3:20). A recent study notes that the similarity
between Eve's and Mami's titles is emphasized because Eve gets
her name at the same point in the Israelite story as Mami does
in *Atrahasis*, suggesting that the figure of the mother goddess
was "probably hidden" behind Eve.[10] But the possible relationship between Eve and Mami is complicated by the Israelite's
belief in one God. The biblical writer, even if he was using
polytheistic sources, would have expunged all gods and goddesses
except Yahweh from his story. Even if Eve did descend from an

earlier goddess figure, her portrayal in the biblical story was
probably not an intentional demotion. In the monotheistic
system she must be a mortal woman. The story as we have it,
however, does depict Eve as Adam's subordinate after the disobedience. According to Carol Meyers, this reflects the Israelites'
social and economic situation at the time they settled in the
promised land (about 1250 B.C.). Meyers argues that wars,
famines, and plagues had reduced the Israelite population,
placing added emphasis on woman's role as childbearer to the
detriment of her other roles. By the time this crisis had
passed, however, an ideology of woman as almost exclusively
mother had become entrenched, and hence her inferior social
position.[11] It seems ironic that Eve is given the title which
indicates her formerly exalted position as mother goddess at
the same place in the story as she is subordinated to Adam.

Although evidence for historical matriarchy is unconvincing--
at least in the Greek world--these portraits of demoted goddesses
suggest that the idea of a prehistoric matriarchy was prevalent
in early historical times. This has prompted the theory of
"a myth of matriarchy." According to this theory many cultures
believed that women ruled in an earlier, prehistoric time, but
their reigns were so violent that men had to wrench power from
them and subordinate them for society's well-being. According
to Joan Bamberger, "the point of the myth is not the recording
of some historical or prehistorical state of affairs, but rather
that women are not fit to rule, only to be ruled."[12] Froma
Zeitlin has shown that the "myth of matriarchy" fits the central
myth of Aeschylus' *Oresteia*: the violent queen's abuse of
power leads to women's subordination and a recognition that it
is "necessary, natural and just" that they be subordinated in
marriage (Zeitlin, p. 153). Both Bamberger and Zeitlin argue
that the "myth of matriarchy" is not a memory of history but
a "social charter," effectively subordinating women down the
ages. More study is needed to demonstrate the applicability of
this theory to a wide range of myths in various cultures. If it
does apply, it would lend support to the speculation that the
"myth of matriarchy" may have contributed to the demotion of
mother goddesses. The present state of our knowledge does not
allow us to draw any definitive conclusions, however.

Mesopotamian Women

Whatever status goddesses and women may have had in pre-
historic Mesopotamia, women's place in Mesopotamian society was
generally subordinate by the beginning of recorded history. If
men and women were equal in the struggles against nature in pre-
history, the dawn of history showed most women already shunted
to the side. The information about women in the Antediluvian
("Before the Flood") Age (3100-2900), derived primarily from
myths that survive in a much later form, indicates an age
"almost wholly indifferent to women" (Hallo, p. 24).[13] The
hero of the flood story, for example, is the only antediluvian
whose wife is even mentioned, and she appears only in a late
version of the story. Nameless, she plays no role in the flood
itself, and her only distinction is to bake bread for Gilgamesh.
In the next few hundred years, there was Queen Puabi whose
sumptuous tomb shows her importance during the time when "heroic"
warriors were ruling the Sumerian cities; and Queen Ku-Bau,
reportedly a low-born tavern keeper, who founded the Third
Dynasty of Kish and ruled without benefit of inheritance or
marriage (Hallo, p. 28). But these queens were rare exceptions:
political power in the earliest recorded periods was almost
exclusively in male hands.

The Sargonic Age (2300-2150) clearly showed female deities
and male rulers coexisting. Apparently, it was during the
reign of Sargon the Great that Inanna/Ishtar achieved a position
of preeminence in the pantheon. Originally a fertility goddess
with her consort Dumuzi, she becomes a goddess of war and of
love as well as the "Queen of Heaven." She is an aristocratic,
proud, short-tempered and often vindictive goddess whose influence has been variously interpreted. For Kramer, for instance,
she should be "soothing balm to the resentful wounds of liberated
women" since her power was "glorified and extolled throughout
Sumer's existence" ("Poets", p. 16);[3a] for Jacobsen, however, she
embodies all the female roles except those "which call for
maturity and a sense of responsibility" (p. 141). Perhaps her
irresponsibility accounts for the fact that she was the only
goddess whose power grew in the third millennium since her
prestige was not a threat to male political power.

Her rise seems to have been tied to that of her protege,
Sargon. During his ascendancy, hymns written by Sargon's
daughter hail Inanna as "Inanna of battle" and as a storm
goddess able to teach men the art of war. They celebrate her

omniscience, her omnipotence and her parity with An, the supreme god. Moreover, they trace Inanna's struggles and victories over foreign and domestic enemies as a divine counterpart of the struggles and victories of Sargon (Hallo, p. 29). These hymns not only contributed to Inanna's exaltation but also secured the power of Inanna's favorite, King Sargon.

The often contradictory traditions about Sargon agree that he rose to power with the help of women. As a youth he "won the love of" the goddess Inanna, which may mean he was loved by a priestess of Inanna. His most important female help, however, came from his daughter, Enheduanna, whom he appointed high priestess of the moongod at Ur and of An at Uruk. Her talent as a poet and "a systematic theologian" produced the hymns that propagated "a new theology" and made her "the first non-anonymous author in literature" (Hallo, p. 29). She also became the first in a long line of royal daughters to be named high priestess at Ur and Uruk and she was later even identified with the goddess Inanna. She thus achieved a rank perhaps unequaled by any woman in the ancient Near East, but her accomplishments were a consequence of male patronage.

There were also classes of aristocratic women who exercised considerable political, religious or economic power. The "nuns" of Sippar, for instance, acquired importance in the business community despite their cloistered lives (Harris, p. 962).[3a] And some aristocratic women of Mari held prestigious positions during the "enlightened" rule of Zimri-Lim (eighteenth century B.C.). His wife was his deputy in his absence; his daughters held real authority; and many other women held important cultic positions as scribes, prophets and priests. Still, the structure of society at Mari was patriarchal: the ruler and most of the administrators were male, and although women had legal rights denied them elsewhere, they suffered the typically disparaging remarks about the "weak, unheroic character of women" (Batto, p. 136).[3a]

There were, then, important Mesopotamian goddesses and royal women, but the pattern seems clear. The goddesses generally supported male rule; and although evidence suggests that aristocratic women achieved more power and responsibility in Mesopotamia than elsewhere, few held political power independent of men.

Israelite Women

One might presume that women would have fared better in
Israel than elsewhere in the ancient Near East since its religion
recognized that both men and women are made in the "image and
likeness of God" (Genesis 1:27). In practice, however, Israel
rarely lived according to this ideal. Phyllis Bird has shown
that the coincidence of male-dominated religion and social
custom gave women "a double liability in Israel" ("Images of
Women" p. 50).[3b] In theory, Yahweh may be a God beyond sexuality,
but the Israelites understood him primarily as a father figure.[14]
Since Yahweh was their only deity, all goddesses, as well as
other gods, were suppressed as part of the general campaign
against false deities. The mother goddess, for instance, emerges
within the Old Testament only in a disguised form. Yahweh's
spouse is not the mother goddess "who encompasses her son-lover"
but Israel whom he "creates and elects as his bride" (Ruether,
p. 41).[6]

If the image of God as father created a subtle liability,
woman's status in society provided a more obvious one. Only in
her role as mother did an Israelite woman have any consistent
respect. "Mother" was an honorific title. The judge and prophet
Deborah, for instance, is called "a mother in Israel" (Judges
5:7), a title reminiscent of Eve's "mother of all who live."
When King Solomon enters his mother's presence, he rises from
his throne and bows before her. Bathsheba then "sat down at his
right hand" (1 Kings 2:19).

A mother, however, had nothing like the authority of a father.
She seems to have had charge of her child's education and to have
had a voice in decisions about his religious future (1 Samuel
1:11), but the sequel to Solomon's respectful bow to Bathsheba
illustrates how meaningless such deference could be. Bathsheba
has come to ask a favor for Solomon's half-brother, Adonijah,
but Solomon fears a coup. In response to her request, therefore,
he announces: "Adonijah shall be put to death this very day"
(1 Kings 2:24). A later queen, however, pursues power more
directly and ruthlessly. When Athaliah learns that her son the
king is dead, she promptly "did away with all those of royal
stock," and she herself ruled for six years (2 Kings 11:1-3).
But Athaliah was the exception. Mothers generally lacked power
and achieved only such prestige and influence as their sons
accorded them.

If the title mother assured a woman respect, the title wife did not. The sterile woman suffered from Yahweh's sanction, the jibes of fertile women, and sometimes her husband's rejection. But most important, she was deprived of her only sure avenue to respect in her society, the bearing of sons. A wife, after all, was a possession which a man acquired in a business transaction from her father (Exodus 20:17; Deuteronomy 4:21). The common use of *baal*, master, instead of *ish*, man, to describe the male "partner" in marriage underscores this view of marriage. The entire story of Jacob and his wives illustrates the plight of his wives, Rachel and Leah. Because he loves Rachel, Jacob promises to work for her father, Laban, for seven years in order to secure her as his wife. But on his wedding night, Laban tricks Jacob and substitutes Leah, her "dull-eyed" older sister (Genesis 29:17-24). When Jacob complains, Laban promises to give him Rachel too, "in return for a further seven years' work" (29:27). Although Jacob shows his love by working the other seven years, the story emphasizes the two sisters' help-lessness. Each sister, for instance, tries to outwit the other by providing more sons to Jacob. When Rachel cannot conceive, she substitutes her slave girl. At one point, when Rachel wants some plants that one of Leah's sons has, she barters for them with her most valuable currency: "Very well," she concedes. "Let him sleep with you tonight in exchange for your sons' mandrakes" (Genesis 30:15).

Subsequently, a whole chapter is devoted to the rape of Jacob's daughter, Dinah. When her brothers hear that a non-Israelite neighbor, Shechem, has raped their sister, they are "grieved and angry" because in lying with Jacob's daughter, he has committed "an outrage, an intolerable thing" (Genesis 34: 7-8). There is no mention, however, of Dinah's feelings or of her response to Shechem who "loved the young girl and comforted her" (34:3). Her brothers do not rest until they kill him and all the males of his town in retaliation. When Jacob objects, they retort: "Is our sister to be treated as a common whore?" (34:31). The ultimate fame of Jacob's wives rests, of course, on the importance of their sons, the twelve sons of Israel. Still, Dinah is assured her own place in history because her rape was an insult to the community.

Although the wife had a precarious position in Israel, more often than not she is treated with great respect in these stories (Bird, pp. 52-55, 71).[3b] The famous description of the "capable wife" shows the stature a noble woman could achieve

(Proverbs 31:11-23). This idealized portrait indicates many possible occupations open to a noble woman: buying and selling property, working the fields, managing the household, and weaving for
trade as well as for the family. Although her industry is praised
as her husband's asset rather than her own, she is nevertheless
a force to be reckoned with. Many women in the Old Testament
embody this description: for instance, Moses' sister Miriam, the
prophet and leader who presided at the victory song at the Red
Sea (Exodus 15:20); and Deborah, the prophet and judge who settled
disputes in Yahweh's name and was the inspirational leader credited with delivering Israel from the Canaanites (Judges 4-5).

But probably the best biblical examples of "capable" women
are Naomi and her daughter-in-law, Ruth, whose courageous manage-
ment of their difficult lives is told in the Book of Ruth. The
tale of these two women, widowed in Moab, Ruth's native land, is
variously interpreted as an allegory of God's kindness working
through their suffering and strength, as a story of the love of
strong women for each other, and as a love story of Ruth and her
husband. In any case, the strength of the two women is the dominant thread: Naomi daring to rage against God for her misfortunes
(Ruth 1:13-21) and urging Ruth to return home even though her departure would further isolate Naomi in a foreign country; and
Ruth's decision to leave her own family, country and gods in order
to be loyal to her aging mother-in-law: "where you go, I will
go...where you die, I will die" (1: 16-17). Whether or not this
tale can serve as a "theological interpretation of feminism,"
since its women are "working out their salvation with fear and
trembling" (Trible, p. 196), it does show two female protagonists
taking the initiative in shaping their own lives in a way that few
stories do even today. (See Heilbrun.)[17] Ironically, however,
the event that makes the story end happily is the birth of Ruth's
son, who will provide the protection these women need to survive
in a patriarchal world.

If the "capable" woman is the "good" woman in the Book of
Proverbs, its "bad" woman is the adulteress whom men are admon-
ished to avoid (e.g., 5:23; 2:16-17). These passages roundly
condemn female sexuality outside marriage, especially because of
its evil effects on young men. Interestingly enough, the Song of
Songs suggests a much more positive view of female sexuality, even
extolling the woman for her sexual initiatives (Songs 3:1-4). The
discrepancy between the view of sexuality in the Song of Songs and

in Proverbs encouraged commentators to allegorize these poems.
Trible, however, analyzes the Song as a simple story of redeeming
erotic love in which there is "no male dominance, no female subordination, and no stereotyping of either sex."[15] Although different interpretations of the Song still abound, scholars agree that
the author of the Song reveals a much more open view of female
sexuality than other texts in the Old Testament.

Finally, we may compare the creation stories with the Song of
Songs for evidence of women's status. Several scholars share
Trible's view that the story of Adam and Eve depicts the creation
of man and woman as equal beings: the male(*ish*) and the female
(*ishshah*) emerge in the same verse and provide identity for each
other (2:22). It is only in the second half of the story that
the woman is shown as subject to the man, reflecting the status
of woman in the author's own period.[16] According to this view,
the author of this story meant to reflect the same equality in
creation as is stated in the Creation Hymn (Genesis 1:27) and is
implied in the Song of Songs. The biblical ideal of sexual equality contained in these texts did not, however, prevail in everyday Israel. The discrepancy between the ideal and the practice
has led Bird to conclude that the Old Testament is "a collection
of writings by males from a society dominated by males" (p. 41).

Israel and Mesopotamia, then, were both patriarchal societies. Neither Mesopotamian goddesses nor Israelite ideals led
to sustained sexual equality in historical times. This is a
point that feminist scholars do not always realize when they
search ancient cultures for new models of equality. Some feminists who object to the Israelite God as patriarchal assume that
Mesopotamia provides models for a new religion.[17] The evidence
suggests, however, that historical Mesopotamia was almost as male-
dominated as Israel.

Greek Women

Male-domination was also firmly established in the Ionian
Greek world of Homer and that of Hesiod on the predominantly
Dorian mainland. These two poets are our chief sources of early
Greek attitudes towards women, and yet they reflect two surpris-
ingly different attitudes towards women in early Greek literature.
Homer's is a sympathetic attitude and Hesiod's a misogynistic one.
Since Hesiod's woman as a booby-trap and drone is amply illus-
trated in his myths (in Chapter 6) and since we discuss possible

explanations for his misogyny in Chapter 9, we will focus here
on Homeric portraits of women and return to Hesiod only in the
conclusion. Still, we cannot be sure how representative either
Homer's sympathetic view or Hesiod's misogyny were of ordinary
Greeks. The abuse of women was a regular literary theme from
Hesiod on, sometimes in a satiric vein as in Semonides, sometimes
in the serious vein that Hesiod himself employed. One of Hesiod's
points which Semonides echoes is that woman is the mother not of
all humanity but only of women. In this view, Hesiod's Pandora
is both the first woman and the sign of a disunity in the human
race, a fitting expression of woman's exclusion from political
life; but others contend that Hesiod's misogyny was not typical of
his society, which was patriarchal but not misogynist.[18]

Hesiod's predecessor, Homer, however, draws women with sen-
sitive insight in the earliest extant Greek literature. Helen,
Andromakhe, and Penelope each represent different types of women
which were to become traditional in western thought. Helen is
the aloof and enticing *femme fatale*, the woman whose terrible
beauty was the mythical cause of the hideous, destructive Trojan
War. Homer never describes this beauty except in its effects; for
instance, it fascinates King Priam and the elders whose civilization was crumbling because of her. This same beauty causes her
loneliness and self disgust as she regrets having forsaken her
home and friends. She has no respect for her lover, Paris, and
she calls herself an evil, contriving bitch (*Iliad* 6.344). Although she has left her husband for Paris, she does not have to
fear slavery as the other women do. When her husband wins, she
returns to her palace at Sparta without undergoing the usual female plight of concubinage. But her security comes at the cost
of intimacy and harmony. All the glitter of Sparta cannot disguise the emptiness of her life with an unimaginative, carping
husband. (*Odyssey* 4.120-305). Still, it is her self-conscious-
ness and her concern for the anguish that she has inflicted on
others that ultimately redeem her character. She is trapped by
her own beauty, the prey of Aphrodite (*Iliad* 3.390 ff.).

Andromakhe, on the other hand, is everything that Helen is
not. In the whole epic, she talks to no one but her beloved
husband, Hektor, and is never far from her loom and hearth except
when she goes up to the ramparts to see how Hektor is faring.
Her farewell to her husband illustrates that she has found happiness in a traditional life as wife and mother (*Iliad* 6.390 ff.).

There is a moving tenderness in the mingled laughter and tears as
Hektor's war-helmet frightens his little son when the family
shares its last moments together. But the scene ends with Hektor's reminder of the division of life into husband's and wife's
spheres:

> Go inside the house and attend to your work, your loom
> and your spindle, and direct your serving-women to be about
> their tasks. It is up to the men to fight the war--
> to all the men in Troy--but especially to me.
> (*Iliad* 6.490-93)

In most ways Andromakhe accepts this "divided world" but she
nevertheless does not hesitate to give Hektor military advice that
might have saved his life (6.431-39). His pursuit of heroic
honor, however, prevents him from heeding her plan for defense
and plunges him instead into a foolhardy offensive that ultimately
destroys both him and Troy. This scene, then, shows more interaction between the male and female spheres than there would be in
later Greek literature, but also a tragic inability on Hektor's
part to heed a woman's advice. (See Arthur's analysis of the
scene, "The Divided World of *Iliad* VI," *Women Studies* 8 [1981]
21-46.)

Helen and Andromakhe, then, are two impressive women depicted in the dire circumstances of the *Iliad*. The *Odyssey*, an epic
of possiblity and hope, shows Penelope, the wife of Odysseus, as
ingenious, resilient, sceptical, and charming. Still, she is
not his equal since her sphere of influence is as limited to the
domestic as Andromakhe's is. During Odysseus' absence, Penelope
copes by sleeping, dreaming, and weaving the web that postpones
the day of an unwanted second marriage. Once there is the faint-
est hope that Odysseus may return, her native guile suggests new
strategies. Intuitive hope transcends her steady skepticism.
Inertia gives way to action when she questions the beggar (Odysseus in disguise), reprimands her son, deceives the suitors with
hints at marriage, beguiles them of gifts, and "enchants their
spirits with blandishing words, while her own mind has other intentions" (*Odyssey* 18.282-83). Intuitively, she realizes this
is the time to set up a contest in which she will marry the suitor
who can string Odysseus' bow (19.575ff.). Even though she does
not consciously recognize her husband in his beggar's disguise,
she sets in motion the events that lead to his victory over the
suitors.

The circumspect Penelope proves, subsequently, to be a
proper match for "the resourceful Odysseus." Hearing that

Odysseus has been victorious, Penelope leaps up in joy but immediately draws back. Is it Odysseus who has killed the suitors
or are the gods deceiving her? Always on guard against deception,
she devises an infallible test. When Odysseus comes to her,
"striding forth from his bath like an immortal" (*Odyssey* 23.163),
Penelope directs her handmaid: "Lay out a thick, firm bed for
him outside the well-fashioned chamber, that very bed that my
husband built" (177-79). Odysseus explodes in rage. What man
dared move their wedding bed which he had built from a living oak,
leaving one leg anchored in the earth? Penelope rejoices at his
torrent of words. She knows he is Odysseus because he has revealed their secret. She flies to him like a shipwrecked sailor
joyfully reaching port. Like him, she has completed a long,
treacherous voyage and Homer pictures them both as weary sailors.
Together, they share their concerns about trials yet to come and
retire to sweet sleep in their firmly rooted bed.

Homer's choice of the sailor as the image for both spouses
is part of a larger pattern of similes and descriptions of the
couples. In this pattern, the poet pictures both Penelope and
Odysseus as transcending their traditional sexual roles. Odysseus, for example, is once compared to an old woman weeping over
the body of a husband lost in war (8.523-31) while Penelope is a
beleaguered lion (4.791-93). Odysseus is more diplomatic, gentle,
and compassionate than other heroes while Penelope is sometimes
described in traditionally "masculine" terms. The pattern is so
pervasive that Odysseus' description of the ideal marriage in
which the man and woman keep a "harmonious household with sweet
agreement in all things" (6.180-83) reminds us of his marriage
with Penelope. Helen Foley asserts that Homer is depicting complementary male and female spheres in Ithaka. Men are in charge
of agriculture and war; women are in charge of the textile industry and the maintenance of the household. In weaving the web
that deceives the suitors, then, Penelope is not only avoiding an
unwelcome marriage but is astutely maintaining the household in
very difficult circumstances. As long as she weaves, her home
remains intact.[19]

Because men and women here seem to complement each other, it
is particularly jarring to our modern sensibilities that Penelope
is not allowed even to be a spectator at the contest which will
decide her future husband. When Penelope suggests that the unknown beggar be given a try at the bow, her son Telemakhos sends

her off summarily to tend her spindle and to direct her serving
women in her own hall: "It is up to the men," he asserts, "to
settle the question of the bow--especially to me. For I am master
in this house" (21.350-53). We notice immediately that Telemakhos, in the manner of oral epic, repeats the same formulae that
Hektor used when he sent Andromakhe back to the woman's sphere.
But at least in that context, Andromakhe was clearly inserting
herself into the male sphere of war. Here Penelope is making a
suggestion in her own home. Her immediate withdrawal after her
son's rebuke indicates that she apparently does not share our
perception of his command.

So, the complementary spheres of man and woman in Ithaka are
quite different from the modern idea of sexual equality. Penelope
has great respect and responsibility in her household and evidently is an ideal marriage partner in her society's terms. She
waits patiently and chastely at home, doing all her sailing in
the turbulent seas of her mind while Odysseus sails the world
and experiences many women; and she waits in her women's chambers
while men in her own home exclude her from the decisions about
her future. If she feels any anger at her unequal treatment, she
does not show it.

In these three portraits Homer shows little evidence of that
strain of misogyny whose effects were to be so demeaning to women
in Hesiod and Semonides. Even so, the myth underlying the *Iliad*
makes woman the cause of man's pain. Helen is introduced weaving
a great web on which she embroiders the sufferings both sides
endured for her sake (3.128). The elders of Troy want her sent
home so she will not be a *pēma*, " a cause of pain," to them and
their children (3.160). Hektor calls Paris' abduction of Helen
mega pēma, "a big pain" (3.50; see also Hesiod's *Works and Days*
56). So even in Homer we do not totally escape the view that
woman causes man's pain.

In this brief survey, we have seen images of women (though
mostly aristocratic women) from three different cultures and from
more than three millennia. In legend or history, each of these
societies produced valiant women who left lasting marks on their
respective cultures: in Mesopotamia's third millennium, a former
tavern-keeper turned queen founded a dynasty at Kish and a brilliant poet-theologian graced Sargon's court; in Israel, the "capable wife" was a cultural ideal and the two women of the Book
of Ruth are unique in being protagonists in their own story; and
in Homer's Greece, Andromakhe and Penelope each illustrate the

strong influence that women could achieve from within a "divided
world" in which there was some communication from one sector to
the other; yet Andromakhe especially shows the tragic limitations
of such a division. Overall, Mesopotamian aristocratic women seem
to have achieved more political power than their counterparts
elsewhere, but in all three cultures, women were denied lasting
political power and full social equality.

We have also seen the consistent demotion of the goddesses
in the three societies. The Mesopotamian goddess of productivity,
an important divine figure in the third millennium, is reduced to
a secondary birth-goddess by the second millennium. In Israel,
the goddess of an earlier setting becomes the woman of the Adam
and Eve Story, created equal to the man in Genesis 2 but subordinated to him in Genesis 3. In Homer's Ionian Greek tradition,
Hera, evidently an independent mother goddess in the pre-Homeric
scheme of things, degenerates into Zeus' nagging wife. Finally,
in Hesiod's Dorian Greek tradition, Ge Pandora, Earth the Giver
of All Gifts, becomes the booby-trap and drone, the source of
man's woes.

We have noted that these demotions probably reflect the growing security of male rulers who no longer felt themselves at the
mercy of Mother Nature. Any further judgments on the overall
pattern are premature, given our limited knowledge of Mesopotamian
religion. We may, however, make an educated guess about the
reasons why Eve tumbled gracefully whereas Pandora fell flat on
her face. The religious belief of the Israelites that God is,
theoretically at least, beyond sexuality and that all humans are
created in God's image assures Eve dignity despite her subordination. In Greece, however, religious power swung totally from
mother earth to Zeus and the male-dominated Olympians. Even
Athena, born fully armed from Zeus' head, was sufficiently male
to fit the Olympian pattern. So, despite the fact that the
Greeks continued to revere Earth as an earlier deity, her power
and woman's claim to position were effectively destroyed.

Economic conditions on the Dorian mainland might have denied
women the complementary role they had in Homer's Ithaka and the
maternal reverence that they enjoyed in Israel. Hesiod's rural
setting with its poverty, over-used land and overpopulation produced conditions conducive to the images of woman as a drone whom
the farmer cannot support and as a booby-trap tricking him with
unwanted children. (See Sussman, p. 33 and Chapter 9). The

Israelites, however, particularly treasured their children because they wanted heirs to possess the land and perhaps also because wars, famines and plagues decimated the population in the late Bronze Age. This naturally gave a socio-economic reason for the exaltation of Eve, "the Mother of all who live." So we can speculate that in the formative periods for the story of Adam and Eve and the story of Pandora (pre-950 B.C. in Israel and pre-700 B.C. on the Greek mainland), socio-economic conditions were somewhat more favorable to Israelite women than to Dorian Greek women. While Israelite women had a double liability from the patriarchal social order and patriarchal religious order, women in Hesiod's Greece seem to have had a triple liability: social, religious and economic. Not only were the social order and the Olympian religious order male-dominated in Hesiod's world, but economic conditions militated against woman's receiving respect either as mother or as worker. Thus, it is at least understandable why Pandora lost any shred of dignity in Hesiod's portrait whereas Eve was subordinate but revered.

Our speculation on the different worlds of Eve and Pandora would seem to corroborate the conclusions we have drawn from our overview of woman in the three civilizations. Male dominance interacted with religious beliefs, politics, and socio-economic conditions to produce a world in which the feminine images of divinity were virtually snuffed out and in which extraordinary women were unable to effect any lasting political or social equality for their sex. It appears, too, that once these inferior social roles became embedded in memorable myths, the myths themselves served to perpetuate and sanctify the social charter. Much work remains to be done if we are to understand the complex interrelationship of politics, social history, and myth in any given culture. If myths are constantly modified by changes of narrators, as Lévi-Strauss claims, we may soon expect drastic changes in some myths. With every fresh re-telling, the narrator's personal selections and embellishments will work surface changes on story and meaning.

Notes

[1]Bronislaw Malinowski, *Sex, Culture and Myth* (New York: Harcourt, Brace and World, 1962), p. 251. See also his seminal work on the relationship between myth and social history, *Myth in Primitive Pyschology* (New York: Norton, 1962).

[2]See Froma Zeitlin, "Dynamics of Misogyny: Myth and Myth-making in the *Oresteia*," *Arethusa* 11 (1978), 149-84, for a similar argument. In her analysis of Aeschylus' *Oresteia*, she argues that once misogyny is embedded in a great work of art, the work legitimates a "social and political ideology whose mythic basis is neither recognized nor acknowledged" (p. 174).

[3]The evidence from the three societies is quite different:

a) The Mesopotamian is limited mostly to short references in historical or mythical material, and we rely especially on articles by Samuel Noah Kramer and William W. Hallo in *The Legacy of Sumer: Invited Lectures of the Middle East at the University of Texas at Austin*, ed. Denise Schmandt-Besserat, Bibliotheca Mesopotamia IV (Malibu, California: Undena Publications, 1976): Kramer's "Poets and Psalmists: Goddesses and Theologians; Literary, Religious and Anthropological Aspects of the Legacy of Sumer," 3-21, and Hallo's "Women of Sumer," 23-40, 129-38. See also Kramer's *The Sacred Marriage Rite* (Bloomington: Indiana University Press, 1969); Bernard Frank Batto, *Studies on Women at Mari* (Baltimore: Johns Hopkins University, 1974); Rivvah Harris, "Woman in the Ancient Near East," *Interpreter's Dictionary of the Bible*, Supplementary Volume (Nashville: Abington, 1976), 960-63; Julian Pitt-Rivers, *The Fate of Shechem or the Politics of Sex: Essays in the Anthropology of the Mediterranean* (New York: Cambridge University Press, 1977); and Judith Ochshorn's forthcoming study, *The Female Experience and the Nature of the Divine* (Bloomington: Indiana University Press, 1981). Although we have not seen Ochshorn's study, we are grateful for her criticism of this chapter.

b) The Israelite material is culled mainly from the Old Testament, and we rely especially on Phyllis Bird, "Images of Women in the Old Testament," in *Religion and Sexism: Images of Women in the Jewish and Christian Religious Traditions*, ed. Rosemary Ruether (New York: Simon & Schuster, 1963), pp. 41-88 who explores the multiple images of women in the Old Testament: woman is usually a non-person in the laws since their chief aim was the stability of the patriarchal family; in the historical writings, women are prominent in the early, patriarchal family-stories but appear rarely in the later political books; in Proverbs, women are considered as the ones who can make or break men; she treats women in the creation accounts last to emphasize the relative unimportance of these stories in the whole Old Testament. In *God and the Rhetoric of Sexuality* (Philadelphia: Fortress Press, 1978), Phyllis Trible studies the Hebrew text of the Adam and Eve Story, the Book of Ruth, and the Song of Songs as a biblical theologian and a feminist. We rely heavily on her analysis of the story of Adam and Eve. See also Roland De Vaux, "Family Institutions," in *Ancient Israel I: Social Institutions*, English Translation, New York: McGraw Hill, 1976, pp. 19-61; and Krister Stendahl, *The Bible and the Role of Women: A Case Study in Hermeneutics*, English Translation by Emilie T. Sander (Philadelphia: Fortress Press, 1966).

c) The Greek material is limited to the epics of Homer and Hesiod. For a general study, see Sarah B. Pomeroy, *Goddesses, Whores, Wives, and Slaves: Women in Classical Antiquity* (New York: Schocken Books, 1975), chapters 1-3, where she examines evidence of the existence of the Amazons, of concubinage, of economic, political and military considerations that affected women's lives. On Matriarchy, see Pomeroy's "A Classical Scholar's Perspective on Matriarchy," in Berenice A. Carroll, ed., *Liberating Women's History* (Urbana: University of Illinois Press, 1976), pp. 217-23, and Marylin B. Arthur, "Classics," *Signs* 2 (1976), 382-403, and Note 5 below. In "Early Greece: The Origins of the Western Attitude toward Women," *Arethusa* 6 (1973), 7-58, Arthur has written an "abbreviated history of the emergence of the Greek city-state, with special emphasis on the position of women and with special attention to those cultural documents that are relevant to an assessment of the status of women." She studies such items as the Pythagorean Table of Opposites in which "the female is associated with the boundless, dark and bad, etc., and the male with limit, light, and good, etc." (p. 48). She notes the persistence of the idea from Hesiod on that progress in civilization is identified with the triumph of male forces over female. On the status of Spartan women after Hesiod, see Paul Cartledge, "Spartan Wives: Liberation or License?" *Classical Quarterly* 31 (1981), 84-105. They enjoyed a much higher status than other Greek women (for instance, in their clothes and property rights). Still, the modern reader is not impressed by their being trained to act and look like men, by their restricted marital choices or "by the overriding emphasis placed on their child-bearing potential and maternal roles by men who monopolized the political direction of a peculiarly masculine society" (p. 105). For an important though seriously flawed sociological study of the Greek gods, see Philip E. Slater, *The Glory of Hera* (Boston: Beacon Press, 1968). See also Note 19. Most other studies of Greek women, for instance, Mary F. Lefkowitz and Maureen Fant, *Women in Greece and Rome* (Toronto: Samuel-Stevens, 1977) deal with the later classical age.

[4]John P. Gould, "Law, Custom and Myth: Aspects of the Social Position of Women in Classical Athens," *Journal of Hellenic Studies* 100 (1980), 38. For a good formulation of the anthropological problem see Rayna R. Reiter, "Men and Women in the South of France: Public and Private Domains," in *Toward an Anthropology of Women* (New York: Monthly Review Press, 1975), pp. 252-82. Studying a French village, she finds "segregation of domains between the sexes along public and private lines" as if the people were dissected into somewhat hostile groups (p. 268).

[5]See Johann Jakob Bachofen, *Myth, Religion, and Mother Right* (Princeton, N.J.: Princeton University Press, 1861, rpt. 1967). See also C. G. Thomas, "Matriarchy in Early Greece: The Bronze and Dark Ages," *Arethusa* 6 (1973), 173-95; Jon-Christian Billigmeier and Judy A. Turner, "The Socio-Economic Roles of Women in Mycenaean Greece: A Brief Survey from Evidence of the Linear B Tablets," *Women's Studies* 8 (1981), 3-20; and Arthur, "Classics," cited in Note 3c.

[6]Rosemary Radford Ruether, *New Woman, New Earth: Sexist Ideologies and Human Liberation* (New York: Seabury Press, 1975), pp. 40-42. We rely heavily on Ruether for her theological and historical overview of sexism. See Note 18.

[7]W. K. C. Guthrie, *The Greeks and Their Gods* (Boston: Beacon Press, 1955), p. 69. See Guthrie for various versions of Hera's pre-Homeric history.

[8]Kramer, "Poets," p. 14 where he cites some similar demotions.

[9]Thorkild Jacobsen, *The Treasures of Darkness* (New Haven: Yale University Press, 1976), p. 110. This is Jacobsen's theory but some scholars dispute it.

[10]Isaac Kikawada, "Two Notes on Eve," *Journal of Biblical Literature* 9 (1972), 33-37. See also Theodor Reik, *The Creation of Woman* (New York: George Braziller, 1960) who does an "archeological psychoanalysis" of the story of Adam and Eve, using historical and psychological tools to understand why the Israelite culture revised the earlier pattern and subordinated the woman. For the tradition of Lilith as Adam's first wife and for a short history of what happened to Eve in later Jewish and early Christian thought, see "Eve" in *Encyclopaedia Judaica* 6 (1971), 979-83. For survivals of the Canaanite mother goddesses in Israelite thought, see Raphael Patai, *The Hebrew Goddess* (Philadelphia: Ktav, 1967), pp. 45-50.

[11]See Carol Meyers, "The Roots of Restriction: Women in Early Israel," *Biblical Archeologist* 41 (1978), 91-103. Not all scholars are convinced by Meyers' evaluation.

[12]Joan Bamberger, "The Myth of Matriarchy: Why Men Rule in Primitive Society," in Michelle Zimbalist Rosaldo and Louise Lamphere, eds., *Woman, Culture, and Society* (Stanford, California: Stanford University Press, 1974), pp. 263-80.

[13]Kramer gives another viewpoint in "Poets," Note 3a. He suggests that woman's second class status may have been true only from about 2000 B.C. on.

[14]On feminine images of God in the Old Testament, see Phyllis Trible, "God, Nature of in the Old Testament," *Interpreter's Dictionary*, Supplementary Volume, 368-69.

[15]Trible, p. 161; see also Marvin H. Pope, "Interpretations of the Sublime Song," in *Song of Songs: A New Translation with Introduction and Commentary*, Anchor Bible Series (New York: Doubleday, 1977), pp. 89-229, especially pp. 205-10; Frances Landy in "The Song of Songs and the Garden of Eden," *Journal of Biblical Literature* 94 (1979), 513-28, suggests the poet of the Song was bitterly critical of existing social mores in which the woman is far more vulnerable to shame than the man. He notes that all references to shame come from her; see also Pitt-Rivers cited in Note 3a.

[16]See Leonard Swidler, *Women in Judaism*, pp. 25-27, who quotes such scholars as George Tavard, *Women in Christian Tradition* (South Bend: Notre Dame, 1973).

[17]Ruether, "A Religion for Woman: Sources and Strategies," *Christianity and Crisis* 39 (1979), 307-11 argues that the ancient cultures that had goddesses were nevertheless sexist and therefore are not appropriate archetypes for a religion for women. In *New Woman*, she traces sexist ideology and social structure in the ancient world and makes suggestions about adequate myths for our own age. On the inadequacy of the portrayal of women in traditional stories and the need for women to learn to identify with the protagonists in stories, see Carolyn Heilbrun, *Reinventing Womanhood* (New York: Norton, 1979); see also Naomi Goldenberg, *The Changing of the Gods: Feminism and the End of Traditional Religions* (Boston: Beacon Press, 1979); Carol P. Christ, "Women's Stories, Women's Quest," *Diving and Surfacing: Women Writers on Spiritual Quest* (Boston: Beacon Press, 1980).

[18]Nicole Loraux, "Sur la race des femmes at quelques-unes de ses tribus," *Arethusa* 11 (1978), 43-87. Hugh Lloyd-Jones, *Females of the Species: Semonides on Women* (Park Ridge, New

Jersey: Noyes Press, 1975) translates Semonides' satire comparing woman to such animals as a sow, bitch, ass, and a busy bee. See the commentary especially on line 1, p. 63. Lloyd-Jones also includes a translation of a new misogynistic fragment of Archilochus. Linda S. Sussman, "Workers and Drones: Labor, Idleness and Gender Definition in Hesiod's Beehive," *Arethusa* 11 (1978), 27-41 analyzes Semonides' bee-woman alongside Hesiod's woman as drone (*Theogony* 590ff.) in the light of the socio-economic conditions of early Greece. She also has a helpful bibliography on socio-economic questions.

[19] Helene P. Foley, "'Reverse Similes' and Sex Roles in the *Odyssey*," *Arethusa* 11 (1978), 7-26. See also Anne Amory, "The Reunion of Odysseus and Penelope," in Charles H. Taylor, ed., *Essays on the Odyssey*, (Bloomington, Indiana: Indiana University Press, 1963), and John H. Finley, Jr., *Homer's Odyssey* (Cambridge, Harvard University Press, 1978), chapters 1 and 8. For a discussion of the traditional "masculine" and "feminine" strengths, see "Androgyny in the *Antigone*, in J. O'Brien, *Bilingual Selections from Sophocles' Antigone* (Carbondale: Southern Illinois University Press, 1977).

CONCLUSION ON COMPARING MYTHS

One of the most striking features of the creation myths in this book is their frequent use of similar patterns. All of the stories of human creation, for instance, describe human beings as a combination of earthly and divine elements, and these new creatures have the potential to both serve the gods and disrupt the divine order imposed on the world. In our Introduction, we suggested some of the reasons for these similarities. Creation myths, like so many other products of human imagination, advocate moral and social beliefs, reflect human psychology, and embody religious paradoxes in everyday symbols. It is equally true, however, that the differences in these stories reveal the distinctive experiences of their individual cultures. The Mesopotamians, for instance, saw the act of creating the human race as an elaborate combination of magic rituals and physical labor as the gods form statues out of clay and recite incantations to bring them to life. The Israelites thought the creative act was essentially a much simpler process in which Yahweh merely breathes life into a lifeless form. Different cultural perspectives, then, are embodied in these creative acts. But both cultures assume that the process of creation helps define human nature. On the other hand, Hesiod's Greek accounts of human creation emphasize the introduction of evil with the birth of woman and generational decline with each new age causing its own destruction.

Some creation myths show a similarity in style as well as content. Both *Enuma Elish* and the Israelite Creation Hymn, for instance, introduce the first creative act by describing the formless world which existed prior to creation, and both describe this chaotic condition in a clause beginning with "when." *Enuma Elish* begins "when on high the heaven had not been named, firm ground below had not been called by name" (I:1-2). Similarly, the Creation Hymn begins "when . . . the earth was without form

and void" (1:1). In both cases, creation is preceded by a time
when the familiar features of the world did not yet exist. Both
stories also assume that the primordial world is composed of
water—in *Enuma Elish*, the first gods are generated in the waters
of Apsu and Tiamat; and in the Creation Hymn, Yahweh spends two
days separating the waters. The gods of both traditions, however, have totally different relationships to this primitive,
watery world. The gods in *Enuma Elish* are waters themselves
and begin the natural process in which the world gradually forms
itself. In the Creation Hymn, Yahweh clearly stands outside
of and above the world which he forms according to his own pre-
conceived plan.

   Although these assumptions can be found in many creation
myths, many others express different views. Hesiod's *Theogony*,
for instance, assumes that the world originally consisted of dry
land. Gaia, Mother Earth, is the most prolific of the four
forces which predate creation, and she generates the rivers and
oceans after she has created the sky and mountains. The land is
also pre-eminent in *Atrahasis*, where the gods dig canals to
provide themselves with water; and in the story of Adam and Eve,
Yahweh makes a garden even before there is any rain. As different as these stories are in other respects, all three share a
farmer's view that the world is essentially land, while *Enuma
Elish* and the Creation Hymn assume a sailor's view of the world
as primarily water.

   This comparison illustrates how many myths from different
cultures may share common patterns and still reveal significant
features which distinguish one from the other. We have included
below a chart showing some general parallels as an aid to the
study of mythic patterns. It contains only a few examples rather
than a comprehensive system since we assume that students will
find many more on their own. One of the joys of studying myths
is the discovery of how people who differ from each other can
share ideas and find diverse ways of expressing them.

THE COSMOS

	MESOPOTAMIAN ACCOUNT *ENUMA ELISH*	ISRAELITE ACCOUNT CREATION HYMN	GREEK ACCOUNT HESIOD'S *THEOGONY*
1. CREATOR(S) AND CREATIONS	TIAMAT--ELEVEN MONSTERS ANU--FOUR WINDS EA--THE APSU (HIS HOUSE) MARDUK--SKY, HUMANITY, EARTH'S SURFACE, ORDER IN UNIVERSE	YAHWEH--COMPLETE ORDERLY UNIVERSE	GAIA--SKY, MOUNTAINS, SEAS, MANY DEITIES AND MONSTERS CHAOS--EREBOS, NIGHT NIGHT--AITHER, DAY ZEUS--ORDER IN UNIVERSE
2. METHODS	SEXUAL GENERATION, CRAFTSMANSHIP	WORD	SEXUAL AND NONSEXUAL GENERATION
3. SEQUENCE OF CREATION	MARDUK'S SEQUENCE: 1. SKY AND EARTH 2. ARRANGEMENT OF STARS, PLANETS 3. DUTIES FOR THE GODS 4. HUMAN BEINGS	1. LIGHT 2. VAULT DIVIDING WATERS 3. DRY LAND, SEAS 4. SUN, MOON, STARS 5. FISH AND BIRDS 6. LAND ANIMALS, HUMANS	SEVERAL SEQUENCES: 1. CHAOS--NIGHT--DAY 2. EARTH--SKY-- MOUNTAINS--SEAS

HUMANITY

	MESOPOTAMIAN ACCOUNT *ATRAHASIS*	ISRAELITE ACCOUNT ADAM AND EVE	GREEK ACCOUNT PANDORA AND THE AGES
1. CREATOR(S) AND MOTIVES	EA AND MAMI--TO FREE THE GODS FROM HARD WORK	YAHWEH--TO TILL AND CARE FOR THE GARDEN	FIVE AGES KRONOS AND ZEUS-- NO REASON GIVEN PANDORA ZEUS--TO BALANCE A GOOD WITH AN EVIL
2. MATERIALS	CLAY, FLESH AND BLOOD OF A SLAIN GOD, SPITTLE	DUST FROM THE GROUND AND YAHWEH'S BREATH	FIVE AGES--NOT EXPLAINED PANDORA--SEE BELOW
3. WOMAN CREATED SEPARATELY	NONE--MALES AND FEMALES CREATED TOGETHER	FORMED FROM MAN'S RIB TO BE HIS PARTNER	PANDORA--MADE OF A GIFT FROM EACH GOD TO BE AN EVIL TO MEN
4. DECLINE OF HUMAN RACE	TOO MUCH NOISE, GODS CANNOT REST	SERPENT'S DECEPTION, ADAM AND EVE BREAK GOD'S LAW	FIVE AGES GENERATIONS DECLINE BECAUSE OF INNATE FLAWS AND *HIBRIS* PANDORA EXTERNAL EVIL, *KAKON*, CAUSES TROUBLE

SELECTED BIBLIOGRAPHY AND APPENDIX

SELECTED BIBLIOGRAPHY

No attempt is made here to cover the literature that is
available in any book on Classical or Comparative Mythology.
It is presumed that the teacher and student will have access to
annotated bibliographies like John Perodotto's *Classical
Mythology: An Annotated Bibliography* (Urbana: American
Philological Association, 1973), nor do we list standard references, e.g., encyclopedias like the *Jewish Encyclopedia* or
dictionaries like *Oxford Classical Dictionary*. We have limited
our listings to a few general works mostly on mythology and to
selected books on the Babylonian and Hebrew backgrounds. For
Greece, we include only selected books on Hesiod. The books
cited in Chapter 10 are not included here. Those marked with
an asterisk are cited in the text.

General

Barbour, Ian G. *Myths, Models and Paradigms: A Comparative
   Study in Science and Religion*. New York: Harper and Row,
   1974. Barbour discusses the two different models through
   which the human mind interprets the world: the scientific
   and the religious. He also gives a good explanation of the
   idea of myths as useful fictions.

Doria, Charles and Harris Lenowitz, ed. and trans. *Origins:
   Creation Texts from the Ancient Mediterranean*. Garden City,
   New York: Anchor Press/Doubleday, 1976. This text provides
   translations of creation stories from all over the ancient
   Mediterranean.

Eliade, Mircea. *Gods, Goddesses, and Myths of Creation*. New
   York: Harper and Row, 1974. This anthology of creation
   myths from many cultures is especially useful for students
   who want to look at myths of cultures other than those of
   Greece, Israel, and Mesopotamia.

--------------. *Myth and Reality*. Trans. Willard R. Trask.
   New York: Harper and Row, 1963. Here, Eliade explores the
   meaning of creation and destruction myths, but mainly those
   of very "primitive" and pre-literate cultures. He finds
   patterns common to myths of many different cultures.

--------------. *Patterns in Comparative Religion*. Trans.
   Rosemary Sheed. New York: Sheed and Ward, 1958.

Frankfort, H. and H. A., et. al. *The Intellectual Adventure of
   Ancient Man*. Chicago: University of Chicago Press, 1946.
   This collection of lectures attempts to interpret the
   societies of ancient Egypt, Mesopotamia, and Israel. The
   first essay, "Myth and Reality," explains why ancient thought
   is mythical and how the "logic" of the ancient world differs

from that of the modern. These standard, seminal essays are
for both specialist and general reader who is prepared to do
some strenuous thinking.

Girard, René. *Violence and the Sacred*. Trans. Patrick Gregory.
Baltimore: Johns Hopkins University Press, 1977. Girard
suggests that violence is at the heart of the sacred, that
religion, myth and ritual seek to explain fundamental
violence.

*Galinsky, G. Karl. "Ovid's Metamorphosis of Myth." in his
Perspectives of Roman Poetry: A Classical Symposium.
Austin: University of Texas Press, 1974. pp. 105-27.

*Hughes, Merritt Y., ed. *John Milton: Complete Poems and Major
Prose*. Indianapolis: Bobbs-Merrill Co., Odyssey Press,
1957.

*Huizinga, J. *Homo Ludens: A Study of the Play Element in
Culture*. Trans. R. F. C. Hull. Boston: Beacon Press, 1950.

*Kierkegaard, Soren. *The Concept of Dread*. Trans. Walter
Lowrie. Princeton: Princeton University Press, 1957.

*Lévi-Strauss, Claude. "Structuralism and Myth." *Kenyon Review*
N. S. III 2 (Spring, 1981), 64-88. This article is a brief
summary of Lévi-Strauss' structuralist approach to the study
of myth.

*Macquarrie, John. *God Talk: An Examination of the Language and
Logic of Theology*. New York: Harper and Row, 1967.
Macquarrie examines the problems of theological terminology
and semantics. The eighth chapter concerns myth and its
relationship to theological language.

*Malinowski, Bronislaw. *Myth in Primitive Psychology*. New York:
Norton, 1926. This cultural anthropologist discusses how
strongly sacred tradition and myth control the moral and
social behavior of the Melanesian tribes. The work is a
seminal study of the relation between myth and social
organization and includes a separate chapter on "Myths of
Origin."

--------------------. *Sex, Culture, and Myth*. New York:
Harcourt, Brace & World, 1962.

*Stone, Lawrence. *The Family, Sex, and Marriage in England.
1500-1800*. New York: Harper and Row, 1977.

*Tillich, Paul. *Dynamics of Faith*. New York: Harper and Row,
1957. The third chapter deals with symbols and myths as the
necessary "language of faith." Tillich's concept of "broken
myth" suggests the existence of three stages in a person's
or a culture's understanding of myth.

*Tracy, David. *Blessed Rage for Order: The New Pluralism in
Theology*. New York: Seabury, 1979. In a chapter on
"Limit-Language" this theologian discusses the limitations
of conceptual analysis to express our deepest human experience and the universal need to find metaphors and myths to
express the inexpressible.

Mesopotamian Background

Bermant, Chaim and Michael Weitzman. *Ebla: An Archaeological Enigma*. London: Weidenfeld and Nicolson, 1979. This work is an account of the excavations at Ebla, an ancient city from the third millennium B.C.; tablets from Ebla may shed light on the origins of Israel. The book contains a detailed and fascinating chapter on the history of the deciphering of cuneiform.

Brandon, S. G. F. *Creation Legends of the Near East*. London: Hodder and Stoughton, 1963. This book presents interpretations of creation legends from five cultures.

Cross, Frank Moore. *Canaanite Myth and Hebrew Epic*. Cambridge, Mass.: Harvard University Press, 1973.

*Frymer-Kensky, Tikva. "The Atrahasis Epic and Its Significance for Our Understanding of Genesis 1-9." *Biblical Archaeologist* 40 (1977), 147-55.

*Hallo, William W. and J. J. A. Van Dijk. *The Exaltation of Inanna*. New Haven, Conn.: Yale University Press, 1968.

*----------------- and William Kelly Simpson. *The Ancient Near East: A History*. New York: Harcourt, Brace, and Jovanovich, 1971. This history of political and cultural development of pre-classical antiquity, relying throughout on texts and documentary remains, is a good overview of Ancient Near Eastern and Egyptian History. Although the book focuses both on Mesopotamia and Egypt, the section on Mesopotamia is of course here more relevant.

*Heidel, Alexander. *The Babylonian Genesis*. 2nd ed. Chicago: University of Chicago Press, 1951. Although dated, especially on its view of *Enuma Elish*, this book is important in presenting various creation stories from the Ancient Near East and showing parallels to the Old Testament.

*Jacobsen, Thorkild. *The Treasures of Darkness*. New Haven, Conn.: Yale University Press, 1976. Jacobsen traces the development of Mesopotamian religious models and thought through more than four millennia, examining each age's conception of the gods. He posits original and interesting theories about *Enuma Elish* and about Mesopotamian gods. This is a fascinating, well-documented analysis of major religious concepts, accessible to the general reader.

----------------. *Toward the Image of Tammuz and Other Essays on Mesopotamian History and Culture*. Ed. William L. Moran. Cambridge, Mass.: Harvard University Press, 1970. This collection of essays by an eminent Near Eastern scholar concentrates on formative patterns in Mesopotamian religion, politics, and economy. The title essay is a difficult but penetrating exploration of Babylonian mythology, attempting to analyze the psychology of ancient religion. The essay on the gods is particularly fascinating.

*Kragerud, A. "The Concept of Creation in Enuma Elish." in *Ex Orbe Religionum. Studies in the History of Religion*, 21 (Leiden: E. J. Brill, 1972). I, 39-49.

*Kramer, Samuel Noah. *History Begins at Sumer*. Garden City,
     New York: Doubleday and Co., Anchor Books, 1959. Twenty-
     five essays present "firsts" in recorded history, these
     are entertaining and absorbing selections on a wide variety
     of topics. The Essay "Man's First Cosmogony and Cosmology"
     is a valuable introductory summary of Sumerian ideas about
     the universe.

     ------------------. *Sumerian Mythology: A Study of Spiritual
     and Literary Achievement in the Third Millennium, B. C.*
     Philadelphia: University of Pennsylvania Press, 1972.
     Written in 1944, this book is a useful compendium of
     Sumerian myths. The 1971 preface brings the contents up
     to date with the help of new translations. The introduction
     is a summary of the history of the decipherment and interpre-
     tation of the Sumerian tablets.

Lambert, W. G. "A New Look at the Babylonian Background of
     Genesis." *Journal of Theological Studies*. N. S. 16.2
     (1965), 287-300.

*--------------. "The Reign of Nebuchadnezzar I: A Turning
     Point in the History of Ancient Mesopotamian Religion."
     in *The Seed of Wisdom: Essays in Honor of T. J. Meek*.
     Ed. W. S. McCullough. Toronto: University of Toronto
     Press, 1964, 3-13.

*-------------- and A. R. Millard. *Atra-Hasis: The Babylonian
     Story of the Flood*. With *The Sumerian Flood Story* by M.
     Civil. Oxford: Oxford University Press, 1969. This is the
     definitive study of the text of *Atrahasis*. See articles in
     such journals as *Journal of Near Eastern Studies* for
     criticisms of Lambert's position.

*Oppenheim, A. Leo. *Ancient Mesopotamia: Portrait of a Dead
     Civilization*. Chicago: University of Chicago Press, 1964.
     Oppenheim presents a general introduction to the history of
     Mesopotamia. The section on religion includes a warning
     against facile interpretations, an examination of image-
     worship, and reflections on the psychology of Mesopotamian
     religion and on divination.

*Pritchard, James B., ed. *Ancient Near Eastern Texts Relating to
     the Old Testament*. 3rd ed. with Supplement. Princeton,
     New Jersey: Princeton University Press, 1969. This volume
     contains many mythological texts from the Ancient Near East.

Thomas, D. Winton, ed. *Documents from Old Testament Times*.
     London: Thomas Nelson and Sons, 1958.

Greek Background

*Brenk, Frederick. "Hesiod: How Much a Male Chauvanist?" *The
     Classical Bulletin* 49.5 (1973), 73-76.

*Fontenrose, Joseph. "Work, Justice, and Hesiod's Five Ages."
     Classical Philology 69 (1974), 1-16.

Lattimore, Richmond. *Hesiod: The Works and Days, Theogony, The
     Shield of Herakles*. Ann Arbor, Michigan: University of
     Michigan Press, 1959.

*Panofsky, Dora and Erwin. *Pandora's Box: The Changing Aspects of a Mythical Symbol*. New York: Harper and Row, 1965. This study traces the Pandora myth from Hesiod to modern times.

*Phillips, F. Carter. "Narrative Compressions and the Myths of Prometheus in Hesiod." *Classical Journal* 68 (1973), 289-305.

*Pucci, Pietro. *Hesiod and the Language of Poetry*. Baltimore: Johns Hopkins University Press, 1977.

*Solmsen, F. *Hesiod and Aeschylus*. Ithaca, New York: Cornell University Press, 1949. The book contains a close philosophical analysis of such problems as good and evil in Hesiod.

*Walcot, Peter. *Hesiod and the Near East*. Cardiff: Wales University Press, 1966.

*West, M. L., ed. *Hesiod: Theogony*. Oxford: Oxford University Press, 1966. This is the standard Greek text, with excellent commentary.

*-----------, ed. *Hesiod: Works and Days*. Oxford: Oxford University Press, 1978. This is the standard Greek text. Its commentary is excellent.

Israelite Background

Bright, John. *A History of Israel*. 2nd ed. Philadelphia: Westminster Press, 1972. This book traces the history of Israel from the Stone Age to the end of the Old Testament period, with a large section devoted to religious history. Accessible to the undergraduate as well as the specialist, this book includes helpful maps, indexes, bibliography, and chronological data.

De Vaux, Roland. *Ancient Israel*. 2 vols. Vol. 1: Social Institutions. Vol. 2: Religious Institutions. New York: McGraw Hill Co., 1965. The first volume examines nomadism and family, economic, state, legal, and religious institutions in the Old Testament. The second volume deals with those institutions directly connected with worship, such as sacrifice, and priesthood, and feasts. Both volumes provide valuable information for the non-specialist although they are somewhat difficult to read. The bibliography and indexes are extensive.

*Gilkey, Langdon. *Maker of Heaven and Earth: A Study of the Christian Doctrine of Creation*. Garden City, New York: Doubleday and Co., Anchor Books, 1965. Gilkey studies the theological importance of the Genesis creation accounts, within a larger study of the meaning of creation.

Karban, Roger, ed. *The Sources of Genesis*. Belleville, Illinois: Llama Publications, 1976.

*The New English Bible with the Apocrypha. New York: Oxford University Press, 1971.

*Pope, Marvin H. Song of Songs. Vol. VIIC of The Anchor Bible. Garden City, New York: Doubleday and Co., 1977.

Sarna, Nahum M. *Understanding Genesis: The Heritage of Biblical Israel*. New York: Jewish Theological Seminary of America, 1966, Schocken Paperback Edition, 1974. Written from a traditional Jewish viewpoint, this book focuses on ethical issues in Genesis and on comparisons between Israelite literature and Near Eastern cultures.

*Speiser, E. A. Genesis. Vol. I of The Anchor Bible. Garden City, New York: Doubleday and Co., 1964.

*Trible, Phyllis. "Depatriarchalizing in Biblical Interpretation." *Journal of the American Academy of Religion*, 41 (1973), 30-46.

*---------------. *God and the Rhetoric of Sexuality*. Philadelphia: Fortress Press, 1978. This contains a close analysis of the Adam and Eve story in terms of its view of sexuality.

*Vawter, Bruce. *On Genesis: A New Reading*. Garden City, New York: Doubleday and Co., 1977. This recent commentary is by a Roman Catholic theologian.

Von Rad, Gerhard. *Genesis: A Commentary*. Trans. John H. Marks. Philadelphia: Westminster Press, 1961. This commentary for the general reader holds that the first six books of the Old Testament should be considered together as the fundamental unity of Israelite theology, rather than the first five as is commonly held.

*Westermann, Claus. *Creation*. Trans. John J. Scullion, S. J. Philadelphia: Fortress Press, 1974. In his exposition of Genesis 1-3, this Lutheran theologian defends the importance of the Biblical creation story for modern society by viewing it as a reflection of Israel's understanding of the Creator-creation relationship rather than as history.

Introduction

Ovid, one of the world's most entertaining storytellers, lived in a far more sophisticated, rich world than any of the other mythographers included in this book. He was born in a small town near Rome in 43 B.C., the same year that Cicero, the last champion of the Roman Republic, was murdered. Julius Caesar was assassinated the previous year; and by the time Ovid was a young man studying rhetoric in Rome, Caesar's nephew Augustus had already inaugurated the Augustan Age. This richly creative era saw Horace writing his satires and odes, Virgil carving out his great epic of Rome the *Aeneid*, and younger poets producing love elegies.

Ovid's father planned a life of public service for his son and sent him to the best schools of rhetoric; but Ovid's interests and talents lay elsewhere. Much to his father's disgust, he soon gave up the idea of a public career and became a poet. He wrote a series of "how-to" manuals on love and sex for Rome's ultrafashionable social set. Like an ancient Fellini, he gave advice through his poetry on how to fall in and out of love, how to seduce and jilt, and even how to use cosmetics to the best advantage. Writing in a period when women were taking a prominent place in society, Ovid went so far as to recommend adultery to the liberated woman. In his more mature narrative poems, Ovid relied heavily on Greek mythology. His *Metamorphoses* retold some two hundred and fifty myths; his *Fasti* was a Roman calendar into which he weaved myths and traditions associated with the days of each month; and his *Heroides* were letters from mythical women to their absent husbands or lovers.

Although he was a popular and successful poet, he eventually ran into trouble with Augustus. In his mid-fifties, he was banished by imperial decree to Tomi, a miserable, deserted out-post on the western shore of the Black Sea. Ovid blamed his exile on *carmen et error*, "a song and a mistake"; but modern scholars have not been able to determine the exact meaning of this cryptic comment. The subject matter of Ovid's poems was certainly at odds with Augustus' program of moral reform, but the specific charge against him was not recorded. Whatever the reasons for his exile, he spent his last ten years vainly plead-ing through poetic laments, such as *Tristia* and *Epistulae ex Ponto*, for his return to civilization. But his requests went unanswered; and he died at Tomi in 18 A.D., survived by his third wife.

Ovid is best remembered for his *Metamorphoses*, an epic in fifteen books, which contains some of the best known Greco-Roman myths. As its title suggests, the epic is united by the theme of change. Ovid celebrates the constant flux "from the beginning of the world to the present" (Metamorphoses 1.4) in a way which no previous poet had. Like many of our contemporaries, Ovid and his bored, aristocratic audience were ever in search of novelty. He loved the old stories but always strove to tell them with a new, unexpected twist. So the *Metamorphoses* is filled with changes of plot, changes of tone, changes of design, and quick changes of mood. Many of the stories tell of physical transformations; Io, for example, is changed into a cow, Arachne into a spider. But all transform the old stories as Ovid retells them in an unforgettable, often playful way.

Ovid's playfulness is not apparent in the creation story which opens the *Metamorphoses*. Rather, with a majesty which rivals the opening of Genesis, the poet depicts the discordant chaos from which "a god or kinder Natural Order" (21) separates the universe. Although Ovid does not know the identity of the creator, his creation is an ordered, beautiful, meaningful whole with human beings at its pinnacle. This impression of order and meaning is reinforced in the subsequent passages. His account of the world's creation is followed by the story of the four ages, the birth of the giants, the sin of Lycaon, the flood, and the survival of Deucalion and Pyrrha. These tales, which are contained in the first half of Book One, form a pattern reminiscent of *Atrahasis* and the opening chapters of Genesis: creation of the world and the human race, problem with the creation, destruction, and renewal. In these tales, too, the majestic tone continues as a morally justified Jupiter punishes Lycaon for his sin and rewards Deucalion and Pyrrha for their piety.

Then, suddenly, Ovid shifts from the majestic mood to a playful, comic tone; and the moral order which he described disintegrates. Jupiter turns into a fatuous, immoral lover, off in hot pursuit of Io, the lovely daughter of a river god. He catches the unwilling girl; but his jealous wife Juno, in turn, catches him. In a series of episodes, embarrassing for Jupiter and disastrous for Io, the all-seeing god is reduced to a henpecked husband who changes Io into a milk-white cow so that he can claim innocence. Although Juno is fully aware of his ruse, Jupiter will not admit to any indiscretion and is eventually forced to give the cow to his wife rather than return Io to her human form. The rest of the story concentrates on the pathetic Io as she wanders along the river's banks and tries to paw her name in the sand. Here Ovid contrasts the triviality of Jupiter's plight with the human suffering which his indiscretion causes. But even then Ovid is not content to leave the situation unchanged. Eventually, Jupiter confesses, Juno relents, and Io is transformed to her original state in which she is honored as a goddess.

Ovid, then, delights in depicting the ever shifting river of life in which the only constant is the poet's *perpetuum carmen*, "continuous song." As his poem goes on, everything and everyone in it, including gods and human beings, change. Strong gods are deflated into fatuous lovers or cruel despots; human beings now love, now suffer, now are changed into other forms. Like the waters of a river, nothing is lost, nothing dies, but nothing is stable. All is transformed by the poet's playful art. To some readers, this playfulness and transfer of power from the gods to the poet's art seems sacriligeous. If myths are serious attempts to come to grips with human mortality, Ovid divests them of their mythic dimension. For him, there is no death and no power strong enough or stable enough to destroy life; there is only life and the poet's humerous, ironic song about it. Other readers, however, see Ovid as the restorer of myth's power because he reintroduces humor into myths on a far larger scale than anyone else. (See Galinsky, *Perspectives in Roman Poetry*, p. 127.) If

primitive myths were "tinged with a certain element of humor,"
Ovid surely recaptures that element. (See Huizinga, *Homo
Ludens*.) Whether he is ultimately myth's destroyer or myth's
restorer, his art kept the Greco-Roman myths alive.

Metamorphoses 1.1-150

translated by Craig McVay

Changes: I want to tell you about shapes
that change to new shapes. Gods, you made these changes,
so lead me in my continuous song
from the beginning of the world to the present!

Before the sea and the land had formed,   5
there was one face of nature, called Chaos;
it was just a rough and inharmonious mass.
There was no sun to shine,
no moon to wax and wane.
The earth did not hang in mid-air,   10
and the sea had no shores.
Although there were land and sea and air,
no one could live on the earth or swim in the sea,
and there was no light in the sky.
Nothing had its own shape,   15
and everything got in the way
of everything else.
Cold things fought against hot,
moist against dry, gentle against harsh,
and heavy against light.   20

A god, or a kinder Natural Order, settled this strife;
he cut the land from the sky,
the sea from the land, and the air from the sky.
Then, after he had separated these things
from the chaotic heap, he put each in its proper place   25
and united them all in peaceful harmony.

Weightless fire leapt up
and lived in the top of the sky.
Air, not quite as light, settled just below the fire.
The earth, still heavier with its large elements,   30
fell to the bottom.
Water was the last to be placed.
It encircles the ends of the earth.

Then the god, whoever it was,
molded the earth into the shape of a large ball.   35
He poured out the seas, ordered them to swell
with rushing winds and to surround the shores;
he added springs and pools and lakes,
and he belted rivers with slanting banks.
Some of the rivers disappeared into the earth itself;   40
some ran to the sea, where they joined the waves
that beat on the shore. He ordered the vast plains
to stretch out, the valleys to settle,
the woods to be clothed with foliage,
and the rocky mountains to rise.   45

Just as he had already divided the sky into five zones,
he then made five divisions on the earth.
The middle zone was too hot for anyone to live in,
and deep snow covered the outer two.

The other two had temperate climates,   50
with mixture of hot and cold.
Over all these hangs the air, which is as much heavier
than fire as water is lighter than earth.
The god ordered clouds of mist to settle in the air;
he ordered storm winds and thunder and lightning,   55
which would one day terrify mankind.
The maker of the world did not allow the winds
to blow anywhere they wanted but gave to each wind
its own region to rule with its blasts.
Even so, they can scarcely be restrained   60
from tearing apart the world,
so great is the discord between brother winds.

Eurus retired to rule in the east,
where the light of dawn shines on mountain ridges;
Zephyr joined the setting sun which warms the shores   65
in the west. Bristly Boreas invaded the far north,
and the south grew damp from the constant clouds
of rainy Auster. Over all these winds, the god placed a clear,
weightless ether, unburdened by any earthly dregs.

As soon as the god made these fixed divisions,   70
the stars which had been crushed and obscured
in the darkness, began to shine throughout the sky.
Then the god gave each region its own living creatures;
the floor of the sky held the stars and divine planets,
the water became the home of the glittering fishes,   75
the earth received wild animals, and the air took the birds.

The world still needed a creature more noble and intelligent,
one that could rule everything else.
So humanity was born. Perhaps it was the maker,
starting a better world, who made humanity   80
from a divine seed. Or maybe it was Prometheus.
Since the earth had just been severed from her brother
the sky and still held some of his seeds,
maybe Prometheus mixed the seeds with rain
and molded them into the likeness of the ruling gods.   85
Although the other animals only faced downward
toward the earth, human beings were given a face
that looked upward and were ordered to stand tall
and look toward the heavens. So what before was just a rough
and formless mass was changed; it was clothed with figures
    of something utterly new: human beings.   90

The Golden Age was first. It freely honored fidelity
and righteousness. There were no threatening laws
cast on bronze tablets, and no one feared punishment
by a stern judge. Everyone felt safe, even without police.
Mountain pines had not yet been cut to make ships   95
which sail to foreign lands; people knew no shores
but their own. There were no deep trenches surrounding
and protecting the towns, no war-trumpets or bronze bugles
to order men to battle, no helmets or swords.
People enjoyed leisurely lives free from care,
    free from wars.   100

The earth herself, unwounded by any plow,
provided all the food people wanted.
All were content with the food they got without force;
they would pick strawberries, blackberries, and acorns
from the spreading oak of Jupiter. Spring was eternal;   105
flowers were growing even though no one planted them,

and they waved in the west wind.
Soon even the unplowed earth was bearing grain,
and fields were growing white and ready for harvest.
The rivers were flowing with milk or with wine,   110
and honey was dripping from the oak.

After Saturn had been banished to gloomy Tartaros
and Jupiter ruled the world, the Silver Age followed.
It was inferior to the Golden Age
but more worthy than the age of bronze.   115
Jupiter shortened the springtime
and cut the year into four seasons.
Then for the first time, the air was hot and thirsty,
and ice hung frozen in the winds.
For the first time, human beings sought out shelter,   120
caves and thick bushes and branches
bound together by strips of bark.
For the first time, seeds were buried in furrows,
and young oxen labored under yokes.

Third came the Bronze Age;   125
its nature was more fierce, quicker to yield rough weapons,
but it was not evil.

Last was the age of hard iron.
Immediately this Iron Age burst forth with every abomination.
Shame, truth, and trust fled; deceit, fraud, snares,   130
force, and wicked greed took their place.
Sailors set sail by winds they hadn't known before;
trees that had stood tall on the mountains
were now ships prancing insolently on foreign seas.
The land, which like the sunlight and the air belonged   135
to everyone, was now chopped by boundaries
made by timid surveyors. Men demanded crops from the earth,
and they dug into her guts and gouged out the wealth
that the gods had stored deep inside her.
This, then, spurred men to further crimes.   140

Guilty iron and guiltier gold were mined. Wars burst out,
and in their blood-stained hands, men wielded clashing arms
of iron and gold. Men lived by plunder.
Guest was not safe from host, nor father from son.
Even among brothers, little love was lost.   145
Men lusted for the deaths of their wives,
who craved the same for their husbands.
Step-mothers brewed ghastly poisons, and sons longed
for their fathers' early deaths. Loyalty lay conquered.
The maiden Justice, the last deity on earth,
    flew away from the blood-soaked land.   150